PENGUIN BOOKS

An Inspector Calls and Other Plays

J. B. Priestley was born in Bradford in 1894. After leaving school, he spent some time as a junior clerk in a wool office and a lively account of his life at this period may be found in his volume of reminiscences, *Margin Released* (1962). He joined the army in 1914, and in 1919, on receiving an ex-officers' grant, went to Trinity Hall, Cambridge. He settled in London in 1922, where he soon earned a reputation as an essayist and critic. His third and fourth novels, *The Good Companions* (1929) and *Angel Pavement* (1930), were a great success and established an international reputation. This was increased by the plays he wrote in the 1930s and 1940s, notably *Dangerous Corner* (1932), *Time and the Conways* (1937) and *An Inspector Calls* (1947). During the Second World War he was exceedingly popular as a broadcaster and published collections of his broadcasts in the volumes *Britain Speaks* (1940) and *All England Listened* (1968). His most important novels during the post-war period include *Bright Day* (1946), *Festival at Farbridge* (1951), *Lost Empires* (1965) and *The Image Men* (1968). His more ambitious literary and social criticism can be found in *The Art of the Dramatist* (1957) and *Literature and the Western Man* (1960). With his third wife, Jacquetta Hawkes, a distinguished archeologist and a well-established writer herself, he collaborated on *Journey Down a Rainbow* (1955) and a play, *Dragon's Mouth* (1952). His other books include *English Journey* (1934), *The Edwardians* (1970), *The English* (1973), *Particular Pleasures* (1975) and *Lost and Found* (1976). J. B. Priestley was awarded the Order of Merit in 1977. He died in 1984.

J. B. PRIESTLEY

An Inspector Calls
and Other Plays

PENGUIN BOOKS

PENGUIN BOOKS

Published by the Penguin Group
Penguin Books Ltd, 80 Strand, London WC2R 0RL, England
Penguin Putnam Inc., 375 Hudson Street, New York, New York 10014, USA
Penguin Books Australia Ltd, 250 Camberwell Road, Camberwell, Victoria 3124, Australia
Penguin Books Canada Ltd, 10 Alcorn Avenue, Toronto, Ontario, Canada M4V 3B2
Penguin Books India (P) Ltd, 11 Community Centre, Panchsheel Park, New Delhi – 110 017, India
Penguin Books (NZ) Ltd, Cnr Rosedale and Airborne Roads, Albany, Auckland, New Zealand
Penguin Books (South Africa) (Pty) Ltd, 24 Sturdee Avenue, Rosebank 2196, South Africa

Penguin Books Ltd, Registered Offices: 80 Strand, London WC2R 0RL, England

www.penguin.com

The plays in this book were published by William Heinemann Ltd
in *The Plays of J. B. Priestley*, volumes 1–3, 1948–50
This collection published in Penguin Books 1969
Reprinted in Penguin Classics 2000

062

Time and the Conways copyright 1937, 1939 by J. B. Priestley
I Have Been Here Before copyright 1937 by J. B. Priestley
An Inspector Calls copyright 1947 by J. B. Priestley
The Linden Tree copyright 1947 by J. B. Priestley
All rights reserved

Printed in England by Clays Ltd, St Ives plc
Set in Monotype Plantin

ISBN-13: 978-0-141-18535-4

www.greenpenguin.co.uk

CONTENTS

Time and the Conways

A PLAY IN THREE ACTS

CHARACTERS

Conways
MRS CONWAY
ALAN
MADGE
ROBIN
HAZEL
KAY
CAROL

Others
JOAN HELFORD
ERNEST BEEVERS
GERALD THORNTON

Act One
That Night. Kay's Twenty-first Birthday

Act Two
Another Night. And Another Birthday

Act Three
That Night Again. Her Twenty-first Birthday

Act Three is continuous with Act One

The Scene throughout is a sitting-room in MRS CONWAY's house, a detached villa in a prosperous suburb of a manufacturing town, Newlingham. Acts One and Three take place on an autumn night in 1919. Act Two on an autumn night at the present time (1937).

'Time and the Conways' was first produced in London on 26 August 1937, at the Duchess Theatre, with the following cast:

HAZEL	Rosemary Scott
CAROL	Eileen Erskine
ALAN	Raymond Huntley
MADGE	Molly Rankin
KAY	Jean Forbes-Robertson
MRS CONWAY	Barbara Everest
JOAN HELFORD	Helen Horsey
GERALD THORNTON	Wilfred Babbage
ERNEST BEEVERS	Mervyn Johns
ROBIN	Alexander Archdale

Produced by Irene Hentschel

ACT ONE

There is a party at the Conways, this autumn evening of 1919, but we cannot see it, only hear it. All we can see at first is the light from the hall coming through the curtained archway on the right of the room, and a little red firelight on the other side. But we can hear young voices chattering and laughing and singing, the sharp little explosion of a cracker or two, and a piano playing popular music of that period. After a moment or two, a number of voices begin to sing the tune we hear on the piano. It is all very jolly indeed.

Then we hear a girl's voice (it is HAZEL CONWAY'S) *calling, loud and clear:* 'Mother, where shall we put them?' *The voice that replies, farther off, can only be* MRS CONWAY'S, *and she says:* 'In the back room. Then we'll act out here.' *To this,* HAZEL, *who is obviously very excited, screams:* 'Yes, marvellous!' *and then calls to somebody still farther away, probably upstairs:* 'Carol – in the back room.'

And now HAZEL *dashes in, switching on the light. We see at once that she is a tall, golden young creature, dressed in her very best for this party. She is carrying an armful of old clothes, hats, and odds and ends, all the things that happy people used to dress up in for charades. The room looks very cosy, although it has no doorway, only the large curtained archway on the right. At the back is a window with a step up to it, and a cushioned seat. The curtains are drawn. On the left is a fireplace or an anthracite stove, glowing red. There are several small bookcases against or in the walls, some pieces of fairly good furniture, including a round table and a small bureau, and some passable pictures. It is obviously one of those nondescript rooms, used by the family far more than the drawing-room is, and variously called the Back Room, the Morning Room, the School-room, the Nursery, the Blue, Brown or Red Room. This might easily have been called the Red Room, for in this light it seems to range from pink to plum colour, and it makes a fine cosy setting for the girls in their party dress.*

Another one has arrived, while HAZEL *is dumping her charade things on a round settee in the middle of the room. This is* CAROL, *the youngest of the Conways – perhaps sixteen – and now terrifically excited, breathless, and almost tottering beneath a load of charade stuff, including a cigar-box gloriously filled with old false whiskers and noses, spectacles, and what not. With all the reckless haste of a child she bangs down all this stuff, and starts to talk, although she has no breath left. And now – after adding that* CAROL *is an enchanting young person – we can leave them to explain themselves.*

CAROL [*gasping but triumphant*]: I've found – the box – with all the false whiskers and things in –

HAZEL [*triumphantly*]: I knew it hadn't been thrown away.

CAROL: Nobody'd *dare* to throw it away. [*Holds it out, with lid open.*] Look! [HAZEL *makes a grab at it.*] Don't *snatch*!

HAZEL [*not angrily*]: Well, I must *look*, mustn't I, idiot? [*They both, like children, eagerly explore the contents of the box.*] Bags I this one. [*She fishes out a large drooping moustache.*] Oo – and this! [*Fishes out very bulbous false nose.*]

CAROL [*an unselfish creature*]: All right, but don't take *all* the good ones, Hazel. Kay and Madge will want some. I think Kay ought to have *first* choice. After all, it's *her* birthday – and you know how she adores charades. Mother won't want any of these because she'd rather look grand, wouldn't she? Spanish or Russian or something. What are you doing?

[HAZEL *has turned aside to fasten on the nose and moustache, and now has managed it, though they are not very secure. She now turns round.*]

HAZEL [*in deep voice*]: Good morning, good morning.

CAROL [*with a scream of delight*]: Mr Pennyman! You know, Hazel, at the paper shop? The one who hates Lloyd George and wags his head very slowly all the time he tells you Lloyd George is no good. Do Mr Pennyman, Hazel. Go on.

HAZEL [*in her ordinary voice, incongruous*]: I couldn't, Carol. I've only seen him about twice. I never go to the paper shop.

[ALAN *looks in, grinning when he sees* HAZEL. *He is a shy, quiet, young man, in his earlier twenties, who can have a slight stammer. He is dressed, rather carelessly, in ordinary clothes.* CAROL *turns and sees him.*]

CAROL: Alan, come in, and don't let the others see. [*As he does.*] Isn't she *exactly* like Mr Pennyman at the paper shop, the one who hates Lloyd George?

ALAN [*grinning shyly*]: She is – a bit.

HAZEL [*in a fantastic deep voice*]: 'I hate Lloyd George.'

ALAN: No, he doesn't talk like that, Hazel.

CAROL: Not the least little bit. He says [*with a rather good imitation of a thick, semi-educated man's voice*]: 'I'll tell you what it is – Mish Conway – that there Lloyd George – they're going to be shorry they ever put 'im where they did – shee?'

ALAN [*grinning*]: Yes, that's him. Very good, Carol.

CAROL [*excitedly*]: I think I ought to be an actress. They said at school I was the best Shylock they'd ever had.

HAZEL [*taking off the nose and moustache*]: You can have these if you like Carol.

CAROL [*taking them*]: Are you sure you don't want them? I don't think you ought to dress up as a silly man because you're so pretty. Perhaps I could wear these and do Mr Pennyman. Couldn't we bring him into the third syllable somehow? Instead of a general. I think we've had enough generals.

ALAN: We have. Ask Kay to work in Mr Pennyman instead.

HAZEL: Kay ought to be here now, planning everything.

ALAN: She's coming in. Mother told me to tell you not to make too much of a mess in here.

CAROL: You *must* have a mess with charades. It's part of it.

HAZEL: And just wait till mother starts dressing up. She makes more mess than anybody. [*To* ALAN] I hope some of the old ones are going now. Are they?

ALAN: Yes.

HAZEL: It's much more fun without them. And mother daren't let herself go while they're still here. Tell Kay and Madge to come in, Alan.

ALAN: Right.

[*Goes out. The two girls begin turning the clothes over.* HAZEL *picks out some old-fashioned women's things and holds them up or against herself.*]

HAZEL: Look at these! Could you believe people *ever* wore such ridiculous things?

CAROL: I can just remember mother in that, can't you?

HAZEL: Of course I can, infant!

CAROL [*more soberly, looking at a man's old-fashioned shooting or Norfolk coat*]: That was Daddy's, wasn't it?

HAZEL: Yes. I believe he wore it – that very holiday.

CAROL: Perhaps we ought to put it away.

HAZEL: I don't think mother would mind – now.

CAROL: Yes she would. And I know I would. I don't want any-body to dress up and be funny in the coat father wore just before he was drowned. [*She has now folded the coat, and puts it on the window-seat. Then, as she returns*] I wonder if it's very horrible being drowned.

HAZEL [*impatiently*]: Oh, don't start that all over again, Carol. Don't you remember how you used to go on asking that – until mother was furious ?

CAROL: Yes – but I was only a kid then.

HAZEL: Well, now that you think you aren't a kid any longer, just stop it.

CAROL: It was the coat that made me remember. You see, Hazel, to be talking and laughing and all jolly, just the same as usual – and then, only half an hour afterwards – to be drowned – it's so horrible. It seemed awfully quick to us – but perhaps to him, there in the water, it may have seemed to take ages –

HAZEL: Oh, stop it, Carol. Just when we're having some fun. Why do you ?

CAROL: I don't know. But don't you often feel like that ? Just when everything is very jolly and exciting, I suddenly think of something awfully serious, sometimes horrible – like Dad drowning – or that little mad boy I once saw with the *huge head* – or that old man who walks in the Park with that great lump growing out of his face –

HAZEL [*stopping her ears*]: No, I'm not listening. I'm not listening.

CAROL: They pop up right in the middle of the jolly stuff, you know, Hazel. It happens to Kay, too. So it must be in the family – a bit.

> [*Enter* MADGE. *She is a year or two older than* HAZEL, *not so pretty, and a far more serious and responsible person. She has been to Girton, and already done a little teaching, and you feel all this in her brisk, decided, self-confident manner. She is, too, an earnest enthusiast.*]

MADGE: You found them ? Good. [*Looks over the things.*] I didn't think we'd have so many old things left. Mother ought to have given them away.

HAZEL: I'm glad she didn't. Besides, who'd have had them ?

MADGE: Lots of people would have been glad of them. You never realize, Hazel, how wretchedly poor most people are. It just doesn't occur to you, does it?

HAZEL [*not crossly*]: Don't be schoolmistressy, Madge.

CAROL [*who is trying things on, turning to point at* MADGE *impishly*]: Has Gerald Thornton arrived?

MADGE: As a matter of fact, he has – a few minutes ago.

CAROL [*triumphantly*]: I knew it. I could see it in your eye, Madge.

MADGE: Don't be absurd. He's brought another man with him, a new client of his, who's desperately anxious to know this family.

HAZEL: So he ought to be. Nice?

MADGE: Oh – a funny little man.

CAROL [*dancing about*]: That's just what we want – a funny little man. Perfect for charades.

MADGE: No, not that kind. In fact, he probably hasn't any sense of humour. Very shy, so far, and terrified of mother. Very much the little business man, I should think.

CAROL: Is he a profiteer – like the ones in *Punch*?

MADGE: He looks as if he might be, some day. His name's Ernest Beevers.

HAZEL [*giggling*]: What a silly name! I'm sorry for his wife, if he has one.

MADGE: I gather he hasn't. Look here, we ought to be starting. [*Enter* KAY, *whose twenty-first birthday party this is. An intelligent, sensitive girl, who need not be as pretty as* HAZEL. *She has a sheet of paper.*] Kay, we ought to be starting.

KAY: I know. The others are coming. [*Begins rooting among the things.*] Some good costumes here, ladies. Oo – look! [*She has fished out some absurd old-fashioned woman's cape, cloak or coat, and hat, and throws them on ridiculously, then stands apart and strikes absurd melodramatic attitude and speaks in false stilted tone.*] One moment, Lord What's-your-name. If I am discovered here, who will believe that my purpose in coming here tonight – visiting your – er – rooms – er unaccompanied – was solely to obtain the – er papers – that will enable me to clear – er – my husband's name, the name of a man who – er – has asked nothing better than the – er privilege of serving his country – and ours too, Lord Thingumtibob – one who – that is – to whom – [*In ordinary tone*] No, I'm getting all tied up. You know, we ought to have had a scene like that, all grand and dramatic and full of *papers*.

MADGE: Well, what *are* we to have?

HAZEL [*coolly*]: I've forgotten the word.

CAROL [*indignantly*]: Hazel, you're the *limit*! And we spent hours working it out!

HAZEL: I didn't. Only you and Kay, just because you fancy yourselves as budding authoresses and actresses.

KAY [*severely*]: The word – idiot! – is *Pussyfoot*. Puss. See. Foot. Then the whole word.

MADGE: I think four scenes are too many. And they'll easily guess it.

KAY: That doesn't matter. It makes them happy if they guess it.

CAROL [*rather solemnly*]: The great thing is – to *dress up*.

[*Enter* MRS CONWAY. *She is a charming woman in her middle forties, very nicely dressed, with an easy, vivacious manner.*]

MRS C: Now I'm ready – if you are. What a mess you're making. I knew you would. Let me see. [*Dives into the clothes, and scatters them far more wildly than the others have done. She finally fishes out a Spanish shawl and mantilla.*] Ah – here they are. Now I shall be a Spanish beauty. I know a song for it, too. [*Begins putting the Spanish things on.*]

HAZEL [*to* KAY]: What did I tell you?

MRS C [*who is specially fond of* HAZEL]: What did you tell her, darling?

HAZEL: I told Kay, whatever she arranged, you'd insist on doing your Spanish turn.

MRS C: Well, why not?

KAY: It doesn't come into the scenes I'd thought of, that's all.

MRS C [*busy with her costume*]: Oh – you can easily arrange that, dear – you're so clever. I've just been telling Dr Halliday and his niece how clever you are. They seemed surprised, I can't imagine why.

HAZEL: It's the first time I've seen Monica Halliday out of her land girl costume. I'm surprised she didn't turn up tonight in her trousers and leggings.

KAY: She looks quite queer out of them, doesn't she? Rather like a female impersonator.

MADGE: Oh, come on, Kay. What do we do?

KAY: The first scene, *Puss*, is an old lady who's lost her cat. She's really a kind of witch.

CAROL [*happily*]: I'm to be the old lady.

[CAROL *begins finding suitable clothes – an old shawl, etc. – and some white hair – for the old lady. And during following dialogue, converts herself into a very creditable imitation.*]

KAY: Mother, you and Hazel are her two daughters who are visiting her –

HAZEL: I know my bit. I keep saying 'I always hated that terrible cat of yours, Mother.' What can I wear ? [*Pokes about.*]

MRS C [*now Spanish*]: Well, that's all right, dear. I'll be the Spanish daughter, you see.

KAY [*resignedly*]: She didn't have a Spanish daughter, but I suppose it doesn't matter.

MRS C: Not in the least. Nobody cares. And then I think I'd better not appear in the others, because I suppose you'll be wanting me to sing afterwards.

KAY: Of course. But I'd put you down for two more. Madge and Joan Helford will have to do those.

MRS C: What a pity Robin isn't here! You know, Madge, he wrote and said he might be demobbed any day now, and it seems such a shame just to miss Kay's party. Robin loves parties. He's like me. Your father never cared for them much. Suddenly, right in the middle, just when everything was getting along, he'd want to be quiet – and take me into a corner and ask me how much longer people were staying – just when they were beginning to enjoy themselves. I never could understand that.

KAY: I can. I've often felt like that.

MRS C: But why, dear, why ? It isn't sensible. If you're having a party, you're having a party.

KAY [*earnestly*]: Yes, it isn't that. And it isn't that you suddenly dislike the people. But you feel – at least I do, and I suppose that's what father felt too – you feel, quite suddenly, that it isn't *real* enough – and you want something to be *real*. Do you see, Mother ?

MRS C: No I don't, my dear. It sounds a little morbid to me. But your father could be quite morbid sometimes – you mightn't think so, but he could – and I suppose you take after him.

KAY [*very gravely*]: Do you think that sometimes, in a mysterious sort of way, he *knew*?

MRS C [*not too attentive to this*]: Knew *what*, dear? Look at Hazel, doesn't she look rather sweet? I can remember where I first wore those things. Absurd! Knew *what*?

KAY: Knew what was going to happen to him. You know, Alan said that some of the men he knew who were killed in the trenches seemed to know sometimes that they were going to be killed, as if a kind of shadow fell over them. Just as if – now and then – we could see round the corner – into the future.

MRS C [*easily*]: You have the most extraordinary ideas. You must try and put some of them into your book. Are you happy, darling?

KAY: Yes, Mother. Very happy.

MRS C: That's all right then. I want you to have a lovely birthday. I feel we all can be happy again, now that the horrible war's all over and people are sensible again, and Robin and Alan are quite safe. I forgot to ask – did Robin send you anything, Kay?

KAY: No. I didn't expect him to.

MRS C: Oh – but that isn't like Robin, you know, Kay. He's a most generous boy, much too generous really. Now that may mean he thinks he's coming home very soon.

[*Enter* ALAN *with* JOAN HELFORD, *who is* HAZEL'*s friend and the same age, pretty and rather foolish.*]

KAY: Alan, tell them we're beginning – and it's three syllables.

[ALAN *goes.*]

JOAN: I think you all look marvellous. I'm rotten at this, you know, Kay. Don't say I didn't warn you.

KAY: Now then, Carol, you start. And remember, only say 'Puss' once. Don't you two say it – only Carol. [ALAN *returns.* CAROL *goes out – and there can be the sound of distant laughing and clapping.*] Good old Carol. Now then – you two. [*Almost pushes them off.*] Now the next syllable is S.Y. So I thought it wouldn't be cheating too badly if we called that 'sy'. Y'know, Cockney – 'I sy, Bert.' So this is an East End scene. Madge, you're the old mother.

MADGE [*who has started putting on very droll shabby clothes*]: Yes, I remembered.

ALAN: What am I? I forget.

KAY: You're Bert. Just put something silly on. Is there anything here you can wear, Joan?

[*During following dialogue, they all dress up.*]

JOAN: I was in London last week, staying with my uncle, and we went to the theatre *three times*. We saw *Tilly of Bloomsbury* and *Cinderella Man* and *Kissing Time*. I liked *Cinderella Man* best – Owen Nares, y'know. I thought Robin was coming home soon.

KAY: He is.

JOAN: He's an officer, isn't he? You weren't an officer, were you, Alan?

ALAN: No, I was a lance-corporal. One stripe, y'know. Nothing at all.

JOAN: Didn't you want to be anything better than that?

ALAN: No.

KAY: Alan has no ambition at all. Have you, my pet?

ALAN [*simply*]: Not much.

JOAN: If I were a man, I'd want to be very important. What are you doing now, Alan? Somebody said you were at the Town Hall.

ALAN: I am. In the Rate Office. Just a clerk, y'know.

JOAN: Isn't it dull?

ALAN: Yes.

KAY: Alan never minds being dull. I believe he has tremendous long adventures inside his head that nobody knows anything about.

JOAN: Hazel says you've started to write another novel, Kay. Have you?

KAY [*rather curtly*]: Yes.

JOAN: I don't know how you can – I mean, I think I'd be all right once I'd started properly – but I can't see how you start. What did you do with the last one?

KAY: Burnt it.

JOAN: Why?

KAY: It was putrid.

JOAN: But wasn't that an awful waste of time?

KAY: Yes, I suppose so.

ALAN: Still, look at the time you and I waste, Joan.

JOAN: Oh – no – I'm always doing *something*. Even though I

haven't to go to the canteen any more, I'm always busy. [MADGE, *who has withdrawn herself a little, now laughs.*] Why do you laugh, Madge?

MADGE: Can't a girl laugh?

JOAN [*humbly*]: You always did laugh at me, Madge. I suppose because I'm not clever, like you.

> [HAZEL *returns, letting in noise – laughing and clapping – from outside.*]

HAZEL: Well, you can imagine what happened. Mother let herself go, and of course it became all Spanish. I don't believe they'll ever remember hearing 'puss' mentioned. What are you supposed to be, Joan?

JOAN [*hopefully*]: A sort of Coster girl.

HAZEL: You look a sort of general mess. Oh – [*to* KAY] Carol wants to do Mr Pennyman at the paper shop instead of a general for the third syllable.

KAY: How can she? If it's soldiers drilling, you can't have Mr Pennyman. Unless we make him another soldier – and get Gerald Thornton or somebody to be a general.

> [CAROL *returns, very hot and flushed, and begins taking off her old woman's disguise.*]

CAROL: Mother's still on. Golly! – it's baking being an old witch.

KAY: Do you insist on being Mr Pennyman in the third syllable?

CAROL [*brightening up*]: Oo – I'd forgotten that. Yes, please let me do Mr Pennyman, Kay – my lamb, my love, my precious –

KAY: All right. But he'll have to be a soldier. Just joined up, you see.

> [*Enter* MRS C *very grand, flushed, triumphant. She is carrying a glass of claret cup.*]

MRS C: Well – really – that was *very* silly – but they seemed to enjoy it, and that's the great thing. I thought you were very good, Carol. [*To* KAY] Carol was sweet, Kay. Now don't ask me to do any more of this, because really I mustn't, especially if you want me to sing afterwards. So leave me out, Kay. [*Begins to sip cup.*]

KAY: All right. Now come on. [*Begins shepherding her players,* MADGE, ALAN, JOAN.]

JOAN: Honestly, Kay, I'll be *awful*.

KAY: It doesn't matter. You've nothing to do. Now then – Madge.

MADGE [*loudly, in laborious imitation of Cockney mother*]: Nah then, Bert. End yew, Dy-sy. Cem along or we'll be lite. [*Leads the way off, followed by other three.*]

HAZEL: How on earth did you get that claret cup, Mother?

MRS C [*complacently*]: Got Gerald Thornton to hand it to me – and it rounded off my little scene nicely. I don't want any more. Would you like it?

[HAZEL *takes it, and sips while removing things. They are all removing things.*]

CAROL: Mother, you weren't going to be an *actress*, were you – just a singer?

MRS C: I don't know what you mean by *just* a singer. I was a singer certainly. But I did some acting too. When the Newlingham Amateur Operatic first did *Merrie England*, I played Bess. And I'd had all you children then. *You* were only about two, Carol.

HAZEL: Mother, Joan *did* stay in London last week, and she went to three theatres.

MRS C: She has relatives there, and we haven't. That makes a great difference.

HAZEL: Aren't we *ever* going?

MRS C: Yes, of course. Perhaps Robin will take us – I mean, just you and me – when he comes back.

CAROL [*solemnly*]: It says in the paper this morning that We Must All Get On With Our Jobs. This Mere Rush For Amusement has gone on long enough now. There's Work Waiting To Be Done.

HAZEL [*indignantly*]: A fat lot of rushing for amusement we've done, haven't we? I think that's frightfully unfair and idiotic. Just when we *might* have some fun, after washing up in canteens and hospitals and queueing for foul food, with *nobody* about at all, they go and say we've had enough amusement and must get on with our jobs. What jobs?

CAROL: Rebuilding a shattered world. It said that too.

MRS C [*half lightly, half not, to* HAZEL]: Your job will be to find a very nice young man and marry him. And *that* oughtn't to be difficult – for you.

CAROL [*now getting into trousers to play Mr Pennyman*]: Hurry up, Hazel, and then I can be a bridesmaid. I believe you're my *only* chance. Kay says she won't get married for *ages*, if ever, because her Writing – Her Work – must come first.

MRS C: That's nonsense, my dear. When the proper young man comes along, she'll forget about her writing.

CAROL: I don't believe she will, Mother. And anyhow, she won't have bridesmaids. And if Madge ever marries, I know it will be to some kind of Socialist in a tweed suit, who'll insist on being married in a Register Office –

HAZEL: I'm not so sure about that. I've had my eye on Madge lately.

CAROL [*now as Mr Pennyman*]: And I've 'ad my eye on Lloyd George. An' what for, Mish Conway? Bee-corsh yew can't trusht that little Welshman. Yew watch 'im, that'sh all I shay –

MRS C: That's *very* good, dear. You're rather like Mr Worsnop – do you remember him – the cashier at the works? Every New Year's Eve, your father used to bring Mr Worsnop here, after they'd done all the books at the office, and used to give him some port. And when I went in, Mr Worsnop always stood and held his glass like this [*she holds glass close to herself in a rather cringing attitude*] and said 'My respects, Mrs Conway, my deepest respects.' And I always wanted to laugh. He's retired now, and gone to live in South Devon.

[*After slight pause*, MADGE, *still in absurd old Costerwoman disguise, enters with* GERALD THORNTON. *He is in his early thirties, a solicitor and son of a solicitor, and is fairly tall and good-looking, and carefully dressed. He has a pleasant, man-of-the-world air, very consciously cultivated.* MADGE *is arguing hotly, with all the fiery slapdash of enthusiastic youth.*]

MADGE: But what the miners want and ask for is simply nationalization. They say, if coal is as important as you say it is, then the mines shouldn't be in the hands of private owners any longer. Nationalize them, they say. That's the fairest thing.

GERALD: All right. But supposing we don't want them nationalized. What then? Some of us have seen enough of Government mismanagement already.

MRS C: Quite so, Gerald. Everybody knows how ridiculous they were. Sending bags of sand to Egypt!

MADGE [*hotly*]: I don't believe half those stories. Besides they had to improvise everything in a hurry. And anyhow it wasn't a *Socialist* Government.

GERALD [*mildly*]: But you don't know they'd be any better. They might be worse – less experience.

MADGE [*same tone*]: Oh – I know that *experience*! We're always having that flung in our faces. When all that's wanted is a little intelligence – and enthusiasm – and – and decency.

GERALD [*to* MRS C *rather as one adult to another at children's party*]: I've been conscripted for the next scene. To be a general or something.

HAZEL: We haven't fancy dress for you.

GERALD: Good!

MRS C: I really mustn't neglect them any longer, must I? And most of them will be going soon. Then we can have a nice cosy little party of our own. [*Goes out.*]

CAROL [*to* GERALD]: Well, you must look different somehow, you know. You could turn your coat inside out.

GERALD: I don't think that would be very effective.

CAROL [*impatiently*]: Wear an overcoat then. Oh – and – [*Fishes out a large false moustache and gives it to him.*] Put this on. That's a *very* good one.

[GERALD *takes and looks at it dubiously.* JOAN *rushes in, more animated now her ordeal is over.*]

JOAN [*excitedly, girlish*]: Hazel, d'you know who's here? You'll never guess!

HAZEL: Who?

JOAN [*ignoring this*]: That *awful* little man who always stares at you – the one who followed us once all round the Park –

HAZEL: He's *not*!

JOAN: He is, I tell you. I distinctly saw him, standing at the side, near the door.

GERALD: This sounds like my friend Beevers.

HAZEL: Do you mean to say the man you brought is *that* awful little man? Well, you're the absolute limit, Gerald Thornton! He's a *dreadful* little creature. Every time I go out, he's somewhere about, staring and staring at me. And now you bring him here!

GERALD [*not worried by this outburst*]: Oh – he's not so bad. He insisted on my bringing him, and your mother said it was all right. You shouldn't be so devastating, Hazel.

JOAN [*giggly*]: I told you he must be mad about you, Hazel.

HAZEL [*the haughty beauty now*]: I swear I won't speak to him. He just would butt in like this!

CAROL: Why shouldn't he, poor little manny?

HAZEL: Shut up, Carol, you don't know anything about him.

[*Enter* KAY *and* ALAN.]

KAY: That wasn't much good. The Costers were a wash-out. Oh – that's all right, Carol. Now you're a general, Gerald, and the others are recruits. Hurry up, Alan, and put something different on. Gerald, you're inspecting them – you know, make up something silly – and then say to one of them: 'Look at your *foot*, my man.' Anyhow, bring in 'foot'.

GERALD: Have I only two recruits, Carol and Alan?

KAY: No, mother's sending in another man. They aren't guessing anything yet, but that's simply because it's all such a muddle. I don't think I like charades as much as I used to do. Dad was marvellous at them. [*To* GERALD] He always did very fat men. You'd better be a fat general. And you can be fat, too, Alan.

[*Piano can be heard playing softly off. As the men are stuffing cushions under coats, and* JOAN *and* KAY *and* MADGE *are finishing removing their last things,* ERNEST BEEVERS *enters slowly and shyly. He is a little man, about thirty, still socially shy and awkward, chiefly because his social background is rather lower in the scale than that of the* CONWAYS, *but there is a suggestion of growing force and self-confidence in him. He is obviously attracted towards the whole family, but completely fascinated by* HAZEL.]

ERNEST [*shyly, awkwardly*]: Oh – er – Mrs Conway told me to come in here.

KAY: Yes, of course. You've to be one of the recruits in this next bit.

ERNEST: I'm – not much good – at this sort of thing – you know –

KAY: It doesn't matter. Just be silly.

GERALD: Oh – Beevers – sorry! I'd better introduce you. [*Carries off slightly awkward situation with determined light touch.*] This – is Mr Ernest Beevers, a rather recent arrival in our – er – progressive city. Now all these are Conways, except this young lady – Miss Joan Helford –

ERNEST [*seriously*]: How d'you do?

JOAN [*faintly giggly*]: How d'you do?

GERALD: This is Kay, who decided to be twenty-one today so that we could have this party –

ERNEST: Many happy returns.

KAY [*nicely*]: Thank you.

GERALD: She's the literary genius of this distinguished family. Over there is Madge, who's been to Girton and will try to convert you to Socialism.

ERNEST: I'm afraid she won't succeed.

GERALD: This strange-looking middle-aged person is young Carol –

CAROL [*nicely*]: Hello!

ERNEST [*grateful for this, smiling*]: Hello!

GERALD: Alan I think you've met already. [*Teasing*] Oh – and let me see – yes, this is Hazel. She creates such havoc that when the Leicesters were stationed here the Colonel wrote and asked her to stay indoors when they had route marches.

ERNEST [*solemnly*]: How d'you do?

HAZEL [*crossly*]: Don't be idiotic, Gerald. [*Very quickly to* ERNEST] How d'you do?

[*Faint giggle from* JOAN.]

ALAN [*to* ERNEST]: You'd better do something funny to yourself. Is there anything here you'd like?

[ERNEST *pokes about in the things, while* HAZEL *looks disdainfully on and* JOAN *wants to giggle.* ERNEST *is very clumsy now.*]

KAY: Carol and Alan, you start. You're recruits. Carol can do bits of Mr Pennyman to fill in.

[CAROL, *followed by* ALAN, *goes out.* GERALD *is waiting for* BEEVERS. KAY *goes out.*]

JOAN: What did your mother say, Hazel, about removing?

HAZEL: Oh, of course, she won't think of it. And she's been offered five thousand pounds – *five thousand* – for this house!

ERNEST [*the business man*]: Tell her to take it. I'll bet in ten years she couldn't get two thousand. It's only this temporary shortage that's forced prices of property up. You'll see 'em come down with a bang yet.

HAZEL [*snubbing him*]: But she adores being here, of course, and so it's hopeless.

[ERNEST *realizes he has been snubbed. He has now made a few ridiculous changes in his clothes. He looks hard at* HAZEL, *who will not return his look.* JOAN *still giggly.*]

ERNEST [*with dignity which ill assorts with his appearance*]: If I spoke out of my turn, I'm sorry.

KAY [*looking in*]: Hurry up, Mr Beevers.

ERNEST [*hurrying forward*]: I'm no good at this, you know, Miss Conway, and it's no use pretending I am –

[*But she rushes him and* GERALD *off, and follows them.* JOAN *bursts into a peal of laughter.*]

HAZEL [*indignantly*]: I don't think it's funny, Joan. I'm *furious.*

JOAN [*between gurgles and gasps*]: He – looked – so – silly.

[HAZEL *begins laughing, too, and they laugh together, rocking round.*]

HAZEL [*hardly distinguishable*]: Did you hear him? 'If I spoke out of my turn, I'm sorry.'

JOAN [*hardly distinguishable*]: We ought to have said 'Pleased to meet you,' and then he'd have said 'Granted.'

[KAY *comes back, and looks rather severely at these two.*]

KAY [*severely*]: I think you were rather beastly to that little man.

[*They still laugh, and as she looks at them* KAY *begins to laugh too. They all laugh.*]

HAZEL [*coming to*]: Oh – dear! Oh – dear! But that's the little man I told you about, Kay, who always stared, and once followed us round.

KAY: Well, now he'll be able to raise his little hat.

HAZEL [*vehemently*]: And that's all he'll jolly well get out of this, I'll tell you. And I think Gerald Thornton had the cheek of the devil to bring him here. Just because he's a new client.

JOAN [*still giggly*]: You don't think you'll marry him then, Hazel?

HAZEL: Ugh! I'd just as soon marry a – a ferret.

KAY [*rather loftily*]: I don't believe you two ever think or talk about anything but clothes and going to London and young men and marriage.

HAZEL [*not too rudely*]: Oh, don't you start being so grand! [*Quotes dramatically*] The Garden of Stars.

KAY [*hastily*]: Now, shut up, Hazel!

HAZEL [*to* JOAN]: That's what she called the last novel she started. *The Garden of Stars.* And there were so many bits of paper with the opening words on that I know them off by heart.

[*Quotes dramatically. As soon as she begins* KAY *makes a rush at her, but she dodges, still quoting.*] 'Marion went out into the still smooth night. There was no moon but already – already – the sky was silver-dusted with stars. She passed through the rose garden, the dying scent of the roses meeting the grey moths – '

KAY [*shouting her down*]: I know it's all wrong, but I tore it up, didn't I ?

HAZEL [*mildly*]: Yes, my duck. And then you cried.

KAY [*fiercely*]: I've just begun a real one. With some *guts* in it. You'll see.

HAZEL: I'll bet it's about a girl who lives in a town just like Newlingham.

KAY [*still fierce*]: Well, why shouldn't it be ? You wait, that's all.
[GERALD, *plus false moustache,* ALAN *and* ERNEST *in their absurd get-up come in slowly and solemnly.*]

GERALD: That's true, Alan.

ERNEST [*seriously*]: But they can't expect people to behave differently when they've still got their war restrictions on everything. They can't have it both ways.

GERALD: Well, there's still a lot of profiteering.

ERNEST: You've got to let business find its own level. The more interference the worse it is.

ALAN: The worse for everybody ?

ERNEST [*decidedly*]: Yes.

ALAN [*stoutly, for him*]: I doubt it.

ERNEST [*not too unpleasantly*]: You're working in the Town Hall, aren't you ? Well, you can't learn much about these things there, y'know.

KAY [*with tremendous irony*]: I say! You three must have been terribly good in the charade, weren't you ?

ALAN: No, we weren't very amusing.

CAROL [*who has just entered*]: Oh – they were awful. No, you weren't *too* bad, Mr Beevers, especially for a man who was doing a charade in a strange house.

ERNEST: Now I call that handsome, Miss Carol.

KAY [*briskly*]: The whole word now. *Pussyfoot.* It's supposed to be a party in America, and we can't have anything to drink. We won't bother dressing up for this. Just some good *acting*. I'll say the word. Joan, tell Madge, she's in this. Just the girls, for the grand finale.

[JOAN *goes.*]

GERALD [*now normal again*]: So we're sacked?

KAY: Yes. No good.

GERALD: Then we can give ourselves a drink. We've earned a drink. Any dancing afterwards?

KAY: There might be, after mother's done her singing.

GERALD: Do you dance, Beevers?

ERNEST: No, never had time for it.

HAZEL [*significantly, in loud clear tone*]: Yes, we *must* have some dancing, Gerald.

[ERNEST *looks hard at her. She gives him a wide innocent stare of complete indifference. He nods, turns and goes.* GERALD, *after distributing a smile or two, follows him.* CAROL *is busy getting out of her Mr Pennyman disguise.*]

CAROL [*excitedly*]: Kay, we could have done the Prince of Wales in America for this last scene. Why didn't we think of it? You could be the Prince of Wales, and you could fall in love with Hazel, who could turn out to be Pussyfoot's daughter.

KAY [*laughing*]: Mother'd be shocked. And so would some of the others.

CAROL: I'd hate to be a Prince of Wales, wouldn't you?

HAZEL [*with decision*]: I'd *love* it.

CAROL: Old Mrs Ferguson – you know, the one with the queer eye – the rather frightening one – told me there was an old prophecy that when King David came to the throne of Britain everything would be *wonderful.*

[*Sound off of a loud shout, then confused voices and laughter.*]

KAY: What's that?

HAZEL [*excitedly*]: It's Robin.

[*They all look up with eager interest.* HAZEL *moves, but before she gets very far,* ROBIN *dashes in. He is twenty-three, and a rather dashing, good-looking young man in the uniform of an RAF officer. He is in tremendous spirits. He carries a small package.*]

ROBIN [*loudly*]: Hello, kids! Hazel! [*Kisses her.*] Kay, many happies! [*Kisses her.*] Carol, my old hearty! [*Kisses her.*] Gosh! I've had a dash to get here in time. Did half the journey on one of our lorries. And I didn't forget the occasion, Kay. What about that ? [*Throws her the parcel, which she opens and finds is a silk scarf.*] All right, isn't it ?

KAY [*gratefully*]: It's lovely, Robin. Lovely, lovely!

ROBIN: That's the stuff to give 'em. And I've finished. Out! Demobbed at last!

HAZEL: Oo – grand! Have you seen mother ?

ROBIN: Of course I have, you chump. You ought to have seen her face when I told her I was now a civilian again. Golly! we'll have some fun now, won't we ?

KAY: Lots and lots.

CAROL: Have you seen Alan ?

ROBIN: Just for a second. Still the solemn old bird, isn't he ?

CAROL [*very young and solemn*]: In my opinion, Alan is a very wonderful person.

ROBIN [*rattling on*]: I know. You always thought that, didn't you ? Can't quite see it myself, but I'm very fond of the old crawler. How's the writing, Kay ?

KAY: I'm still trying – and learning.

ROBIN: That's the stuff. We'll show 'em. This is where the Conways really begin. How many young men, Hazel ?

HAZEL [*calmly*]: Nobody to speak of.

CAROL: She'd worked her way up to Colonels, hadn't you, Haze ?

KAY [*affectionately*]: Now that it's civilians, she's having to change her technique – and she's a bit uncertain yet.

ROBIN: All jealousy that, isn't it, Hazel ? [MRS C *appears, carrying a tray laden with sandwiches, cake, etc., and some beer.*] A-ha, here we are! [*Rushes to take the tray from her.* MRS C *is very happy now.*]

MRS C [*beaming*]: Isn't this nice! Now we're *all* here. I knew somehow you were on your way, Robin, even though you didn't tell us – you naughty boy.

ROBIN: Couldn't, Mother, honestly. Only wangled it at the last minute.

MRS C [*to* KAY]: Finish your charade now, dear.

ROBIN: Charade! Can I be in this ? I used to be an ace at charades.

MRS C: No, dear, they're just finishing. We can have as many charades as we want now you're home for good. Have something to eat and talk to me while they're doing the last bit.

KAY [*to* HAZEL *and* CAROL]: Come on, you two. We can collect

Madge out there. Remember, it's an American party, and we can't have anything to drink, and then, after kicking up a row, you ask who's giving the party, and then I'll say *Pussyfoot*.

[*She is going off and the others following her as she is saying this.* MRS C *hastily puts some of the old clothes together, while* ROBIN *settles down to the tray.* MRS C *then comes and watches him eat and drink with maternal delight. Both are happy and relaxed, at ease with each other.*]

MRS C: Is there anything you want there, Robin?

ROBIN [*mouth full*]: Yes thanks, Mother. Gosh, you don't know what it feels like to be out at last!

MRS C: I do, you silly boy. What do you think I feel, to have you back at last – for good?

ROBIN: I must get some clothes.

MRS C: Yes, some really nice ones. Though it's a pity you can't keep on wearing that uniform. You look so smart in it. Poor Alan – he was only a corporal or something, y'know, and had the most hideous uniform, nothing seemed to fit him – Alan never looked *right* in the Army.

ROBIN: He's got a piffling sort of job at the Town Hall, hasn't he?

MRS C: Yes. He seems to like it, though. And perhaps he'll find something better later on.

ROBIN [*eagerly*]: I've got all sorts of plans, y'know, Mother. We've all been talking things over in the mess. One of our chaps knows Jimmy White – you know, *the* Jimmy White – you've heard of him – and he thinks he can wangle me an introduction to him. My idea is something in the car and motor-bike line. I understand 'em, and I've heard people are buying like mad. And I have my gratuity, you know.

MRS C: Yes, dear, we'll have to talk about all that. There's plenty of time now, thank goodness! Don't you think all the girls are looking well?

ROBIN [*eating and drinking away*]: Yes, first-rate, especially Hazel.

MRS C: Oh – of course Hazel's the one everybody notices. You ought to have seen the young men. And Kay – twenty-one – I can hardly believe it – but she's *very* grown-up and serious now – I don't know whether she'll make anything out of this writing of hers – but she is trying very hard – don't tease her too much, dear, she doesn't like it –

ROBIN: I haven't been teasing her.

MRS C: No, but Hazel does sometimes – and I know what you children are. Madge has been teaching, you know, but she's trying for a much better school.

ROBIN [*indifferently*]: Good old Madge. [*With far more interest*] I think I ought to go up to town for my clothes, Mother. You can't get anything really decent in Newlingham, and if I'm going to start selling cars I've got to look like somebody who knows a good suit when he sees one. Lord! – it's grand to be back again, and not just on a filthy little leave. [*Breaks off, as he looks at her, standing quite close to him.*] Here, Mother – steady! – nothing to cry about now.

MRS C [*through her tears, smiling*]: I know. That's why. You see, Robin – losing your father, then the war coming – taking you – I'm not used to happiness. I've forgotten about it. It's upsetting! And Robin, now you are back – don't go rushing off again, *please*! Don't leave us – not for years and years. Let's all be cosy together and happy again, shall we ?

[JOAN *enters, then stands awkwardly as she sees them together.* MRS C *turns and sees her. So does* ROBIN, *and his face lights up.* MRS C *sees* ROBIN'S *face, then looks again at* JOAN. *This should be played for as long as it will stand.*]

JOAN [*rather nervously*]: Oh – Mrs Conway – they've finished the charade – and some people are going – and Madge asked me to tell you they're expecting you to sing something.

MRS C: Why didn't she come herself ?

JOAN [*rather faltering*]: She and Kay and Carol began handing people sandwiches and things as soon as they finished the charade.

ROBIN [*rising*]: Hello, Joan!

JOAN [*coming forward, thrilled*]: Hello, Robin! Is it – nice to be back again ?

ROBIN [*smiling, rather significantly*]: Yes, of course.

MRS C [*rather irritably*]: Really this room's a dreadful mess. I knew it would be. Hazel and Carol brought all these things down here. Joan, go and tell them they must take these things upstairs at once. I can't have this room looking like an old clothes' place. Perhaps you'd like to help them, dear.

JOAN: Yes – rather.

[*Smiles at* ROBIN *and goes.* MRS C *turns and looks at him. He smiles at her. She has to smile back.*]

ROBIN: You're looking very artful, Mother.

MRS C: Am I? I'm not feeling very artful. [*Carefully just.*] Joan's grown up to be a very nice-looking girl, hasn't she?

ROBIN [*smiling*]: Quite.

MRS C [*same careful tone*]: And I think she's got a pleasant easy disposition. Not very clever or go-ahead or anything like that. But a thoroughly *nice* girl.

ROBIN [*not eagerly*]: Yes, I'll bet she is.

[HAZEL *sails in, to begin packing up the things. This should be done as quickly as possible.*]

HAZEL: They're all panting for a song, Mother. They don't even mind if it's German.

MRS C: Thank goodness, I was never so stupid as to stop singing German songs. What have Schubert and Schumann to do with Hindenburg and the Kaiser?

[CAROL *comes in, followed by* JOAN. HAZEL *goes with her armful.* ROBIN *helps* JOAN *to collect her lot.* MRS C *stands rather withdrawn from them.*]

CAROL [*loudly and cheerfully as she collects her stuff*]: Everybody guessed the charade, just because it was Pussyfoot – though they hadn't guessed *any* of the syllables. All except Mr James, who thought it was *Kinema*. [*Hard 'k'.*] When they say 'Kinema' I can't believe I've ever been to one. It sounds like some other kind of place. Robin, have you seen William S. Hart?

ROBIN: Yes.

CAROL [*pausing with her armful, very solemnly*]: I *love* William S. Hart. I wonder what 'S.' stands for.

ROBIN: Sidney.

CAROL [*turning in horror*]: Robin, it *doesn't*! [*Goes out.*]

[JOAN *now has the remainder of the things.*]

MRS C: Come along, Robin, I may want you and Alan to move the piano for me.

ROBIN: Righto.

[*They all go out. Nearly all the things have been cleared now. Sounds of the party – vague applause and laughter – off. Then* KAY *enters quickly and eagerly, and finds a bit of paper and*] *pencil in some convenient drawer or cupboard. She frowns and thinks, then makes some rapid notes, not sitting down but standing against table or bookshelf. A few chords and runs can be heard from the piano.* CAROL *looks in, to remove the last of the charade things.*]

CAROL [*with awe, very charming*]: Kay, have you suddenly been inspired?

KAY [*looking up, very serious*]: No, not really. But I'm bursting with all kinds of feelings and thoughts and impressions – you know –

CAROL [*coming close to her favourite sister*]: Oh – yes – so am I. Millions and millions. I couldn't possibly *begin* to write them.

KAY [*that eager young author*]: No, but in my novel, a girl goes to a party – you see – and there are some things I've been feeling – very subtle things – that I *know* she'd feel – and I want my novel to be very real this time – so I had to scribble them down –

CAROL: Will you tell me them afterwards?

KAY: Yes.

CAROL: Bedroom?

KAY: Yes, if you're not too sleepy.

CAROL: I couldn't be. [*She pauses happily, one earnest young creature staring at the other. And now we can just hear* MRS CONWAY *in the drawing-room beginning to sing Schumann's 'Der Nussbaum'.* CAROL *is now very solemn, a little awed.*] Kay, I think you're *wonderful*.

KAY [*awed herself*]: I think *life's* wonderful.

CAROL: Both of you are.

[CAROL *goes out, and now we can hear the lovely rippling Schumann better than before.* KAY *writes for another moment, then moved by both the music and the sudden ecstasy of creation, she puts down pencil and paper, drifts over to the switch and turns out the lights. The room is not in darkness because light is coming in from the hall.* KAY *goes to the window and opens the curtains, so that when she sits on the window-seat, her head is silvered in moonlight. Very still, she listens to the music, and seems to stare not at but into something, and as the song goes soaring away, the curtain creeps down.*]

END OF ACT ONE

ACT TWO

When the curtain rises, for a moment we think nothing has happened since it came down, for there is the light coming in from the hall, and there is KAY sitting on the window-seat. But then ALAN comes in and switches on the central light, and we see that a great deal must have happened. It is the same room, but it has a different wall-paper, the furniture has been changed round, the pictures and books are not altogether the same as before. We notice a wireless set. The general effect is harder and rather brighter than it was during the party in 1919, and we guess at once that this is present day [1937]. KAY and ALAN are not quite the same, after nearly twenty years. KAY has a rather hard, efficient, well-groomed look, that of a woman of forty who has earned her own living for years. ALAN, in his middle forties, is shabbier than he was before – his coat does not match the rest of his suit and really will not do – but he is still the rather shy, awkward, lovable fellow, only now there is about him a certain poise, an inward certainty and serenity, missing from all the others we shall see now.

ALAN [*quietly*]: Well – Kay.
KAY [*happily*]: Alan!
   [*She jumps up and kisses him. Then they look at one another, smiling a little. He rubs his hands in embarrassment, as he always did.*]
ALAN: I'm glad you could come. It was the only thing about this business that didn't make me hate the thought of it – the chance *you* might be able to come. But mother says you're not staying the night.
KAY: I can't, Alan. I must get back to London tonight.
ALAN: Work?
KAY: Yes. I have to go to Southampton in the morning – to write a nice little piece about the newest little film star.
ALAN: Do you often have to do that?
KAY: Yes, Alan, quite often. There are an awful lot of film stars and they're always arriving at Southampton, except when they arrive at Plymouth – damn their eyes! And all the women

readers of the *Daily Courier* like to read a bright half-column about their glamorous favourites.

ALAN [*thoughtfully*]: They look very nice – but all rather alike.

KAY [*decidedly*]: They *are* all rather alike – and so are my bright interviews with 'em. In fact, sometimes I feel we're all just going round and round, like poor old circus ponies.

ALAN [*after a pause*]: Are you writing another novel?

KAY [*very quietly*]: No, my dear, I'm not. [*Pauses, then gives short laugh.*] I tell myself too many people are writing novels.

ALAN: Well, it does look like that – sometimes.

KAY: Yes. But that's not the real reason. I still feel mine wouldn't be like theirs – anyhow, not the next, even if the last was. But – as things are – I just can't . . .

ALAN [*after a pause*]: The last time you wrote, Kay – I mean to me – you sounded rather unhappy, I thought.

KAY [*with self-reproach*]: I was. I suppose that's why I suddenly remembered you – and wrote. Not very flattering – to you – is it?

ALAN [*with cheerful modesty*]: In a way it is, y'know. Yes, Kay, I'd take that as a compliment.

KAY [*with a sudden burst of affection*]: Alan! And I loathe that coat you're wearing. It doesn't match the rest of you, does it?

ALAN [*stammering, apologetic*]: No – well, you see – I just wear it in the house – an old coat – just as a house coat – it saves my other one – I oughtn't to have put it on tonight. Just habit, y'know. I'll change it before the others come. . . . Why were you so unhappy then – the last time you wrote?

KAY [*in broken painful phrases*]: Something – that was always ending – really did come to an end just then. It had lasted ten years – off and on – and eating more of one's life away when it was off than when it was on. He was married. There were children. It was the usual nasty muddle. [*Breaks off.*] Alan, you don't know what day it is today?

ALAN [*chuckling*]: But I do, I do. And, of course, Mother did, too. Look! [*He pulls small package out of his pocket and holds it out to her.*]

KAY [*after taking it and kissing him*]: Alan, you're an angel! I never thought I'd have another single birthday present. And you know how old I am now? Forty. *Forty!*

ALAN [*smiling*]: I'm forty-four. And it's all right, y'know. You'll like it. [*Front door bell rings.*] Look at your present. I hope it's all right. [*Goes to front door.*]

   [KAY *hastily unwraps her parcel and takes out a hideous cheap little handbag. She looks at it and does not know whether to laugh or cry over the thing. Meanwhile* ALAN *has brought in* JOAN, *now Joan Conway, for she married* ROBIN. *Time has not been very kind to her. She is now a rather sloppy, querulous woman of forty-one. Her voice has a very irritating quality.*]

JOAN: Hello, Kay. I didn't think you'd manage to be here – you hardly ever do come to Newlingham now, do you? And I must say I don't blame you. [*Breaks off because she notices the awful handbag.*] Oh – what a –

KAY [*hastily*]: Nice, isn't it? Alan has just given it to me. How are the children?

JOAN: Richard's very well, but the doctor says Ann's tonsils ought to come out – though he doesn't tell me who's going to pay for the operation, never thinks about that. They did enjoy those things you sent at Christmas, Kay – I don't know what they'd have done without them, though I did my best.

KAY: I'm sure you did, Joan.

JOAN: Alan was very good to them, too, weren't you, Alan? Though, of course, it's not like their having a father. [*Breaks off and looks miserably at* KAY.] You know, I haven't seen Robin for months. Some people say I ought to divorce him – but – I don't know – [*With sudden misery*] Honestly, isn't it awful? Oh – Kay. [*Suddenly giggles.*] Doesn't that sound silly – *Oh – Kay.*

KAY [*wearily*]: No, I've stopped noticing it.

JOAN: Richard's always saying Okay – he's heard it at the pictures – and, of course, Ann copies him. [*Breaks off, looks anxiously at them both.*] Do you think it's all right, my coming here tonight? It was Hazel who told me you were having a sort of family meeting, and she thought I ought to be here, and I think so too. But Granny Conway didn't ask me –

KAY [*with a sudden laugh*]: Joan, you don't call mother Granny Conway?

JOAN: Well, I got into the habit, y'know, with the children.

KAY: She must loathe it.

ALAN [*apologetically, to* JOAN]: I think she does, you know.

JOAN: I must try and remember. Is she upstairs?

ALAN: Yes. Madge is here, too.

JOAN [*nerving herself*]: I think – I'll go up and ask her if it's all right – my staying – otherwise I'd feel such a fool.

KAY: Yes, do. And tell her we think you ought to be here – if you *want* to be –

JOAN: Well, it isn't that – but – you see – if it's about money – I must know something, mustn't I? After all, I'm Robin's wife – and Richard and Ann are his children –

ALAN [*kindly*]: Yes, Joan, you tell mother that, if she objects. But she won't, though.

[JOAN *looks at them a moment doubtfully, then goes. They watch her go, then look at one another.*]

KAY [*lowering her voice a little*]: I suppose Robin's pretty hopeless – but really, Joan's such a fool –

ALAN: Yes, but the way Robin's treated her has made her feel more of a fool than she really is. It's taken away all her confidence in herself, you see, Kay. Otherwise she mightn't have been so bad.

KAY: You used to like Joan, didn't you?

ALAN [*looking at her, then slowly smiling*]: You remember when she and Robin told us they were engaged? I was in love with her then. It was the only time I ever fell in love with anybody. And I remember – quite suddenly hating Robin – yes, really hating him. None of this loving and hating lasted, of course – it was just silly stuff. But I remember it quite well.

KAY: Suppose it had been you instead of Robin?

ALAN [*hastily*]: Oh – no, that wouldn't have done at all. Really it wouldn't. Most unsuitable!

[KAY *laughs in affectionate amusement at his bachelor's horror.* MADGE *enters. She is very different from the girl of Act One. She has short greyish hair, wears glasses, and is neatly but severely dressed. She speaks with a dry precision, but underneath her assured schoolmistress manner is a suggestion of the neurotic woman.*]

MADGE [*very decisively, as she bustles about the room, finding an envelope and filling her fountain-pen*]: I've just told mother that if I hadn't happened to be in the neighbourhood today – I've applied for a headship at Borderton, you know, Kay, and had my interview there this afternoon – nothing would have induced me to be here tonight.

KAY: Well, I don't know why you bothered telling her, Madge. You *are* here, that's all that matters.

MADGE: No it isn't. I want her to understand quite clearly that I've no further interest in these family muddles, financial or otherwise. Also, that I would have thought it unnecessary to ask for a day away from my work at Collingfield in order to attend one of these ridiculous hysterical conferences.

KAY: You talk as if you'd been dragged here every few weeks.

MADGE: No I haven't. But I've had a great many more of these silly discussions than you have – please remember, Kay. Mother and Gerald Thornton seem to imagine that the time of a woman journalist in London is far more precious than that of a senior mistress at a large girls' public school. Why – I can't think. But the result is, I've been dragged in often when you haven't.

KAY [*rather wearily*]: All right. But seeing we're both here now, let's make the best of it.

ALAN: Yes, of course.

MADGE: Joan's here. I hope there's no chance of Robin coming too. That's something you've missed so far, I think, Kay. I've had one experience of their suddenly meeting here – Robin half drunk, ready to insult everybody. Joan weeping and resentful – the pair of them discussing every unpleasant detail of their private life – and it's not an experience I want to repeat.

KAY [*lightly, but serious underneath*]: I don't blame you, Madge. But for the Lord's sake be human tonight. You're not talking to the Collingfield common room now. This is your nice brother, Alan. I'm your nice sister Kay. We know all about you –

MADGE: That's just where you're wrong. You know hardly anything about me, any of you. The life you don't see – call it the Collingfield common room if that amuses you – is my real life. It represents exactly the sort of person I am now, and what you and Alan and mother remember – and trust mother not to forget anything foolish and embarrassing – is no longer of any importance at all.

KAY: I'd hate to think that, Madge.

ALAN [*shyly, earnestly*]: And it isn't true. It really isn't. Because – [*Hesitates, and is lost.*]

MADGE: I heard your extraordinary views the last time I was here, Alan. I also discussed them with Herrickson – our senior Maths mistress and a most brilliant woman – and she demolished them very thoroughly.

KAY [*to cheer him up*]: You tell *me*, Alan, if there's time later on. We're not going to be trampled on by any of Madge's Miss What's-her-names. And we don't care how brilliant they are, do we, Alan?

> [ALAN *grins and rubs his hands.* MADGE *deliberately changes the subject.*]

MADGE: I hope you're doing something besides this popular journalism now, Kay. Have you begun another book?

KAY: No.

MADGE: Pity, isn't it?

KAY [*after a pause, looking steadily at her*]: What about you, Madge? Are you building Jerusalem – in England's green and pleasant land?

MADGE: Possibly not. But I'm trying to put a little knowledge of history and a little sense into the heads of a hundred and fifty middle-class girls. It's hard work and useful work. Certainly nothing to be ashamed of.

KAY [*looking hard, speaking very quietly*]: Then – why be ashamed?

MADGE [*instantly, loudly*]: I'm not.

> [HAZEL *enters, from outside. She is extremely well dressed, the best dressed of them all, and has not lost her looks, but there is something noticeably subdued, fearful, about her.*]

HAZEL: Hello, Madge! [*Sees* KAY.] Kay! [*Kisses her.*]

KAY: Hazel, my dear, you're grander every time I see you.

HAZEL [*preening*]: Do you like it?

KAY: Yes – and you didn't get that in Newlingham. At the *Bon Marché*. Do you remember when we used to think the *Bon Marché* marvellous?

HAZEL [*brightening up at this*]: Yes – and now they seem ghastly. Well, that's something, isn't it? [*Realizes that this gives her away, so hastily asks*] Is Joan here?

ALAN: Yes. She's upstairs with mother. Is Ernest coming tonight?

HAZEL [*hesitating*]: I – don't – know.

MADGE: I thought it was understood he was coming. Mother thinks he is. I believe she's rather counting on him.

HAZEL [*hastily*]: Well, she mustn't. I've told her not to. I don't even know yet if he'll be here at all.

MADGE [*annoyed*]: But this is ridiculous. We're told that things are desperate. Kay and I have to leave our work, travel miles and miles, stop thinking about anything else, and now you don't even know if your own husband will walk down the road to be here.

HAZEL: But you know what Ernest is. He said he *might* come tonight. I asked him again only at lunch time today – and he said he didn't know – and then I didn't like –

MADGE [*cutting in sharply*]: Didn't like! You mean you *daren't*. That miserable little –

HAZEL: Madge! Please stop.

[MADGE *looks at her in contempt, then walks off.* HAZEL *looks very miserable.*]

KAY: How are the children?

HAZEL: Peter has a cold again – poor lamb – he's always getting colds. Margaret's all right. Never *any* trouble with her. She's been doing some ballet dancing, y'know, and the teacher thinks she's *marvellous* for her age. Oh – you forgot her last birthday, Kay. The child was *so* disappointed.

KAY: I'm sorry. Tell her I'll make up for it at Christmas. I must have been away on a job or something –

HAZEL [*eagerly*]: I read your article on Glyrna Foss – you know, about three months ago – when she came over from Hollywood. Did she really say all those things to you, Kay, or did you make them up?

KAY: She said some of them. The rest I made up.

HAZEL [*eagerly*]: Did she say anything about Leo Frobisher – her husband, y'know, and they'd just separated?

KAY: Yes, but I didn't print it.

HAZEL [*all eagerness now*]: What did she say?

KAY: She said [*imitating very bad type of American voice*], 'I'll bet that God-forgotten left-over ham husband of mine gets himself poured out o' the next boat.' [*Normal voice, dryly*] You'd like her, Hazel. She's a sweet child.

HAZEL: She sounds awful, but I suppose you can't judge by the

way they talk, using all that slang. And I know you don't think
you're very lucky, Kay –

KAY: I vary. Sometimes when I manage to remember what most
women go through, all kinds of women all over the world, I
don't think, I *know* I'm lucky. But usually – I feel clean out of
luck.

HAZEL: I know, that's what I say. But I think you're *very* lucky,
meeting all these people, and being in London and all that.
Look at me, still in Newlingham, and I *loathe* Newlingham,
and it gets worse and worse. Doesn't it, Alan – though I don't
suppose you notice?

ALAN: I think it's about the same – perhaps we get worse, that's
all.

HAZEL [*looking at him in a sort of impersonal fashion*]: Somebody
was saying to me only the other day how queer they thought you
were, Alan, and you are – really, aren't you? I mean you don't
seem to bother about everything as most people do. I've often
wondered whether you're happy inside or just dull. But I often
wonder about people like that – [*to* KAY] don't you? Though I
suppose being so clever now, and a writer and everything, you
know about them. But I don't. And I simply can't tell from
what people look like. We had a maid, y'know, Jessie, and she
seemed such a cheerful little thing – always smiling and humming – Ernest used to get quite cross with her – she was *too*
cheerful really – and then suddenly she took over twenty
aspirins all at once, we had to have the doctor and everything,
and she said it was simply because she couldn't bear it any
longer – she'd had enough of *everything*, she said. Isn't it
strange?

KAY: But you must feel like that sometimes, don't you?

HAZEL: Yes, I do. But I'm always surprised when other people
do, because somehow they never *look* it. Oh – [*gets up and
lowers her voice*] Robin rang me up yesterday – he's living in
Leicester just now, you know – and I told him about tonight –
and he said he might look in because he wouldn't be far
away.

ALAN: I hope he doesn't.

KAY: What's he doing now, Hazel?

HAZEL: I don't know really – he's always changing, y'know – but it's something to do with commission. Shall I tell Joan he might be coming here?

KAY: No. Risk it.

[*Doesn't say any more because* MRS CONWAY *comes in now, followed by* JOAN. MRS CONWAY *is now a woman of sixty-five, and has not gone neat and modern, but kept to her full-blown Edwardian type.*]

MRS C [*who is still very brisk*]: Now then, Hazel, haven't you brought Ernest with you?

HAZEL: No, Mother. I hope – he'll be here soon.

MRS C: Of course he will. Well, we can't do anything until Gerald arrives. He knows how things are – exactly. Where's Madge?

KAY: I thought she went upstairs.

MRS C [*as she goes to turn on more lights*]: She's probably taking something in the bathroom. I've never known anybody who took so many things as poor Madge. She's given herself so many lotions and gargles and sprays that no man has ever looked twice at her – poor thing. Alan, I think we ought to have both port and whisky out, don't you? I told the girl to leave it all ready in the dining-room. Better bring it in. [ALAN *goes out, returning, during following dialogue, carrying a tray, with port and small glasses, whisky and soda and tumblers.*] Now what I'm wondering is this – should we all sit round looking very stiff and formal – y'know, make it a proper business affair, because, after all, it *is* a business affair – or should we make everybody comfortable and *cosy*? What do you think?

KAY: I think – Mother – you're enjoying this.

MRS C: Well, after all, why shouldn't I? It's nice to see all you children at home again. Even Madge. [MADGE *enters.* MRS C *probably saw her before, but undoubtedly sees her now.*] I say it's nice to see all you children home again – even you, Madge.

MADGE: I'm not a child and this is no longer my home.

MRS C [*sharply*]: You were a child once – and a very troublesome one too – and for twenty years this was your home – and please don't talk in that tone to me. You're not in a classroom now, remember.

HAZEL: Now – Mother – please – it's not going to be easy tonight – and –

MADGE [*coldly*]: Don't worry, Hazel. Mother *enjoys* things not being easy. [*She sits down.*]

[MRS C *observes her maliciously, then turns to* KAY.]

MRS C: Kay, *who* was the man the Philipsons saw you dining with at the – what's the name of that restaurant ?

KAY: The Ivy, Mother. And the man is a man called Hugo Steel. I've told you already.

MRS C [*smoothly*]: Yes, dear, but you didn't tell me much. The Philipsons said you seemed awfully friendly together. I suppose he's an old friend ?

KAY [*sharply*]: Yes.

MRS C [*same technique*]: Isn't it a pity – you couldn't – I mean, if he's a really nice man.

KAY [*trying to cut it short*]: Yes, a great pity.

MRS C: I've so often hoped you'd be settled with some nice man – and when the Philipsons told me –

KAY [*harshly*]: Mother, I'm forty today. Had you forgotten ?

MRS C [*taking it well*]: Of course I hadn't. A mother *always* remembers. Joan –

JOAN [*whose attention has been elsewhere, turning*]: Yes, Grannie Conway ?

MRS C [*crossly*]: Don't call me that ridiculous name.

JOAN: I forgot, I'm sorry.

MRS C: Didn't I tell you it was Kay's birthday ? I've something for you too –

KAY: No, Mother, you mustn't – really –

MRS C [*producing small diamond brooch*]: There ! Your father gave me that, the second Christmas after we were married, and it's a charming little brooch. Brazilian diamonds. It was an old piece then. Look at the colour in the stones. You always get that in the old South American diamonds. There now !

KAY [*gently*]: It's very sweet of you, Mother, but really I'd rather not take this from you.

MRS C: Don't be absurd. It's mine and now I give it to you. Take it or I'll be cross. And many happy returns, of course. [KAY *takes the brooch, then, suddenly rather moved, kisses her mother.*] When you were younger, I never liked you as much as I did Hazel, but now I think I was wrong.

HAZEL: Oh – Mother !

MRS C: I know, Hazel dear, but you're such a *fool* with that little husband of yours. Why, if he were mine –

HAZEL [*sharply for her*]: Well he isn't – and you really know very little about him.

MRS C [*as she looks about her*]: It's time the men were here. I've always hated seeing a lot of women sitting about, with no men. *They* always look silly, and then I feel silly myself. I don't know why. [*Notices* ALAN. *With some malice*] Of course you're here, Alan. I was forgetting you. Or forgetting you were a man.

ALAN [*mildly*]: I must grow a shaggy beard and drum on my chest and ro-o-ar!

JOAN [*doing her best*]: When their Uncle Frank – you know, Freda's husband, they live in London – took the children to the Zoo for the first time, little Richard was only five – and there was an enormous monkey – what Alan said reminded me of it – and –

MRS C [*cutting this ruthlessly*]: Would anybody like a glass of port? Kay? Hazel? What about you, Madge? It's a scholarly wine. You remember what Meredith wrote about it in *The Egoist*. But nobody reads Meredith now and nobody takes port. I used to read Meredith when I was a girl and thought I was very clever. But I didn't like port then. Now I don't care about Meredith, but I rather like port. [*She has poured herself a glass of port, and now sips it.*] It's not good port this – even I know that, though men always say women don't know anything about it – but it's rich and warming, even this – like a handsome compliment. That's gone too. Nobody pays compliments any more – except old Doctor Halliday, who's well over eighty and has no memory at all. He talked to me for half an hour the other day, thinking I was Mrs Rushbury – [*Ring at bell.*] There! That's probably Gerald.

MADGE [*wearily*]: At last!

MRS C [*maliciously*]: Yes, Madge, but you mustn't be so impatient.
[MADGE *glares at her.* ALAN *is now ushering in* GERALD THORNTON, *who carries a brief-case, and* ERNEST BEEVERS. GERALD *is over fifty now, and though careful of his appearance, he looks it. He is grey and wears glasses. He is much drier and harder than he was in Act One.* ERNEST BEEVERS *looks far more prosperous than he did before, and has lost his early shyness.*

With the arrival of these two, the party is apparently complete, so that there is no longer the feeling of waiting about.]

MRS C: Well, Gerald, will you have a drink before you begin talking?

GERALD: No, thank you. [*He turns to* KAY.] How are you, Kay?

KAY: Quite well, thank you, Gerald. [*Stares at him.*] I'm sorry, but it's true.

GERALD: What is?

KAY: I always remember your saying, years ago, that you didn't mind living in Newlingham but you were determined to be as different as possible from the Newlingham type of man.

GERALD [*hastily, frowning a little*]: I don't remember saying that –

KAY: Yes, you did. And now – I'm sorry, Gerald, but it's true – you suddenly look like *all* those Newlingham men rolled into one –

GERALD [*rather shortly*]: What do I do? Apologize? [*Turns away, leaving her regarding him speculatively.*]

HAZEL [*who has managed to get* ERNEST *to herself a moment*]: Oh – Ernest – I'm so glad you're here –

ERNEST [*not pleasantly*]: You are, eh?

HAZEL [*who knows him by this time*]: I suppose that means you won't stay now – just to show me –

ERNEST: I don't need to show you. You know, by this time.

HAZEL [*lowering voice*]: Ernest – please – be nice to them tonight – especially to Mother – you could be such a help if you wanted to be –

ERNEST [*cutting through this*]: I don't know what you're talking about.

[*They both notice then that* MADGE *is quite near, regarding them with a contemptuous smile.* ERNEST *gives her a sharp look, then turns away.* HAZEL *looks deeply embarrassed, then looks as if she was about to appeal to* MADGE.]

MADGE [*coolly*]: I shouldn't say a word, if I were you, Hazel. I mean, to me. It would only make it worse.

MRS C [*loud cheerful tone*]: Now then, everybody, please be quiet and pay attention. We must be very business-like, mustn't we, Gerald? I'm so glad you were able to come, Ernest. You'll help us to be business-like, won't you?

ERNEST [*grimly*]: Yes.

MADGE: And that doesn't mean you're at liberty to make yourself unpleasant.

MRS C [*sharply*]: Be quiet, Madge. [*Turning, with smile and great social air, to* GERALD] Now then, Gerald, we're all waiting. Tell us all about it.

[GERALD, *who has been glancing at his papers, looks up at her and round the waiting circle with a sort of despair, as if to ask what could be done with such people.*]

GERALD [*in dry legal tone*]: Acting under instructions from Mrs Conway, after it was decided you should all meet here, I have prepared a short statement of Mrs Conway's present financial position –

MRS C [*protesting*]: Gerald.

GERALD [*rather despairing*]: Yes?

MRS C: Must you talk in that awful dry inhuman way? I mean, after all, I've known you since you were a boy, and the children have known you all their lives, and you're beginning to talk as if you'd never seen any of us before. And it sounds so horrid.

GERALD: But I'm not here now as a friend of the family, but as your solicitor.

MRS C [*with dignity*]: No. You're here as a friend of the family who also happens to be my solicitor. And I think it would be much better if you told us all in a simple friendly way what the position is.

ALAN: I think that would be better, you know, Gerald.

KAY: So do I. When you turn on that legal manner, I can't take you seriously – I feel you're still acting in one of our old charades.

HAZEL [*with sudden warmth*]: Oh – weren't they fun! And you were so good in them, Gerald. Why can't we have some more –

ERNEST [*brutally*]: What – at your age?

HAZEL: I don't see why not. Mother was older than we are now when she used to play –

GERALD [*not amused by all this*]: You're not proposing to turn this into a charade, are you, Hazel?

KAY: What a pity it isn't one!

ALAN [*very quietly*]: Perhaps it is.

MRS C: Now don't *you* start being silly, Alan. Now then, Gerald, just tell us how things are – and don't read out a lot of figures

and dates and things – I know you've brought them with you
– but keep them for anybody who wants to have a look at them –
perhaps *you*'d like to have a look at them afterwards, Ernest –

ERNEST: I might. [*To* GERALD] Go ahead.

GERALD [*dryly*]: Well, the position is this. Mrs Conway for a long
time now has derived her income from two sources. A holding
in Farrow and Conway Limited. And some property in
Newlingham, the houses at the north end of Church Road.
Farrow and Conway were hit badly by the slump and have not
recovered yet. The houses in Church Road are not worth anything like what they were, and the only chance of making that
property pay is to convert the houses into flats. But this would
demand a substantial outlay of capital. Mrs Conway has received
an offer for her holding in Farrow and Conway Limited, but
it is a very poor offer. It would not pay for the reconstruction of
the Church Road property. Meanwhile that property may soon
be a liability instead of an asset. So, you see, the position is very
serious.

MADGE [*coldly*]: I must say I'm very much surprised. I always
understood that mother was left extremely well provided for.

MRS C [*proudly*]: Certainly I was. Your father saw to that.

GERALD: Both the shares and the property have declined in value.

MADGE: Yes, but even so – I'm still surprised. Mother must have
been very extravagant.

GERALD: Mrs Conway hasn't been as careful as she might have
been.

MRS C: There were six of you to bring up and educate –

MADGE: It isn't that. I know how much *we* cost. It's since then
that the money's been spent. And I know who must have had
most of it – Robin!

MRS C [*angry now*]: That'll do, Madge. It was my money –

MADGE: It wasn't. It was only yours to hold in trust for us. Alan,
you're the eldest and you've been here all the time, why didn't
you do something?

ALAN: I'm afraid – I – haven't bothered much about – these
things –

MADGE [*with growing force*]: Then you ought to have done. I
think it's absolutely wicked. I've been working hard earning
my living for over twenty years, and I've looked forward to

having something from what father left, enough to pay for a few really good holidays or to buy myself a little house of my own – and now it's all gone – just because mother and Robin between them have flung it away –

MRS C [*angrily*]: You ought to be ashamed of yourself, talking like that! What if I have helped Robin? He needed it, and I'm his mother. If you'd needed it, I'd have helped you too –

MADGE: You wouldn't. When I told you I had a chance to buy a partnership in that school, you only laughed at me –

MRS C: Because you were all right where you were and didn't need to buy any partnerships.

MADGE: And Robin did, I suppose?

MRS C: Yes, because he's a man – with a wife and children to support. This is just typical of you, Madge. Call yourself a Socialist and blame people for taking an interest in money, and then it turns out you're the most mercenary of us all.

MADGE: I don't call myself a Socialist – though that's nothing to do with it –

ERNEST [*who has been glancing at an evening paper, breaking in brutally*]: How long does this go on? Because I've something else to do.

MRS C [*trying hard to placate him*]: That's all right, Ernest. Look what you've done now, Madge. Made Joan cry.

JOAN [*suddenly weeping quietly in the background*]: I'm sorry – I just – remembered – so many things – that's all –

GERALD: At the present moment, Mrs Conway has a considerable overdraft at the bank. Now there are two possible courses of action. One is to sell the houses for what they'll fetch, and to hold on to the Farrow and Conway shares. But I warn you that the houses won't fetch much. The alternative is to sell the shares, then to raise an additional sum – probably between two or three thousand pounds – and to convert the houses into flats –

MRS C [*hopefully*]: We've had a sort of scheme from an architect, and really it looks most attractive. There'd be at least thirty nice flats, and you know what people will pay for flats nowadays. Don't you think it's a splendid idea, Ernest? [*He does not reply. She smiles at him and then her smile falters, but she returns hope-*

fully to the theme.] I felt if we all discussed it in a nice friendly way, we could decide something. I know you business men like everything cut-and-dried, but I believe it's better to be nice and friendly. It isn't true that people will only do things for money. I'm always being surprised about that. People are very nice and kind, really – [*Breaks off, then looks at the women, more intimate tone.*] Only last week, I went to old Mrs Jepson's funeral, and I was walking back through the cemetery with Mrs Whitehead – I hadn't been round there for years – and I saw Carol's grave – and, of course, I was rather upset, suddenly coming on it like that – but it was so beautifully kept, with flowers – lovely flowers – growing there. And I thought, now there's an instance – nobody's told them to do that or paid them for it – it's just natural kindness –

MADGE [*harshly*]: No it isn't. Somebody must have been paying for it.

KAY [*turning*]: Alan! It must be you. Isn't it?

ALAN: Well – I do send them something – once every year, y'know – it isn't much.

HAZEL: Oh, Mother – I'd forgotten about Carol – it's sixteen years ago.

ALAN: Seventeen.

HAZEL [*in melancholy wonder*]: Why, my Margaret's nearly as big as she was. Doesn't that seem strange, Kay?

KAY: I'd nearly forgotten about Carol too.

MRS C [*with some emotion*]: Don't think I had – because I was so stupid about that grave. I'm not one of those people who remember graves, it's human beings I remember. Only the other day, when I was sitting upstairs, I heard Carol shouting 'Mo-ther, mo–ther' – you know how she used to do. And then I began thinking about her, my poor darling, and how she came in that awful day, her face quite greyish, and said, 'Mother, I've the most sickening pain,' and then it was too late when they operated –

HAZEL: Yes, Mother, we remember.

ERNEST [*harsh and astonishing*]: I'll tell you what you don't remember – and what some of you never even knew. She was the best of the lot – that one – little Carol – worth all the rest of you put together.

HAZEL [*a shocked wife*]: Ernest!

ERNEST: Yes, and I'm counting you in. You were the one I wanted – that's all right, I got the one I wanted – but it didn't take me two hours to see that little Carol was the best of the lot. [*Adds gloomily*] Didn't surprise me when she went off like that. Out! Finish! Too good to last.

MRS C [*now near to tears*]: Ernest is quite right. She was the best of you all. My darling baby, I haven't forgotten you, I haven't forgotten you. [*Rising.*] Oh, why isn't Robin here? [*Begins weeping, also moves away.*] Go on, Gerald, explaining to them. I shan't be long. Don't move. [*Goes out in tears.*]

[*There is silence for a moment or two.*]

MADGE: Surely, under the circumstances, it's absurd that mother and Alan should continue living in this house. It's much too large for them.

ALAN [*mildly*]: Yes. We could do with something much smaller now.

MADGE: Then this house could be sold, that would help. It's mother's freehold, isn't it?

GERALD: I think it would be better to move into something smaller, just to cut down living expenses. But this house wouldn't fetch very much now.

HAZEL: Why, mother was offered thousands and thousands for it just after the War.

ERNEST [*dryly*]: Yes, but this isn't just after the War. It's just before the next War.

GERALD: How much do *you* think, Ernest?

ERNEST: Take anything you can get for it.

KAY: Well, what are we supposed to do? If the worst comes to the worst, we can club together to keep mother going –

MADGE: But it's monstrous. When I was at home – and knew about things – we were considered quite well off. There were all the shares and property father left, not simply for mother but for all of us. And now not only has it nearly all been frittered away, but we're expected to provide for mother –

KAY [*rather wearily*]: But if the money's gone, it's gone.

GERALD: No, the point is this –

[*He is stopped by a loud ring at bell. They turn and look.* ALAN *moves, then stops.* ROBIN *has marched in. He is wearing an old* raincoat. *He is shabbily smart, and looks what he is, a slackish, hard-drinking unsuccessful man of forty-two.*]

ROBIN: Hello! All here? Where's mother?

ALAN: She'll be back in a minute.

[ROBIN *takes off his raincoat and negligently gives it to* ALAN, *who characteristically accepts it and puts it away.* ROBIN *takes no notice of this, but looks at* JOAN.]

ROBIN: Well, Joan. How are the offspring?

JOAN [*stiffly*]: They're quite well, Robin.

ROBIN: Still telling them what an awful man their father is?

MADGE: Are we going to have this all over again?

ROBIN: No, you're not – dear old Madge. Do I see a drink over there? I do. Have a drink, Gerald. Ernest, have a drink. No? Well, I will. [*Goes and helps himself liberally to whisky and soda. Turns after first quick drink, faces them and grins.*] Hello, Kay. Condescending to visit the provinces again, eh?

KAY: Yes, but I've got to be back sometime tonight.

ROBIN: Don't blame you. Wish I was going back to town. That's the place. I've half a mind to chuck what I'm doing and try my luck there again. Know several decent chaps there.

KAY: What are you doing now, Robin?

ROBIN [*rather gloomily*]: Trying to sell a new heavy motor oil. I ought to have tried your stunt – writing. Might, one day. I could tell 'em something – my oath I could. [*Finishes his drink rather noisily.*] Well, don't let me interrupt the business. Or are you waiting for mother?

MADGE: No, we're better without her.

ROBIN [*belligerently*]: Yes, you would think that! But don't forget, it's her money –

[*He stops because* MRS C *reappears, all smiles.*]

MRS C [*joyfully*]: Robin! Now this is nice! [*Sweeps across and kisses him. There is perhaps a touch of defiance to the others in the warmth of her welcome.*] Are you staying the night?

ROBIN: I wasn't, but I could do – [*with a grin*] in Alan's best pyjamas.

[*They settle themselves.*]

MADGE: We were just saying, Mother, that it was absurd for you to keep on living here. The house is much too big and expensive now.

ROBIN: That's for mother to decide –

MRS C: No, that's all right, dear. It is too big now, and, of course, if I sold it I could probably raise enough to convert the Church Road houses into flats.

ERNEST: No you couldn't. Nothing like.

MRS C [*with dignity*]: Really, Ernest! I was offered four thousand pounds for it once.

ERNEST: You ought to have taken it.

GERALD: I'm afraid you can't count on getting much for this house, though, of course, you'll save money by living in a smaller place.

ROBIN: Not much, though. She'd have to pay rent for the smaller house, and this is hers.

GERALD [*rather impatiently for him, probably because* ROBIN *is here*]: But rates and taxes are fairly heavy on this house. I want you all to understand that the present situation is very unsatisfactory. The overdraft can be paid off, of course, simply by selling shares or some of the houses, but after that Mrs Conway would be worse off than ever. If the money for the conversion scheme could be raised, then the Church Road property would bring in a decent income.

MRS C: And I'm sure that's the thing to do. Flats. I might live in one of them myself – a nice, cosy little flat. Delightful!

GERALD: But after you've sold your shares you've still to find another two or three thousand to pay for the conversion into flats.

MRS C: But couldn't I borrow that?

GERALD: Not from the bank. They won't accept the Church Road houses as security for a loan to convert them into flats. I've tried that.

HAZEL [*hopefully, and a shade timidly*]: Ernest – could lend you the money.

ERNEST [*staggered by this*]: *What!*

HAZEL [*rather faltering now*]: Well, you could easily afford it, Ernest.

MRS C [*smiling*]: From what I hear, you're very well off indeed these days, Ernest.

GERALD: Oh – there's no doubt about that.

MRS C [*hoping this will win him over*]: And it only seems yesterday,

Ernest, that you first came here – a very shy young man from nowhere.

ERNEST [*grimly*]: It's twenty years ago, to be exact – but that's just what I was – a shy young man from nowhere. And when I managed to wangle myself into this house I thought I'd got somewhere.

MRS C: I remember so well feeling that about you at the time, Ernest.

ERNEST: Yes. I was made to feel I'd got somewhere, too. But I stuck it. I've always been able to stick it, when I've had my mind on something I badly wanted. That's how I've managed to get on.

ROBIN [*who doesn't like him, obviously*]: Don't begin to tell us now that you landed here with only a shilling in your pocket –

MRS C [*warning, reproachful, yet secretly amused*]: Now, now Robin!

ERNEST [*in level unpleasant tone*]: I wasn't going to. Don't worry, you're not going to have the story of *my* life. All I was about to say was – that as far as I'm concerned, you can whistle for your two or three thousand pounds. You won't get a penny from me. And I might as well tell you – while I'm making myself unpleasant – that I could lend you the two or three thousand without feeling it. Only, I'm not going to. Not a penny.

HAZEL [*indignation struggling with her fear of him*]: You make me feel ashamed.

ERNEST [*staring hard at her*]: Oh! Why? [*She does not reply, but begins to crumple under his hard stare.*] Go on. Tell 'em why I make you feel ashamed. Tell *me*. Or would you like to tell me later when *I'm* telling *you* a few things?

[HAZEL *crumples into tears.* ROBIN *jumps up, furious.*]

ROBIN: I never did like you, Beevers. I've half a mind to boot you out of this house.

ERNEST [*no coward*]: You do, and I'll bring an action for assault. *And* I'd enjoy it. My money or the boot, eh? I told Hazel a long time ago that not one of you would ever get a penny out of me. And I'm not mean. Ask her. But I swore to myself after the very first night I came here, when you were all being so high and mighty – especially you – that you'd never see a penny that I ever made.

ROBIN [*with a lurking grin*]: I see.

ERNEST [*very sharply*]: What's that mean? By God, she *has*! She's been giving you money – *my* money.

HAZEL [*terribly alarmed now*]: Oh – Robin, why did you?

ROBIN [*irritably*]: What does it matter? He can't eat you.

ERNEST [*very quietly and deadly, to* HAZEL]: Come on. [*Goes out.*]
    [HAZEL *looks terrified.*]

MADGE: Don't go, if you don't want to.

KAY: Hazel, there's nothing to be afraid of.

HAZEL [*sincere, quiet, desperate*]: There is. I'm frightened of *him*. Except right at the first – I've always been frightened of him.

ROBIN [*noisily*]: Don't be silly. This little pipsqueak! What can *he* do?

HAZEL: I don't know. It isn't that. It's just something about him.

ERNEST [*returning with his overcoat on, to* HAZEL]: Come on. I'm going.

HAZEL [*summoning up all her courage*]: N-no.
    [*He waits and looks at her. She slowly moves towards him, fearful and ashamed.* MRS C *moves hastily over towards* ERNEST.]

MRS C [*excitedly*]: You sneaked your way in here, Ernest Beevers, and somehow you persuaded or bullied Hazel, who was considered then one of the prettiest girls in Newlingham, into marrying you –

HAZEL [*imploring her*]: No, Mother – please don't –

MRS C: I'll tell him now what I've always wanted to tell him. [*Approaching* ERNEST *with vehemence.*] I was a fool. My husband wouldn't have had such a bullying mean little rat near the house. I never liked you. And I'm not surprised to hear you say you've always hated us. Don't ever come here again, don't ever let me see you again. I only wish I was Hazel for just one day, I'd show you something. What – you – my daughter – ! [*In a sudden fury she slaps him hard across the face, with a certain grand magnificence of manner.*] Now bring an action for that!
    [*Stands there, blazing at him. He rubs his cheek a little, backs a step or two, looking at her steadily.*]

ERNEST [*quietly*]: You've done a lot of dam' silly things in your time, Mrs Conway, but you'll find that's the dam' silliest. [*Turns and walks to door. At door he turns quickly to* HAZEL.] Come on. [*Goes out.*]

[HAZEL *is wretched.*]

HAZEL: Oh – Mother – you shouldn't.

ROBIN [*rather grandly*]: She did quite right. And you just let me know – if he gives you any trouble.

HAZEL [*tearfully, shaking her head as she wanders towards door*]: No, Robin. You don't understand . . . you don't understand. . . . [*She goes out slowly.*]

[*A strained silence.* MRS C *goes back to her place.*]

MRS C [*with a short laugh*]: Well – I suppose that was a silly thing to do.

GERALD [*gravely*]: I'm afraid it was, y'know.

KAY: You see, it's Hazel who will have to pay for it.

ROBIN: Well, she needn't. She's only to let me know what he's up to.

JOAN [*surprisingly*]: What's the good of talking like that? What could *you* do? He can make her life a misery, and you couldn't stop it.

MADGE: Well, it's her own fault. I've no patience with her. I wouldn't stand it ten minutes.

JOAN [*with plenty of spirit, for her*]: It's no use you talking, Madge. You simply don't understand. You've never been married.

MADGE: No, and after what I've seen here, I think I'm lucky.

MRS C [*with energy*]: You're not lucky – never were and never will be – and as you haven't the least idea what a woman's real life is like, the less you say the better. You're not among schoolgirls and silly teachers now. Robin, give me a glass of port. Won't you have a drink too?

[ROBIN *pours her a port and himself another whisky.*]

GERALD [*rising. He has already put his papers away in case*]: I don't think there's any point in my staying any longer.

MRS C: But we haven't settled anything.

GERALD [*rather coldly*]: I thought there was a chance that Ernest Beevers might have been persuaded to lend you the money. As I don't think anybody else here has three thousand pounds to spare –

ROBIN [*turning on him*]: All right, Thornton, you needn't be so damned supercilious about it. Seems to me you've not made a particularly bright job of handling my mother's affairs.

GERALD [*annoyed*]: I don't think that comes too well from you. For years I've given good advice, and never once has it been acted upon. Now I'd be only too delighted to hand over these affairs.

ROBIN: I believe I could make a better job of it myself.

GERALD [*stiffly*]: I can't imagine a possible worse choice. [*Moves with his case.*] Good night, Kay. Good night, Alan.

JOAN [*moving*]: I think I'll come along too, Gerald.

[GERALD *and* ALAN *go out.*]

ROBIN: You'll be able to have a nice little chat about me on the way.

[JOAN *stands still now and looks across at him.*]

JOAN [*very quietly*]: It doesn't hurt so much as it used to do, Robin, when you say such bitter things. I suppose one day it won't hurt at all.

ROBIN [*who is sorry at the moment*]: Sorry, old girl. And give my love to the kids. Say I'm coming to see them soon.

JOAN: Yes, come and see us soon. Only remember – we're very poor now.

ROBIN: Thanks for that. And then you talk about being bitter.

[*They look at one another for a moment, lost and hopeless. Then* JOAN *moves away, slowly.*]

KAY [*rather painfully*]: Good night, my dear.

JOAN [*painfully turning and producing little social smile*]: Good night, Kay. It's been nice – seeing you again. [*She goes out.*]

[KAY, *who is moved, withdraws herself.*]

ROBIN [*after another drink, an optimist*]: Well, now we ought to be able to settle something.

MADGE [*coldly*]: So far as I'm concerned, this has simply been a waste of time – and nervous energy.

MRS C [*with malice*]: You know, Madge, when I think of Gerald Thornton as he is now, a dreary, conceited middle-aged bachelor, I can't help thinking it's perhaps a pity you *didn't* marry him.

ROBIN [*with a guffaw*]: What, Madge! I never knew you fancied Gerald Thornton.

MRS C [*in light but significant tone*]: She did – once. Didn't you, dear? And I believe he was interested – oh, a long time ago, when you children were all still at home.

KAY [*sharply*]: Mother, if that's not true, then it's stupid silly talk. If it *is* true, then it's cruel.

MRS C: Nonsense! And not so high-and-mighty, please, Kay.

MADGE [*facing them bravely*]: It *was* true, a long time ago, just after the War. When I still thought we could suddenly make everything better for everybody. Socialism! Peace! Universal Brotherhood! All that. And I felt then that Gerald Thornton and I together could – help. He had a lot of fine qualities, I thought – and I believe he had then, too – and only needed to be pulled out of his rut here, to have his enthusiasm aroused. I was remembering tonight – when I was looking at him. It came back to me quite quickly. [*This last was more to* KAY *than the other two. Now she takes her mother in.*] One evening – just one evening – and something you did that evening – ruined it all. I'd almost forgotten – but seeing us all here again tonight reminded me – I believe it was at a sort of party for you, Kay. [*Accusingly to her mother*] Do you remember?

MRS C: Really, Madge, you *are* absurd. I seem to remember some piece of nonsense, when we were all being foolish.

MADGE: Yes, you remember. It was quite deliberate on your part. Just to keep a useful young man unattached or jealousy of a girl's possible happiness, or just out of sheer nasty female mischief. . . . And something went for ever. . . .

MRS C: It can't have been worth very much then.

MADGE: A seed is easily destroyed, but it might have grown into an oak tree. [*Pauses, looks solemnly at her mother.*] I'm glad I'm not a mother.

MRS C [*annoyed*]: Yes, you may well say that.

MADGE [*with deadly deliberation*]: I know how I'd have despised myself if I'd turned out to be a bad mother.

MRS C [*angrily, rising*]: So that's what you call me? [*Pauses, then with more vehemence and emotion*] Just because you never think of anybody but yourselves. All selfish – selfish. Because everything hasn't happened as you wanted it, turn on me – all my fault. You never really think about me. Don't try to see things for a moment from my point of view. When you were children, I was so proud of you all, so confident that you would grow up to be wonderful creatures. I used to see myself at the age I am now, surrounded by you and your own children, so proud of you, so happy with you all, this house happier and gayer even than it was in the best of the old days. And now my life's gone by, and what's happened? You're a resentful soured schoolmistress, middle-aged before your time. Hazel – the loveliest child there ever was – married to a vulgar little bully, and terrified of him. Kay here – gone away to lead her own life, and very bitter and secretive about it, as if she'd failed. Carol – the happiest and kindest of you all – dead before she's twenty. Robin – I know, my dear, I'm not blaming you now, but I must speak the truth for once – with a wife he can't love and no sort of position or comfort or anything. And Alan – the eldest, the boy his father adored, that he thought might do anything – what's he now? [ALAN *has come in now and is standing there quietly listening*.] A miserable clerk with no prospects, no ambition, no self-respect, a shabby little man that nobody would look at twice. [*She sees him standing there now, but in her worked-up fury does not care, and lashes out at him*.] Yes, a shabby clerk that nobody would look at twice.

KAY [*in a sudden fury of loyalty*]: How dare you, Mother, how dare you! Alan of all people!

ALAN [*with a smile*]: That's all right, Kay. Don't you get excited. It's not a bad description. I am a shabby little clerk, y'know. It must be very disappointing.

MRS C: Oh – don't be so forgiving! Robin, you've always been selfish and weak and a bit of a good-for-nothing –

ROBIN: Here, steady, old girl. I've had some rotten bad luck, too, y'know, and a lot of it's just luck. I've come to see that.

MRS C [*exhausted now*]: All right – add the bad luck, too, my dear. The point is, whatever they may say about you, Robin my darling, you're my own boy and my own sort, and a great comfort. So you and I will go upstairs and talk.

ROBIN [*as she takes his arm*]: That's the spirit!

[*They move off together.*]

MADGE [*very quietly*]: Mother! [MRS C *stops but does not turn*.] We've both said what we want to say. There isn't any more to be said. And if you decide to have any more of these family conferences, don't trouble to ask me to attend them, because I shan't. I don't expect now to see a penny of father's money. And please don't expect to see any of mine.

ROBIN: Who wants yours?

MRS C: Come on, my dear, and we'll talk like human beings.

[*They go out. The other three are quiet and still.*]

MADGE: I have an idea I wasn't too pleasant to you, Kay, earlier when we met tonight. If so, I'm sorry.

KAY: That's all right, Madge. Are you going back to Collingfield tonight?

MADGE: No, I can't. But I'm staying with Nora Fleming – you remember her? She's Head of Newlingham High now. I've left my things there. I'll go now. I don't want to see mother again.

KAY: Good-bye, Madge. I hope you collar one of these headships.

MADGE: Good-bye, Kay. And do try and write a good book, instead of doing nothing but this useless journalism.

[*They kiss.* MADGE *goes off, accompanied by* ALAN. KAY, *left to herself, shows that she is deeply moved. She moves restlessly, then hastily pours herself a whisky and soda, lights a cigarette, tastes the whisky, then sits down, ignores the cigarette burning in her hand and the whisky, stares into the past, and then begins to cry.* ALAN *returns, filling his pipe.*]

ALAN [*cheerfully*]: You've a good half-hour yet, Kay, before you need set out for the London train. I'll take you to the station. [*Comes up to her.*] What's the matter? Has all this – been a bit too much for you?

KAY [*ruefully*]: Apparently. And I thought I was tough now, Alan. . . . See, I was doing the modern working woman – a cigarette and a whisky and soda . . . no good, though. . . . You see, Alan, I've not only been here tonight. I've been here remembering other nights, long ago, when we weren't like this. . . .

ALAN: Yes, I know. Those old Christmasses . . . birthday parties . . .

KAY: Yes, I remembered. I saw all of us then. Myself, too. Oh, silly girl of Nineteen Nineteen! Oh, lucky girl!

ALAN: You mustn't mind too much. It's all right, y'know. Like being forty?

KAY: Oh no, Alan, it's hideous and unbearable. Remember what we once were and what we thought we'd be. And now this. And it's all we have, Alan, it's *us*. Every step we've taken – every tick of the clock – making everything worse. If this is all life is, what's the use ? Better to die, like Carol, before you find it out, before Time gets to work on you. I've felt it before, Alan, but never as I've done tonight. There's a great devil in the universe, and we call it Time.

ALAN [*playing with his pipe, quietly, shyly*]: Did you ever read Blake ?

KAY: Yes.

ALAN: Do you remember this ? [*Quotes quietly, but with feeling*]

> Joy and woe are woven fine,
> A clothing for the soul divine;
> Under every grief and pine
> Runs a joy with silken twine.
> It is right it should be so;
> Man was made for joy and woe;
> And when this we rightly know,
> Safely through the world we go. . . .

KAY: Safely through the world we go ? No, it isn't true, Alan – or it isn't true for me. If things were merely mixed – good and bad – that would be all right, but they get worse. We've seen it tonight. Time's beating us.

ALAN: No, Time's only a kind of dream, Kay. If it wasn't, it would have to destroy everything – the whole universe – and then remake it again every tenth of a second. But Time doesn't destroy anything. It merely moves us on – in this life – from one peep-hole to the next.

KAY: But the happy young Conways, who used to play charades here, they've gone, and gone for ever.

ALAN: No, they're real and existing, just as we two, here now, are real and existing. We're seeing another bit of the view – a bad bit, if you like – but the whole landscape's still there.

KAY: But, Alan, we can't be anything but what we are *now*.

ALAN: No ... it's hard to explain ... suddenly like this ... there's a book I'll lend you – read it in the train. But the point is, now, at this moment, or any moment, we're only a cross-section of our real selves. What we *really* are is the whole stretch of ourselves, all our time, and when we come to the end of this life, all those selves, all our time, will be *us* – the real you, the real me. And then perhaps we'll find ourselves in another time, which is only another kind of dream.

KAY: I'll try to understand . . . so long as you really believe – and think it's possible for me to believe – that Time's not ticking our lives away . . . wrecking . . . and ruining everything . . . for ever. . . .

ALAN: No, it's all right, Kay. I'll get you that book. [*Moves away towards door, then turns.*] You know, I believe half our trouble now is because we think Time's ticking our lives away. That's why we snatch and grab and hurt each other.

KAY: As if we were all in a panic on a sinking ship.

ALAN: Yes, like that.

KAY [*smiling at him*]: But you don't do those things – bless you!

ALAN: I think it's easier not to – if you take a long view.

KAY: As if we're – immortal beings?

ALAN [*smiling*]: Yes, and in for a tremendous adventure.

[*Goes out.* KAY, *comforted, but still brooding, goes to the window and stands there looking out, with head raised. No sooner is she settled there than the curtain comes down.*]

END OF ACT TWO

ACT THREE

KAY *is sitting just as we left her at the end of Act One, and we can still hear* MRS CONWAY *singing Schumann's 'Der Nussbaum'. Nothing happens until the song has ended and we have heard some applause and voices from the party, but then* ALAN *enters and switches on the lights. We see that the room and everything in it is exactly as they were before. Only* KAY *herself has changed. Something – elusive, a brief vision, a score of shadowy presentiments – is haunting her. She is deeply disturbed. She throws a look or two at the room, as if she had just seen it in some other guise. She looks at* ALAN, *puzzled. He grins and rubs his hands a little.*

ALAN: Well, Kay?

KAY [*as if to break into something important*]: Alan – [*Breaks off.*]

ALAN: Yes?

KAY [*hurriedly*]: No – nothing.

ALAN [*looking more closely at her*]: I believe you've been asleep – while mother was singing.

KAY [*confusedly*]: No. I was sitting here – listening. I turned the light out. No, I didn't fall asleep – I don't know, perhaps I did – just for a second. It couldn't have been longer.

ALAN: You'd know if you'd been asleep.

KAY [*looking about her, slowly*]: No, I wasn't asleep. But – quite suddenly – I thought I saw . . . we were. . . . Anyhow, you came into it, I think, Alan.

ALAN [*amused and puzzled*]: Came into *what*?

KAY: I can't remember. And I know I was listening to mother singing all the time. I'm – a bit – wuzzy.

ALAN: Most of the people are going now. You'd better go and say good night.

[HAZEL *enters, carrying plate on which is enormous piece of sticky, rich, creamy cake. She has already begun to tackle this as she moves in.*]

KAY [*seeing her*]: Hazel, you greedy pig! [*Deftly swoops up a bit of the cake and eats it.*]

HAZEL [*talking with her mouth rather full*]: I didn't come in here just to eat this.

KAY: Course you did!

HAZEL: They're all saying good night now, and I'm dodging that little horror Gerald Thornton brought.

KAY [*hastily*]: I must say my piece to them. [*Hurries off.*]
    [ALAN *lingers.*]

ALAN [*after a pause*]: Hazel!

HAZEL [*mouth full*]: Um?

ALAN [*with elaborate air of casualness*]: What's Joan Helford going to do now?

HAZEL: Oh – just mooch round a bit.

ALAN: I thought I heard her saying she was going away – I was wondering if she was leaving Newlingham.

HAZEL: She's only going to stay with her aunt. Joan's always staying with aunts. Why can't *we* have aunts planted all over the place?

ALAN: There's Aunt Edith.

HAZEL: And a doctor's house in Wolverhampton! Ghastly! [*Quick change of tone. Teasingly*] Anything else you'd like to know about Joan?

ALAN [*confused*]: No – no. I – just wondered. [*Turns to go and almost bumps into* ERNEST, *who is wearing a very shabby mackintosh-raincoat and carrying a bowler hat. As soon as* HAZEL *sees who it is, she turns away and has another dab at her cake.* ALAN *stops and so does* ERNEST.] Oh! – you going?

ERNEST [*a man who knows his own mind*]: In a minute. [*He obviously waits for* ALAN *to clear out.*]

ALAN [*rather confused*]: Yes – well – [*Makes a move.*]

HAZEL [*loudly and clearly*]: Alan, you're not going?
    [*She looks across, completely ignoring* ERNEST, *who waits, not perhaps quite as cool as he would appear on the surface, for the hat he is clutching moves a bit.*]

ALAN [*not at home in this*]: Yes – have to say good night and get their coats and things – you know – [*Goes out.*]
    [HAZEL *attends to her cake, and then looks, without a smile, at* ERNEST.]

ERNEST: I just looked in to say good night, Miss Conway.

HAZEL [*blankly*]: Oh – yes – of course. Well –

ERNEST [*cutting in*]: It's been a great pleasure to me to come here and meet you all.

[*He waits a moment. She finds herself compelled to speak.*]

HAZEL [*same tone*]: Oh – well –

ERNEST [*cutting in again*]: Especially you. I'm new round here, y'know. I've only been in the place about three months. I bought a share in that paper mill – Eckersley's – out at West Newlingham – you know it?

HAZEL [*no encouragement from her*]: No.

ERNEST: Thought you might have noticed it. Been there long enough. Matter of fact it wants rebuilding. But that's where I am. And I hadn't been here a week before I noticed you, Miss Conway.

HAZEL [*who knows it only too well*]: Did you?

ERNEST: Yes. And I've been watching out for you ever since. I expect you've noticed me knocking about.

HAZEL [*loftily*]: No, I don't think I have.

ERNEST: Oh – yes – you must have done. Come on now. Admit it.

HAZEL [*her natural self coming out now*]: Well, if you must know, I have noticed you –

ERNEST [*pleased*]: I thought so.

HAZEL [*rapidly and indignantly*]: Because I thought you behaved very stupidly and rudely. If you want to look silly yourself – that's your affair – but you'd no right to make me look silly too –

ERNEST [*rather crushed*]: Oh! I didn't know – it'ud been as bad as that –

HAZEL [*feeling she has the upper hand*]: Well, it has.

[*He stares at her, perhaps having moved a little closer. She does not look at him at first, but then is compelled to meet his hard stare. There is something about this look that penetrates to the essential weakness of her character.*]

ERNEST [*coming up again now*]: I'm sorry. Though I can't see anybody's much the worse for it. After all, we've only one life to live, let's get on with it, I say. And in my opinion, you're the best-looking girl in this town, Miss Hazel Conway. I've been telling you that – in my mind – for the last two months. But I knew it wouldn't be long before I got to know you. To tell you properly. [*Looks hard at her. She does not like him but is completely helpless before this direct attack. He nods slowly.*] I expect you're thinking I'm not much of a chap. But there's a bit more in me than meets the eye. A few people have found that out already, and a lot more'll find it out before so long – here in Newlingham. You'll see. [*Changes his tone, because he is uncertain on purely social matters, almost humble now.*] Would it be all right – if I – sort of – called to see you – some time soon?

HAZEL [*coming to the top again*]: You'd better ask my mother.

ERNEST [*jocularly*]: Oh! – sort of *Ask Mamma* business, eh?

HAZEL [*confused and annoyed*]: No – I didn't mean it like that at all. I meant that this is mother's house –

ERNEST: Yes, but you're old enough now to have your own friends, aren't you?

HAZEL: I don't make friends with people very quickly.

ERNEST [*with appalling bluntness*]: Oh! I'd heard you did.

HAZEL [*haughtily, angrily*]: Do you mean to say you've been discussing me with people?

ERNEST: Yes. Why not?

[*They stare at one another,* ERNEST *coolly and deliberately and* HAZEL *with attempted hauteur, when* MADGE *and* ROBIN *enter together, in the middle of a talk.*]

ROBIN [*who is in great form*]: Golly yes! It was a great lark. We weren't in uniform, y'know. I did some stoking. Hard work, but a great stunt.

MADGE [*hotly*]: It wasn't. You ought to have been ashamed of yourselves.

ROBIN [*surprised*]: Why?

MADGE: Because helping to break a strike and being a blackleg isn't a lark and a stunt. Those railwaymen were desperately anxious to improve their conditions. They didn't go on strike for fun. It was a very serious thing for them and for their wives and families. And then people like you, Robin, think it's amusing when you try to do their work and make the strike useless. I think it's shameful the way the middle classes turn against the working class.

ROBIN [*rather out of his depth now*]: But there had to be some sort of train service.

MADGE: Why? If the public had to do without trains altogether, they might realize then that the railwaymen have some grievances.

ERNEST [*sardonically*]: They might. But I've an idea they'd be too busy with their own grievance – no trains. And you only want a few more railway strikes and then half their traffic will be gone for ever, turned into road transport. And what do your clever railwaymen do then ? [*Pauses.* MADGE *is listening, of course, but not quite acknowledging that he had any right to join in.*] And another thing. The working class is out for itself. Then why shouldn't the middle class be out for itself ?

MADGE [*coldly*]: Because the middle class must have already been 'out for itself' – as you call it –

ERNEST: Well, what do you call it ? Something in Latin ?

MADGE [*with chill impatience*]: I say, the middle class must have already been successfully out for itself or it wouldn't be a comfortable middle class. Then why turn against the working class when at last *it* tries to look after itself ?

ERNEST [*cynically*]: That's easy. There's only so much to go round, and if you take more, then I get less.

MADGE [*rather sharply*]: I'm sorry, but that's bad economics as well as bad ethics.

ROBIN [*bursting out*]: But we'd have Red Revolution – like Russia – if we began to listen to these wild chaps like this J. H. Thomas.

HAZEL [*moving*]: Well, I think it's all silly. Why can't people agree ?

ERNEST [*seeing her going*]: Oh! – Miss Conway –

HAZEL [*her very blank sweetness a snub*]: Oh – yes – good night. [*She goes out.*]

> [ERNEST *looks after her, a rather miserable figure. Then he looks towards* ROBIN *just in time to catch a grin on his face before it is almost – but not quite – wiped off.*]

MADGE [*to* ROBIN]: I came in here for something. What was it ? [*Looks about her and through* ERNEST, *whom she obviously dislikes.*]

ROBIN [*still a grin lurking*]: Don't ask me.

> [MADGE *goes, ignoring* ERNEST, *though rather absently than pointedly.* ROBIN, *still looking vaguely mocking, lights a cigarette.*]

ROBIN [*casually*]: Were you in the army ?

ERNEST: Yes. Two years.

ROBIN: What crush ?

ERNEST: Army Pay Corps.

ROBIN [*easily, not too rudely*]: That must have been fun for you.
[ERNEST *looks as if he is going to make an angry retort when* CAROL *hurries in.*]

CAROL: Mr Beevers – [*As he turns, looking rather sullen,* ROBIN *wanders out.*] Oh! – you look *Put Out.*

ERNEST [*grimly*]: That's about it. Put out!

CAROL [*looking hard at him*]: I believe you're all hot and angry inside, aren't you?

ERNEST [*taking it as lightly as he can*]: Or disappointed. Which is it?

CAROL: A mixture, I expect. Well, Mr Beevers, you mustn't. You were very nice about the charade – and very good in it too – and I don't suppose you've ever played before, have you?

ERNEST: No. [*Grimly*] They didn't go in for those sort of things in my family.

CAROL [*looking at him critically*]: No, I don't think you've had enough Fun. That's your trouble, Mr Beevers. You must come and play charades again.

ERNEST [*as if setting her apart from the others*]: *You*'re all right, y'know.

[MRS C'*s voice, very clear, is heard off saying,* 'But surely he's gone, hasn't he?']

CAROL: We're *all* all right, you know. And don't forget that, Mr Beevers.

ERNEST [*liking her*]: You're a funny kid.

CAROL [*severely*]: I'm not very funny and I'm certainly not a kid –

ERNEST: Oh – sorry!

CAROL [*serenely*]: I'll forgive you this time.

[MRS C *enters with* GERALD. *She looks rather surprised to see* ERNEST *still there. He notices this.*]

ERNEST [*awkwardly*]: I'm just going, Mrs Conway. [*To* GERALD] You coming along?

MRS C [*smoothly, but quickly in*]: No, Mr Thornton and I want to talk business for a few minutes.

ERNEST: I see. Well, good night, Mrs Conway. And I'm very pleased to have met you.

MRS C [*condescendingly gracious*]: Good night, Mr Beevers. Carol, will you –

CAROL [*cheerfully*]: Yes. [*To* ERNEST, *who looks bewildered by it, in imitation Western American accent*] I'll set you and your hoss on the big trail, pardner.

> [*She and* ERNEST *go out.* MRS C *and* GERALD *watch them go. Then* GERALD *turns and raises his eyebrows at her.* MRS C *shakes her head. We hear a door slammed to.*]

MRS C [*briskly*]: I'm sorry if your little friend thought he was being pushed out, but really, Gerald, the children would never have forgiven me if I'd encouraged him to stay any longer.

GERALD: I'm afraid Beevers hasn't been a success.

MRS C: Well, after all, he is – rather – isn't he?

GERALD: I did warn you, y'know. And really he was so desperately keen to meet the famous Conways.

MRS C: Hazel, you mean.

GERALD: Hazel, especially, but he was determined to know the whole family.

MRS C: Well, I do think they're an attractive lot of children.

GERALD: Only outshone by their attractive mother.

MRS C [*delighted*]: Gerald! I believe you're going to flirt with me.

GERALD [*who isn't*]: Of course I am. By the way, there *wasn't* any business you wanted to discuss, was there?

MRS C: No, not really. But I think you ought to know I've had another *enormous* offer for this house. Of course I wouldn't dream of selling it, but it's nice to know it's worth so much. Oh! – and young George Farrow would like me to sell him my share in the firm, and says he's ready to make an offer that would surprise me.

GERALD: I believe it would be pretty handsome too. But, of course, there's no point in selling out when they're paying fifteen per cent. And once we're really out of this war-time atmosphere and the government restrictions are off, there's going to be a tremendous boom.

MRS C: Isn't that lovely? All the children back home, and plenty of money to help them to settle down. And, mind you, Gerald, I shouldn't be a bit surprised if Robin doesn't do awfully well in some business quite soon. *Selling* things, probably – people find him so attractive. Dear Robin! [*Pauses. Then change of tone, more depth and feeling*] Gerald, it isn't so very long ago that I thought myself the unluckiest woman in the world. If it hadn't

been for the children, I wouldn't have wanted to go on living.
Sometimes – without *him* – I didn't want to go on living.
And now – though, of course, it'll never be the same without
him – I suddenly feel I'm one of the luckiest women in the
world. All my children round me, quite safe at last, very happy.
[ROBIN's *voice, shouting, off,* 'It's hide and seek all over the
house.'] Did he say 'all over the house'?

GERALD: Yes.

MRS C [*calling*]: Not in my room, Robin, please.

ROBIN'S VOICE [*off, shouting*]: Mother's room's barred.

JOAN'S VOICE [*farther off, shouting*]: Who's going to be It?

ROBIN'S VOICE [*off*]: I am. Mother, come on. Where's Gerald?

MRS C [*as she prepares to move*]: Just to hear him shouting about the
house again – you don't know what it means to me, Gerald. And
you never will know.

    [*They go out. As* MRS C *passes switch, she can switch off half the
lights in the room, perhaps leaving right half unilluminated and
perhaps standard lamp on left half.*]

ROBIN'S VOICE [*loud, off*]: I'll go into the coat cupboard and
count fifty. Now then – scatter.

    [*After a moment* JOAN *enters, happy and breathless, and after
looking about chooses a hiding-place to the right – behind a
chair, end of bookcase or sofa, or curtain. No sooner has she in-
stalled herself than* ALAN *enters and moves across to that end.
She peeps out and sees him.*]

JOAN [*imploring whisper*]: Oh – Alan – don't hide in here.

ALAN [*humbly*]: I came specially. I saw you come in.

JOAN: No, please. Go somewhere else.

ALAN [*wistfully*]: You look so pretty, Joan.

JOAN: Do I? That's sweet of you, Alan.

ALAN: Can I stay, then?

JOAN: No, please. It's *so* much more fun if you go somewhere else.
Alan, don't spoil it.

ALAN: Spoil what?

JOAN [*very hurriedly*]: The game – of course. Go on, Alan, there's
a pet. Oh – you can't go out that way now. You'll have to go out
of the window and then round. Go on.

ALAN: All right. [*Climbs out of window, then looks closely at her a
moment, then softly*] Good-bye, Joan.

JOAN [*whispering, surprised*]: Why do you say that?

ALAN [*very sadly*]: Because I feel it *is* good-bye.

[ROBIN's *voice, humming, is heard off.* ALAN *goes through the curtains at the window.* ROBIN, *half humming, half singing, a popular song of the period, enters slowly. He moves to the edge of the lighted half, looking about him, still singing. Finally he turns away and begins to move, when* JOAN *joins in the song softly from her hiding-place.*]

ROBIN [*with satisfaction*]: A-ha! [*Very quickly he closes the curtains but as he turns his back,* JOAN *reaches out and turns off the switch of the standard lamp in her corner. The room is now almost in darkness.*] All right, Joan Helford. Where are you, Joan Helford, where are you? [*She is heard to laugh in the darkness.*] You can't escape, Joan Helford, you can't escape. No, no. No, no. No escape for little Joan. No escape.

[*They run round the room, then she goes to the window and stands on the seat. He pulls her down, and then, in silhouette against the moonlight we see them embrace and kiss.*]

JOAN [*really moved*]: Oh – Robin!

ROBIN [*mocking, but nicely*]: Oh – Joan!

JOAN [*shyly*]: I suppose – you've been – doing this – to dozens of girls?

ROBIN [*still light*]: Yes, Joan, dozens.

JOAN [*looking up at him*]: I thought so.

ROBIN [*a trifle unsteadily*]: Like that, Joan. But not – like this – [*Now he kisses her with more ardour.*]

JOAN [*deeply moved, but still shy*]: Robin – you *are* sweet.

ROBIN [*after pause*]: You know, Joan, although it's not so very long since I saw you last, I couldn't believe my eyes tonight – you looked so stunning.

JOAN: It was because I'd just heard that you'd come back, Robin.

ROBIN [*who does*]: I don't believe it.

JOAN [*sincerely*]: Yes, it's true – honestly – I don't suppose you've ever thought about me, have you?

ROBIN [*who hasn't*]: Yes, I have. Hundreds of times.

JOAN: I have about you too.

ROBIN [*kissing her*]: Joan, you're a darling!

JOAN [*after pause, whispering*]: Do you remember that morning you went away so early – a year ago?

ROBIN: Yes. But you weren't there. Only mother and Hazel and Kay.

JOAN: I was there too, but I didn't let any of you see me.

ROBIN [*genuinely surprised*]: You got up at that filthy hour just to see me go?

JOAN [*simply*]: Yes, of course. Oh – it was awful – trying to hide and trying not to cry, all at the same time.

ROBIN [*still surprised and moved*]: But Joan, I'd no idea.

JOAN [*very shyly*]: I didn't mean to give myself away.

ROBIN [*embracing her*]: But Joan – oh gosh! – it's marvellous.

JOAN: You don't love me?

ROBIN [*now sure he does*]: Of course I do. Golly, this is great! Joan, we'll have a scrumptious time!

JOAN [*solemnly*]: Yes, let's. But Robin – it's terribly *serious*, y'know.

ROBIN: Oh – yes – don't think I don't feel that, too. But that's no reason why we shouldn't enjoy ourselves, is it?

JOAN [*crying out*]: No, no, no. Let's be happy for ever and ever. [*They embrace fervently, silhouetted against the moonlit window. Now the curtains are suddenly drawn by* CAROL, *who sees them and calls out to people behind her.*]

CAROL [*with a sort of cheerful disgust*]: I thought so! They're in here – *Courting*! I knew there was a catch in this hide-and-seek. [ROBIN *and* JOAN *spring apart but still hold hands as* CAROL *switches on all the lights and comes into the room, followed by* MADGE *and* GERALD. MADGE *is rather excited – and rather untidy, too, as if she had been hiding in some difficult place.*]

ROBIN [*grinning*]: Sorry! Shall we start again?

MADGE [*crossing towards window*]: No, thank you, Robin.

CAROL: You'd better explain to mother. I'm going to make tea. [*She goes.*]

[ROBIN *and* JOAN *look at one another, then go out.* GERALD *watches* MADGE, *who now draws the curtains and then returns to him.*]

GERALD: Well, Madge, it sounds all right. And I know Lord Robert Cecil's a fine chap. But I don't quite see where I come into it.

MADGE: Because in a few weeks' time there'll be a branch of this League of Nations Union here in Newlingham. It's no use my

doing much about it – though I'll join, of course – because I'll
be away. But you could be organizing secretary or something,
Gerald.

GERALD: Don't know that I'd be much good.

MADGE: You'd be perfect. You understand business. You know
how to handle people. You'd make a good public speaker. Oh,
Gerald – you're maddening!

GERALD [*smiling, not without affection*]: Why, Madge ? What have
I done now ?

MADGE: We're friends, aren't we ?

GERALD: I consider you one of my very best friends, Madge, and I
hope I'm not flattering myself.

MADGE [*warmly*]: Of course not.

GERALD [*smiling*]: Good! So ?

MADGE: You're not doing enough, Gerald.

GERALD [*mildly*]: I'm kept pretty busy, y'know.

MADGE: Yes, I don't mean you're lazy – though I'm not sure that
you aren't a bit, y'know, Gerald – I mean you're not doing
enough with yourself. You're not *using* yourself to the utmost. I
could be *tremendously* proud of you, Gerald.

GERALD: That's – almost overwhelming – coming from you,
Madge.

MADGE: Why from me ?

GERALD: Because I know very well that you've got a very good
brain and are a most critical young woman. Rather frightening.

MADGE [*rather more feminine here*]: Nonsense! You don't mean
that. I'd much rather you didn't, y'know.

GERALD: All right, I don't. As a matter of fact, I'm very fond of
you, Madge, but don't often get a chance of showing you that I
am.

MADGE [*lighting up at this*]: I've always been fond of you, Gerald,
and that's why I say I could be tremendously proud of you.
[*With more breadth and sweep and real warm enthusiasm*] We're
going to build up a new world now. This horrible War was
probably necessary because it was a great bonfire on which we
threw all the old nasty rubbish of the world. Civilization can
really begin – at last. People have learned their lesson –

GERALD [*dubiously*]: I hope so.

MADGE: Oh – Gerald – don't be so pessimistic, so cynical –

GERALD: Sorry, but a lawyer – even a young one – sees a lot of human nature in his office. There's a procession of people with their quarrels and grievances. And sometimes I wonder how much people are capable of learning.

MADGE: That's because you have to deal with some of the stupidest. But *the* people – all over the world – have learned their lesson. You'll see. No more piling up armaments. No more wars. No more hate and intolerance and violence. Oh – Gerald – I believe that when we look back – in twenty years' time – we'll be staggered at the progress that's been made. Because things happen quickly now –

GERALD: That's true enough.

MADGE [*begins to orate a little, sincerely*]: And so is all the rest. Under the League, we'll build up a new commonwealth of all the nations, so that they can live at peace for ever. And Imperialism will go. And so in the end, of course, will Capitalism. There'll be no more booms and slumps and panics and strikes and lock-outs, because the people themselves, led by the best brains in their countries, will possess both the political and economic power. There'll be Socialism at last, a free, prosperous, happy people, all enjoying equal opportunities, living at peace with the whole world. [*Quotes with great fervour and sincerity*]

> Bring me my bow of burning gold:
> Bring me my Arrows of desire:
> Bring me my Spear: O clouds unfold!
> Bring me my Chariot of fire.
>
> I will not cease from Mental Fight,
> Nor shall my Sword sleep in my hand
> Till we have built Jerusalem
> In England's green and pleasant Land ...

GERALD [*genuinely moved by her fervour*]: Madge – you're inspired tonight. I – I hardly recognize you – you're –

MADGE [*warmly, happily*]: This is the real me. Oh! – Gerald – in this New World we're going to build up now, men and women won't play a silly little game of cross-purposes any longer. They'll go forward together – sharing everything –

[MRS C *enters with* HAZEL. MADGE *breaks off, looking rather untidy.* GERALD, *who has been genuinely dominated by her, looks round, recovering himself.*]

MRS C [*with maddening maternal briskness*]: Madge dear, your hair's all over the place, you've made your nose all shiny, you're horribly untidy, and I'm sure you're in the middle of a Socialist speech that must be boring poor Gerald.

[*The generous mood is shattered.* MADGE *might have been hit in the face. She looks at her mother, then looks quickly at* GERALD, *reads something in his face – a sort of withdrawal from her – that is somehow final, and then in complete silence walks straight out of the room.*]

MRS C [*lightly, but knowing what has happened*]: Poor Madge!

HAZEL [*with sudden reproach*]: Mother!

MRS C [*with wide innocence*]: What, Hazel?

HAZEL [*significantly, indicating* GERALD]: *You* know!

GERALD [*not half the man he was*]: I think – I'd better be going.

MRS C: Oh – no, Gerald, don't go. Kay and Carol are making some tea and we're all going to be nice and cosy together in here.

GERALD: I fancy it's rather late, though. [*Glances at his watch, while* HAZEL *slips out.*] After eleven. I *must* go. I've an early appointment in the morning, and one or two things to look through before I turn in tonight. So – [*With slight smile.* KAY *enters with folding legs of small Oriental table. She puts them down, to turn to* GERALD, *and* MRS C *arranges them.*] Good night, Kay. Thank you for a very nice party. And now that you're properly grown-up, I hope you'll be happy.

KAY [*with a slight smile*]: Thank you, Gerald. Do you think I will?

GERALD [*his smile suddenly vanishing*]: I don't know, Kay. I really don't know.

[*Smiles again and shakes hands. Nods and smiles at* HAZEL, *who enters with tray of tea things.*]

MRS C: No. I'll see you out, Gerald.

[*They go out.* HAZEL *and* KAY *can rearrange things a little while talking.*]

HAZEL [*thoughtfully*]: I've always thought it must be much more *fun* being a girl than being a man.

KAY: I'm never sure. Sometimes men seem quite hopelessly dull, like creatures made out of wood. And then at other times they seem to have all the fun.

HAZEL [*very seriously for her*]: Kay, just now – this very minute – I wish I wasn't a girl. I'd like to be a man – one of those men with red faces and loud voices who just don't care what anybody says about them.

KAY [*laughingly*]: Perhaps they do, though.

HAZEL: I'd like to be one of those who don't.

KAY: Why all this?

[HAZEL *shakes her head.* CAROL *and* ALAN *enter with the rest of the tea things.*]

CAROL: Alan says he wants to go to bed.

KAY: Oh – no, Alan. Don't spoil it.

ALAN: How could I?

KAY: By going to bed. It's my birthday, and you're not to leave us until I say you can.

CAROL [*severely*]: Quite right, Kay. [*Going up to* ALAN] And that's because we're very very fond of you, Alan, though you are such a chump. You must smoke your pipe too – for cosiness. [*Generally*] Robin and Joan are courting in the dining-room now. I can see they're going to be an awful nuisance.

KAY [*as* HAZEL *and* CAROL *settle down*]: If you had to fall in love with somebody, would you like it to be at home or somewhere else?

HAZEL: Somewhere else. Too ordinary at home. On a yacht or the terrace at Monte Carlo or a Pacific Island. Marvellous!

CAROL: That would be using up too many things at once. Greedy stuff!

HAZEL [*coolly*]: I *am* greedy.

CAROL: I should think so. [*To the other two*] Yesterday morning, she was in the bath, reading *Greenmantle*, and eating nut-milk chocolate.

KAY [*who has been thinking*]: No, it wouldn't be too ordinary, falling in love at home here. It would be best, I think. Suppose you were suddenly unhappy. It would be awful to be desperately unhappy and in love miles away in a strange house. ... [*Suddenly stops, shivers.*]

CAROL: Kay, what's the matter?

KAY: Nothing.

CAROL: Then it must have been a goose walking over your grave.
[KAY *abruptly turns away from them, going towards the window.* HAZEL *looks at her – as the other two do – then raises her eyebrows at* CAROL, *who shakes her head sternly.* MRS C *enters and looks cheerful at the sight of the tea.*]

MRS C [*cheerfully*]: Now then, let's have some tea and be nice and cosy together. Where's Robin?

HAZEL: Spooning with Joan in the dining-room.

MRS C: Oh! – hasn't Joan gone yet? I really think she might leave us to ourselves now. After all, it's the first time we've all been together in this house for – how long? It must be at least three years. I'll pour out. Come on, Kay. What's the matter?

CAROL [*in tremendous whisper, seriously*]: Sh! It's a *Mood*.
[*But* KAY *returns, looking rather strained. Her mother looks at her carefully, smiling.* KAY *manages an answering smile.*]

MRS C: That's better, darling. What a funny child you are, aren't you?

KAY: Not really, Mother. Where's Madge?

ALAN: She went upstairs.

MRS C: Go up, dear, and tell her we're all in here, with some tea, and ask her – very nicely, dear, specially from me – to come down.

HAZEL [*muttering, rather*]: I'll bet she doesn't.
[ALAN *goes.* MRS C *begins pouring out tea.*]

MRS C: This is just like old times, isn't it? And we seem to have waited so long. I ought to tell fortunes again – tonight.

HAZEL [*eagerly*]: Oh – yes – Mother, do.

KAY [*rather sharply*]: No.

MRS C: Kay! Really! Have you had too much excitement today?

KAY: No, I don't think so. Sorry, Mother. Somehow, I hated the idea of you messing about with those cards tonight. I never did like it much.

CAROL [*solemnly*]: I believe only the Bad Things come true.

MRS C: Certainly not. I clearly saw Madge's Girton scholarship, you remember. I said she was going to get one, didn't I? And I always said Robin and Alan would come back. I saw it every time in the cards.
[*Enter* JOAN *and* ROBIN.]

JOAN: I – I think I ought to go now, Mrs Conway. [*To* KAY,

impulsively.] Thank you so much, Kay, it's been the loveliest
party there ever was. [*Suddenly kisses her with great affection,
then she looks solemnly at* MRS C *who is considering the situation.*]
I really have had a marvellous time, Mrs Conway.

[*Standing close to her now,* MRS C *looks quite searchingly at her.*
JOAN *meets her look quite bravely, though a little shaky.*]

ROBIN: Well, Mother?

[MRS C *looks at him, then at* JOAN, *and suddenly smiles.* JOAN
smiles back.]

MRS C: Are you two children *serious*?

ROBIN [*boisterously*]: Of course we are.

MRS C: Joan?

JOAN [*very solemnly, nervously*]: Yes.

MRS C [*with an air of capitulation*]: I think you'd better have a cup
of tea, hadn't you?

[JOAN *flings her arms round* MRS C *and kisses her excitedly.*]

JOAN: I'm so happy.

CAROL [*loudly, cheerfully*]: Tea. Tea. Tea.

[*Passing of cups, etc.* ALAN *enters.*]

ALAN: Madge says she's too tired, Mother. [*Goes and sits down
near* KAY.]

MRS C: Well, I think we can get on very nicely without Madge.
Kay ought to read us some of the new novel she's writing –

[*Exclamations of agreement and approval from* JOAN *and*
ROBIN *and a groan from* HAZEL.]

KAY [*in horror*]: I couldn't possibly, Mother.

MRS C: I can't see why not. You always expect me to be ready to
sing for you.

KAY: That's different.

MRS C [*mostly to* ROBIN *and* JOAN]: Kay's always so solemn and
secretive about her writing – as if she were ashamed of it.

KAY [*bravely*]: I am – in a way. I know it's not good enough yet.
Most of it's stupid, stupid, *stupid*.

CAROL [*indignantly*]: It isn't, Kay.

KAY: Yes, it is, angel. But it won't always be. It *must* come right if
I only keep on trying. And then – you'll see.

JOAN: Is that what you want to do, Kay? Just to write novels and
things?

KAY: Yes. But there's nothing in simply writing. The point is to be *good* – to be sensitive and sincere. Hardly anybody's both, especially women who write. But I'm going to try and be. And whatever happens, I'm never *never* going to write except what I want to write, what I feel is true to me, deep down. I won't write just to please silly people or just to make money. I'll – [*But she suddenly breaks off.*]

   [*The rest wait and stare.*]

ALAN [*encouragingly*]: Go on, Kay.

KAY [*confusedly, dejectedly*]: No – Alan – I'd finished really – or if I was going to say something else, I've forgotten what it was – nothing much –

MRS C [*not too concernedly*]: You're sure you're not over-tired, Kay?

KAY [*hastily*]: No, Mother. Really.

MRS C: I wonder what will have happened to you, Hazel, when Kay's a famous novelist? Perhaps one of your majors and captains will come back for you soon.

HAZEL [*calmly*]: They needn't. In fact, I'd rather none of them did.

ROBIN [*teasingly*]: Thinks she can do much better than them.

HAZEL [*calmly*]: I know I can. I shall marry a tall, rather good-looking man about five or six years older than I am, and he'll have plenty of money and be very fond of travel, and we'll go all over the world together but have a house in London.

MRS C: And what about poor Newlingham?

HAZEL: Mother, I couldn't possibly spend the rest of my life here. I'd die. But you shall come and stay with us in London, and we'll give parties so that people can come and stare at my sister, Kay Conway, the famous novelist.

ROBIN [*boisterously*]: And what about your brother, Robin, the famous – oh! famous something-or-other, you bet your life.

JOAN [*rather teasingly*]: You don't know what you're going to do yet, Robin.

ROBIN [*grandly*]: Well, give me a chance. I've only been out of the Air Force about twelve hours. But – by jingo – I'm going to do *something*. And none of this starting-at-the-bottom-of-the-ladder, pushing-a-pen-in-a-corner business either. This is a time when young men get a chance, and I'm going to take it. You watch.

MRS C [*with mock alarm, though with underlying seriousness*]: Don't tell me you're going to run away from Newlingham, too!

ROBIN [*grandly*]: Oh – well – I don't know about that yet, Mother. I might make a start here – there's some money in the place, thanks to some jolly rotten profiteering, and we're pretty well known here, so that would help – but I don't guarantee to take root in Newlingham, no fear! Don't be surprised, Hazel, if I'm in London before you. Or even before you, Kay. *And* making plenty of money. [*To* HAZEL] Perhaps more than this tall, good-looking chap of yours will be making.

CAROL [*sharply, pointing*]: Hazel will always have plenty of money.

MRS C [*amused*]: How do you know, Carol?

CAROL: I just do. It came over me suddenly then.

MRS C [*still amused*]: Well now! I thought I was the prophetic one of the family. I suppose it wouldn't be fair if I sent my rival to bed.

CAROL: I should jolly well think it wouldn't. And I'll tell you another thing. [*Points suddenly at* ALAN] Alan's the happy one.

ROBIN: Good old Alan!

ALAN: I – rather think – you're wrong there, y'know, Carol.

CAROL: I'm not. I *know*.

MRS C: Now I'm not going to have this. I'm the one who *knows* in this family. Now wait a minute. [*Closes her eyes, then half playfully, half seriously*] Yes. I see Robin dashing about, making lots of money and becoming very important and helping some of you others. And a very devoted young wife by his side. And Hazel, of course, being very grand. And her husband *is* tall and *quite* good-looking, nearly as good-looking as she thinks he is. I believe he comes into a title.

ROBIN: Snob!

MRS C: I don't see Madge marrying, but then she'll be headmistress of a big school quite soon, and then she'll become one of these women who are on all sorts of committees and have to go up to London to give evidence, and so becomes happy and grand that way.

ROBIN: I'll bet she will, too, good old Madge!

MRS C [*gaily*]: I'll go and stay with her sometimes – *very* important, the headmistress's mother – and the other mistresses will be invited in to dine and will listen *very* respectfully while I tell them about my other children –

JOAN [*happily, admiringly*]: Oh – Mrs Conway – I can just imagine that. You'll have a *marvellous* time.

MRS C [*same vein*]: Then there's Carol. Well, of course, Carol will be here with me for years yet –

CAROL [*excitedly*]: I don't know about that. I haven't exactly decided *what* to do yet, there are so many things to do.

JOAN: Oh – Carol – I think you could go on the stage.

CAROL [*with growing excitement*]: Yes, I could, of course, and I've often thought of it. But I shouldn't want to be on the stage *all* the time – and when I wasn't playing a part, I'd like to be painting pictures – just for myself, y'know – daubing like mad – with lots and lots and lots of the very brightest paint – tubes and tubes of vermilion and royal blue and emerald green and gamboge and cobalt and Chinese white. And then making all kinds of weird dresses for myself. And scarlet cloaks. And black crêpe-de-Chine gowns with orange dragons all over them. And cooking! Yes, doing sausages and gingerbread and pancakes. And sitting on the top of mountains and going down rivers in canoes. And making friends with all sorts of people. And I'd share a flat or a little house with Kay in London, and Alan would come to stay with us and smoke his pipe, and we'd talk about books and laugh at *ridiculous* people, and then go to foreign countries –

ROBIN [*calling through*]: Hoy, hoy, steady!

MRS C [*affectionately amused*]: How are you going to *begin* doing all that, you ridiculous child!

CAROL [*excitedly*]: I'd get it all in somehow. The point is – to live. Never mind about money and positions and husbands with titles and rubbish – I'm *going to live*.

MRS C [*who has now caught the infection*]: All right, darling. But wherever you were, all of you, and whatever you were doing, you'd all come back here sometimes, wouldn't you ? I'd come and see you, but you'd all come and see me, too, all together, perhaps with wives and husbands and lovely children of your own, not being rich and famous or anything but just being yourselves, as you are now, enjoying our silly old jokes, sometimes playing the same silly old games, all one big happy family. I can see us all here again –

KAY [*a terrible cry*]: Don't! [*She is standing, deeply moved.*]

[*The others stare in silent consternation.*]

MRS C: But what is it, Kay?

[KAY, *still moved, shakes her head. The others exchange puzzled glances, but* CAROL *hurries across, all tenderness, and puts an arm round her.*]

CAROL [*going to her with the solemnity of a child*]: I won't bother with any of those things, Kay, really I won't. I'll come and look after you wherever you go. I won't leave you ever if you don't want me to. I'll look after you, darling.

[KAY *stops crying. She looks – half-smiling – at* CAROL *in a puzzled, wistful fashion.* CAROL *goes back to her mother's side.*]

MRS C [*reproachful but affectionate*]: Really, Kay! What's the matter?

[KAY *shakes her head, then looks very earnestly at* ALAN.]

KAY [*struggling with some thought*]: Alan . . . please tell me. . . . I can't bear it . . . and there's something . . . something . . . you could tell me. . . .

ALAN [*troubled, bewildered*]: I'm sorry, Kay. I don't understand. What is it?

KAY: Something you know – that would make it different – not so hard to bear. Don't you know *yet*?

ALAN [*stammering*]: No – I don't – understand.

KAY: Oh – hurry, hurry, Alan – and then – tell me – and comfort me. Something – of Blake's – came into it – [*Looks hard at him, then struggling, remembers, saying brokenly*]

> Joy . . . and woe . . . are woven fine,
> A clothing for the . . . soul divine. . . .

I used to know that verse, too. What was it at the end? [*Remembers, as before*]

> And, when this . . . we rightly know,
> Safely through the world we go.

Safely . . . through the world we go. . . .

[*Looks like breaking down again, but recovers herself.*]

MRS C [*almost a whisper*]: Over-excitement. I might have known.

[*To* KAY, *firmly, cheerfully*] Kay, darling, all this birthday excitement's been too much. You'd better go to bed now, dear, and Carol shall bring you some hot milk. Perhaps an aspirin, too, eh ? [KAY, *recovering from her grief, shakes her head.*] You're all right now, aren't you, darling ?

KAY [*in muffled voice*]: Yes, Mother, I'm all right. [*But she turns and goes to the window, pulling back the curtains and looking out.*]

MRS C: I know what might help, it did once before. Robin, come with me.

JOAN [*rather helplessly*]: I ought to go, oughtn't I ?

MRS C: No, stay a few minutes, Joan. Robin.

[*She and* ROBIN *go out.*]

CAROL [*whispering as she moves*]: She's going to sing, and I know what it will be.

[CAROL *switches out the lights and returns to sit with* HAZEL *and* JOAN, *the three girls making a group, dimly but warmly lit by the light coming in from the hall. Very softly there comes the opening bars of Brahms's 'Wiegenlied'.* ALAN *joins* KAY *at the window, so that his face, too, like hers, is illuminated by the moonlight.*]

ALAN [*quietly through the music*]: Kay.

KAY [*quietly*]: Yes, Alan ?

ALAN: There will be – something – I can tell you – one day. I'll try – I promise.

[*The moonlight at the window shows us* ALAN *looking at her earnestly, and we just catch her answering smile, as the song swells out a little. And then the lights begin to fade, and very soon the three girls are no more than ghosts and all the room is dark, but the moonlight – and the faces of* KAY *and* ALAN *– still lingers; until at last there is only the faintest glimmer, and the Conways have gone, the curtain is down, and the play over.*]

END OF PLAY

I Have Been Here Before

A PLAY IN THREE ACTS

CHARACTERS

SALLY PRATT

SAM SHIPLEY

DR GÖRTLER

OLIVER FARRANT

JANET ORMUND

WALTER ORMUND

The Scene throughout is the sitting-room of the
Black Bull Inn, Grindle Moor, North Yorkshire, at
Whitsuntide.

Act One
Friday

Act Two
Saturday

Act Three
Sunday

'I Have Been Here Before' was first produced at the Royalty Theatre, London, on Wednesday, 22 September 1937, with the following cast:

SALLY PRATT	Eileen Beldon
SAM SHIPLEY	William Heilbronn
DR GÖRTLER	Lewis Casson
OLIVER FARRANT	William Fox
JANET ORMUND	Patricia Hilliard
WALTER ORMUND	Wilfrid Lawson

Produced by Lewis Casson

(For some of Dr Görtler's theories of Time and Recurrence, I gratefully acknowledge my debt to P. D. Ouspensky's astonishing book, *A New Model of the Universe*. It must be understood, however, that I accept full responsibility for the free use I have made of these borrowed ideas, and that it does not follow because I make use of them that I necessarily accept them.) — J.B.P.

ACT ONE

Sitting-room of the Black Bull Inn, Grindle Moor, North Yorkshire, a moorland inn of the farmhouse type that serves as the local 'pub' and also takes a few guests. The room is simply furnished in the style of a north-country farmhouse sitting-room. On the left, is a long low window, deeply set, with a cushioned seat, and the sunlight is streaming in through this window. At the back, on the left, is a door that serves as an entrance to the Inn to the people staying there, but not to people who merely go for a drink or a meal. On the right at the back is the door that leads to the dining-room, the bar and the rest of the Inn, including two of the guest bedrooms. Through this door a passage can be seen. Downstage right is a slighter door, leading to two bedrooms; it opens directly on to a steep flight of stairs. Through the main door, when open, can be seen a distant glimpse of high-moorland. The fireplace of the room is presumed to be in the fourth wall. On the right is an old-fashioned sofa, and a table towards centre. A couple of shabby but comfortable easy chairs, not too large, at either side of this table, and two or three smaller chairs near walls. Near door to the dining-room is a telephone attached to the wall. It is an evening in June, about eight o'clock. The room is empty at rise of curtain, but immediately afterwards SALLY PRATT *enters bringing in some flowers. She is a pleasant-looking country-woman in her middle thirties and is nicely dressed, but wears an apron as if she were still busy with household work. She speaks in a rather loud tone and with a north-country accent, but not too broad. After a moment or two,* SAM SHIPLEY *enters. He is a stout, humorous, contented Yorkshireman in his sixties. He is in his shirt-sleeves and is smoking a pipe. His accent is broader than his daughter's, but not very broad.*

SALLY [*as she finishes her task*]: That looks a bit better.

SAM: Ay.

SALLY [*sharply but not unpleasantly*]: Father – get your coat on.

SAM: What for?

SALLY: You know what for, I've told you often enough. Landlord o' the Black Bull in his shirt-sleeves like a barman!

SAM: Long as folk pay me what they owe me – they can tak' me for a barman if they like. I'm not a particular chap.

SALLY: Now go on. We'll have somebody here in a minute. I don't want Miss Holmes and her friends marching in, catching you in your shirt-sleeves.

SAM: If they never see worse nor that, they'll be lucky. [*Pause.*] When's Mr Farrant getting back?

SALLY: Any time. He only wanted some cold meat and salad and cheese left for his supper. I wish they were all as easy to please.

[*He wanders out during this speech, leaving door open behind him. Then he pops his head back.*]

SAM: Butcher's here.

SALLY: An' he's rare an' late. [*As she is going, there is the sound of a car. She hears it and shouts*] Father, I believe there's somebody here.

SAM [*off*]: I'm coming.

[*She hurries out. In the empty room we hear the clock ticking. A moment's pause. Then there is a quiet knocking on the outer door and it opens slowly, and* DR GÖRTLER *enters. The clock chimes. He is a man about sixty, in well-worn darkish clothes of a foreign cut. He has a slight foreign accent, and speaks with precision. Although his appearance and manner suggest the quiet detached scholar, he has a good deal of assurance and authority. He looks about him with eager interest and curiosity, and when he has taken the room in, consults a small notebook, as if comparing its appearance with some notes there. Finally, he nods.* SAM *now returns, wearing his coat. The two men look at one another for a moment.*]

SAM: Good evening, sir.

DR GÖRTLER: Good evening. You are the landlord?

SAM: That's right. Sam Shipley.

DR GÖRTLER: You let rooms to visitors?

SAM: A few.

DR GÖRTLER: Three or four, perhaps?

SAM [*slightly surprised*]: Yes.

[SALLY *bustles in, then stops short in surprise when she sees* DR GÖRTLER.]

SALLY: Oh! – good evening.

DR GÖRTLER [*smiling*]: Good evening.

SALLY: Were you wanting a room?

DR GÖRTLER [*slowly*]: I am not sure.

SALLY [*who does not like this*]: Oh! – well it doesn't matter because I'm afraid we can't oblige you.

DR GÖRTLER: You have no room?

SALLY: We've only four bedrooms and they're all taken for this Whitsuntide. There's a gentleman in one already, and the other three are coming tonight.

DR GÖRTLER: So. These three who are coming tonight – you know them?

SALLY [*surprised*]: Yes.

DR GÖRTLER [*gently, tentatively*]: Two of them – perhaps – are married people – the man older than his wife – he might be rich – and then – perhaps – a younger man – ?

SALLY [*who has listened to this with some surprise*]: No. We're expecting three ladies.

DR GÖRTLER [*rather taken aback*]: Three ladies?

SALLY: Teachers from Manchester.

DR GÖRTLER: Oh! Perhaps there is another inn here, eh?

SAM: Nay, this is t'only one. There's t'Lion at Dale End, but that's eight mile from here.

SALLY: But there's one or two here that lets rooms. You might try Lane Top Farm – Mrs Fletcher – it's just a bit farther on.

SAM: Not five minutes in a car – if you've come in a car.

DR GÖRTLER [*still showing signs of disappointment*]: Yes, I have a little car. I will try this farm but I do not think it will be any use. [*Smiles rather forlornly.*] This must be the wrong year.

SAM: Don't you know what year your friends are coming?

DR GÖRTLER [*with a slight smile*]: They are not my friends. [*He goes to the door.*] How do I find this farm?

SAM [*following him*]: When you get out o' t'yard here, turn sharp to your right, and she has a sign up – you can't miss it. [*By the time he has said this,* DR GÖRTLER *is outside and* SAM *is at the door. There is the sound of small car starting up.* SAM *closes door and comes in.*] There'll be no rain this week-end. We'd have had a smell of it by now.

SALLY: Just fancy! Creeping in like that and asking questions!

SAM: What, yon chap? Well, he's a foreigner o' some sort, you see.

SALLY: What's that got to do with it?

SAM: Well, happen it's foreign style o' doing things. [*Begins to chuckle.*] Nay, what tickled me was him saying he must ha' come at wrong year. Now that's as good as aught I've heard o' some time. If he's going round asking for people – not friends of his, mind you – and he doesn't know where they are nor what year they'll be there – I reckon he's got his work cut out. I must tell that to some of 'em in t'bar.

SALLY: You and your bar!

[*Telephone rings.*]

SALLY [*at telephone*]: Yes, this is the Black Bull. Yes, well I *am* waiting. . . . Oh, Miss Holmes, yes – this is Mrs Pratt – we were wondering what had become of you. . . . Oh dear dear! . . . Well, I never did! . . . No, if your friend's so poorly I don't suppose you could. . . . No, well it can't be helped. . . . Yes, we're sorry too. . . . Oh, we'll manage to get somebody . . . that's right . . . good-bye. [*Puts down telephone. To* SAM] Miss Holmes – ringing up from Manchester – to say they can't come.

SAM: Nay!

SALLY: One of the other two's been suddenly taken poorly, and they don't like to leave her.

SAM: Oh!

SALLY [*indignantly*]: Yes, I should think it is 'oh!' That's all three rooms going begging, at very last minute, an' we could have let 'em four times over. Here we are – Friday night – Whit Saturday tomorrow – an' now only one room taken. We ought to do what everybody else does, an' charge 'em a deposit when they book rooms in advance, and then if they do give backward we're not clean out o' pocket.

SAM: Well, it's happened afore.

SALLY: Does that make it any better?

SAM: Yes, 'cos we know we'll fill 'em up easy. Black Bull's nivver had rooms empty o' Whitsuntide. There'll be some motorists coming. Ay, and happen some business chaps who'll spend more nor them three women teachers. All they want is cups o' tea, an' they'd nivver put their noses into t'bar.

[OLIVER FARRANT *enters. He has been walking and wears a tweed jacket and flannel trousers, and is rather dusty. He is about 28–30, good-looking, with something of the boy left in him and something of the intellectual man. He has a decisive, slightly donnish manner, which shows itself least with these two, with whom he is on pleasant easy terms. He has more personal charm than would appear from his actual words, and though he suffers from the rather priggish conceit of the successful intellectual, there is more of this in the matter than in the manner of his talk.*]

FARRANT: Any sherry left, Sam?

SAM: Yes, Mr Farrant. [*Goes to get it.*]

SALLY [*who obviously likes him*]: Your supper'll be ready when you are.

FARRANT: Good! [*Sitting down and relaxing.*] The last few miles were becoming a bit grim. [*Remembering, with whisper and slightly droll manner*] Oh! – have the three females from Manchester arrived yet?

SALLY: No, they're not coming. One of 'em's poorly.

FARRANT: Well, I can't say I was looking forward to them – but I'm sorry. It's bad news for you, isn't it?

SALLY: It's a nuisance, but we'll fill up tomorrow all right. I only hope, whoever we do have, you can get on with 'em, Mr Farrant.

FARRANT: Now you're not going to suggest I'm hard to get on with.

SALLY [*earnestly*]: No, I don't mean that, Mr Farrant, but you know what it is. If we take people at last minute, we can't be too particular, and when you've all got to sit in here together, it might be a bit awkward.

FARRANT: Oh, don't worry about me. I don't suppose I shall be in much this week-end, anyhow, and if the worst comes to the worst I can always go up to my room and read.

[SAM *enters with a glass of sherry.*]

SALLY: I'll see if you've everything you want in there. Do you like Wensleydale cheese, Mr Farrant, 'cos I've got some?

FARRANT: I don't know. I'd like to try it.

[SALLY *goes out.*]

SAM: Bit o' nice Wensleydale tak's some beating. Have a good walk, Mr Farrant?

FARRANT: Yes, thanks, Sam. I must have done about sixteen miles. Down the dale, then across by the church, up the moor and back over Grindle Top.

SAM: Ay, that'll be all o' sixteen mile. Did you find a bit o' bog again at the top.

FARRANT: No, I'm getting artful, Sam. I dodged it this time –

worked well over to the right. The ordnance map's all wrong about Grindle Top. [*Sips sherry, and talks easily.*] You know, Sam, there must have been three or four times as many people living in this dale two or three hundred years ago.

SAM: I've heard 'em say that.

FARRANT: Look at all those old ruins of byres and barns and sheep pounds – and the miles of old walls on the moor.

SAM: Ay, they built them afore folk went into the towns. I remember me grandfather talking about that when I wor a little lad.

FARRANT: Somebody ought to try and find the old records of these dales. Why, in the Middle Ages, what with all that old moorland farming life, and the abbeys and a castle or two, the whole place must have been humming with people.

SAM: I'll bet it worn't humming wi' folk today.

FARRANT: Didn't see a soul this afternoon over the Top except a couple of shepherds. [*He finishes his sherry, and begins moving towards his bedroom.*]

[SAM *takes glass, and then telephone rings. As* SAM *rather dubiously prepares to answer it,* SALLY *hurries in.*]

SAM: Yes, this is Black Bull. That's right . . .

SALLY [*impatiently*]: Here, I'll answer it, Father.

SAM: Hold on a minute.

[*She takes it from him.*]

SALLY: Yes, who is it? . . . Yes, Mr Ormund. . . . Well, it just happens we have two rooms because somebody's just given us backword. . . . Yes, they're both ready, you can come up as soon as you like. Straight away? . . . Will you be wanting supper tonight? Oh, I see. . . . Well then, you turn to your left just outside Marlingset, and then straight up and you can't miss it. . . . That's right. [*Puts down telephone and is rather excited.*] Now would you believe it?

SAM [*humorously*]: I don't know till you tell me.

SALLY [*excitedly*]: That's a Mr and Mrs Ormund. They rang up from Marlingset to see if they could stay over the week-end – they want a bedroom each – and they're coming straight away – they've just had their dinner at the White Hart – and d'you know what I think?

SAM: No, I don't.

SALLY: I believe this Mr Ormund is one o' them big Ormunds – y'know – Ormunds Limited.

SAM: Nay, he wouldn't come here if he wor.

SALLY: How do *you* know ? And he sounded as if he'd plenty o' money. Wanted two rooms and didn't ask price or anything. I'll bet you he's one of Ormunds Limited. Him and his wife – they'll be company for Mr Farrant.

SAM: I told you we'd have them rooms let i' no time. [*Pauses.*] I wonder if that foreign chap's fixed up at Dale End ?

SALLY: He didn't even know whether he wanted to stay or not.

SAM: No, but happen it'ud suit him here now. We have a married couple for him, if that's what he wants. [FARRANT *returns, having changed his shoes and tidied himself.*] You're having company *tonight*, Mr Farrant. [*Grins and goes out.*]

SALLY: There's a Mr and Mrs Ormund coming tonight, to stay the week-end.

FARRANT [*interested*]: Ormund ?

SALLY: Yes, an' I fancy it's one o' them big Ormunds – Ormunds Limited – manufacturers – I expect you've heard o' them ?

FARRANT: I ought to. They put up most of the money for my school.

SALLY: Well, I'm sure this is one o' 'em.

[*The noise of small car is heard outside.*]

FARRANT: Here already ?

SALLY: No, they couldn't have come from Marlingset so soon.

[*She moves towards door,* OLIVER *watching idly. Before she can open it,* DR GÖRTLER *enters slowly, carrying an old-fashioned bag. He looks at* SALLY, *then sees* OLIVER *and appears to recognize him.* SALLY *looks at him, then at* OLIVER, *rather bewildered.*]

DR GÖRTLER [*to* FARRANT, *with some eagerness*]: You are staying here ?

FARRANT: Yes. [*Pauses.*]

[DR GÖRTLER *carefully puts down his bag. There is something decisive in his manner.*]

DR GÖRTLER: I am Doctor Görtler.

FARRANT [*rather puzzled*]: My name's Farrant, Oliver Farrant.

DR GÖRTLER: A schoolmaster, I think ?

FARRANT: Yes, I'm head of Lamberton.

DR GÖRTLER: I am now an exile from my own university – and my country, Germany – and I have been doing some little work for the University of London. [*Turns to* SALLY.] And still you have no room for me?

[SALLY *gives* OLIVER *a quick questioning look. He nods reassuringly.*]

SALLY: Well, as a matter of fact we have now, because those three ladies aren't coming and we've a room to spare –

DR GÖRTLER: I should very much like to stay here.

SALLY [*businesslike*]: We charge twelve-and-six a day – all in. That's for this holiday time and really we ought to charge more because we could easily get it – but –

DR GÖRTLER [*simply*]: But you do not like to be greedy, eh?

SALLY [*rather taken aback*]: No.

DR GÖRTLER: I will stay. The car will be all right there for a time, eh?

SALLY: Yes. My father can put it away.

DR GÖRTLER: And my room?

SALLY: It's up there.

FARRANT: Next door to me. I'm just going to have some supper, Dr Görtler. You'd better join me.

DR GÖRTLER [*taking* SALLY *in too*]: Thank you, yes. I should like something to eat. Anything.

SALLY: I'll see to it. My father can show you your room. [*Hurries out.*]

FARRANT: It's a simple unpretentious little place – but they're nice people – and I think you'll be comfortable.

DR GÖRTLER: Thank you.

FARRANT: What's your subject? Science?

DR GÖRTLER: It *was* physics and mathematics.

FARRANT: Not now?

DR GÖRTLER [*with a slight shrug*]: I still teach these subjects. But for myself – I go farther –

FARRANT: Research, eh?

DR GÖRTLER: You might say – exploring.

FARRANT [*with a smile*]: I know. Spherical geometry. Two parallel lines meeting. Two angles of a triangle no longer greater than the third angle. Poor old Euclid turned upside down and inside out. I have a maths master who talks like that – for his own

amusement – not ours – [*Pauses, then looks hard at* DR GÖRTLER.]
You know, I must have seen your photograph somewhere.

DR GÖRTLER: No, I do not think so. I am not an Einstein.

FARRANT [*hesitantly*]: I thought I – seemed – to recognize you.

DR GÖRTLER: We often seem to recognize people – and places.

FARRANT: I don't.

DR GÖRTLER: You have been ill?

FARRANT: I was ordered a short rest. [*Pauses, then resumes, rather
hastily*] They say that it's when you're nervously exhausted
that the two halves of your brain don't synchronize. Then they
play that recognition trick on you. Isn't that the explanation?

DR GÖRTLER: Yes. But do not believe it. We are not as simple as
bicycles.

[SAM *enters.*]

SAM: Supper's ready, Mr Farrant.

[FARRANT *moves and* SAM *holds door open for him.*]

FARRANT [*to* DR GÖRTLER *as he goes*]: You'll join me in the
dining-room, eh? [*He goes.*]

SAM [*heartily*]: Now then, sir, you're here, after all. And you'd like
to see your room.

DR GÖRTLER: Please.

[SAM *goes across for* DR GÖRTLER's *bag, talking as he moves,
takes bag and returns, moving towards door to bedrooms.*]

SAM: Ay, not five minutes after you'd gone, them three ladies rang
up to say they couldn't come, so we'd room after all for you.
Just the one left.

DR GÖRTLER: But the other two rooms?

SAM: Oh – we got rid o' them all right. There's a Mr and Mrs
Ormund coming tonight into them.

DR GÖRTLER [*triumphantly, with a touch of wonder, really to
himself*]: So! So! Ich bin glücklich.

SAM [*almost through door now, and climbing stairs*]: What language
is that, sir? German?

DR GÖRTLER: Yes. It means 'I am fortunate'.

[*They go out and their voices die away. The stage is empty. The
light begins to fade slowly, but there is a last glow in it. There is a
pause of a moment or two, then* DR GÖRTLER *and* SAM *return.*]

DR GÖRTLER: You say that because you have been happy here?

SAM: Yes, I can't grumble at all. I've never made much out o' this

place, but I've had all I want. I'd ask for naught better – if I had
my time over again.

DR GÖRTLER [*interested*]: Do you often say that?

SAM: Say what?

DR GÖRTLER [*slowly*]: If you had your time over again.

SAM [*surprised*]: Well – no – not specially. I mean to say – it's just
a way – like – o' putting it. Everybody says it.

[SALLY *enters holding door from bar open behind her.*]

SALLY [*not very cordially*]: Your supper's ready, Dr – er –

DR GÖRTLER: Thank you. [*Turning, rather mischievously, to*
SAM] My friend – perhaps you *will* have your time over
again.

SALLY [*from passage outside*]: In here, that's right. And if you don't
find everything you want, just ring the bell. [*She watches him go,
then comes in, closing the door behind her.*] If four of 'em's going
to sit in here, it wants changing round a bit.

[SALLY *is now busy, with some small assistance from* SAM,
*slightly re-arranging the furniture of the room, changing the
tablecloth on the centre table, and finally switching on the lights
and drawing the curtains.*]

What was that Dr Görtler talking about?

SAM: Nay, I just happened to say 'If I'd my time over again' –
you know how you do? – and he seemed right taken up with it.
[*Repeating it speculatively.*] 'If I'd my time over again.' Nay it's
a common enough saying.

SALLY [*in a slow, grumbling tone, as she moves about*]: Yes, it's
common enough. An' it's silly enough an' all. A lot of use it is
you or anybody else saying what they'd do if they had their time
over again. A fat chance they have, haven't they? Time moves
on and it takes you with it, whatever you say – as I know only
too well.

SAM: Ay. Though it's only same for you as for onnybody else, lass.

SALLY: Well, I'm not so sure about that.

SAM: We all go on getting older, Sally.

SALLY: I didn't mean just that. Y'know, father, it's only four
years since Bob and I were staying here with you over Whitsun.
And Charlie was still a little lad. The three of us here . . .
laughing and talking and going on day long . . . and nothing to
tell us it was nearly all over . . .

SAM [*disturbed and affectionate*]: Ay – I know – lass – but don't think about it.

SALLY: It's not so long since, but time's run on. . . . It's taken Bob from me . . . even Charlie's growing up and doesn't need me like he used to. . . . I almost might be an old woman wondering where they're going to bury me . . .

SAM: Now then, Sally lass, it's not so bad as it might be.

SALLY: I might have thirty years to live yet – and I'd swop the lot for just that week we had here, four years ago. . . . But what's the use ?

SAM: Ay – but give it a chance. You'll forget.

SALLY: I know I'll forget. I'm forgetting now. I can't hear Bob's voice as plain as I could a year or two since. It's taken even that from me now. . . . That's what time does to you . . . and if it's God's idea, He'll get no thanks from me. . . . [*The curtains are drawn, and the lights are on now. She looks critically at the room.*] Well, I don't think I can do any better with it as it is. I've sometimes had an idea we might do better to bring the big table in and make this the dining-room – I mean, just for people who's staying here. But it's too far from the kitchen. [*She is silent a moment, and then is heard the siren of a very large car.*] It'll be Mr and Mrs Ormund. Here, I must nip upstairs and see if their rooms look all right. Go and see to their luggage. [*She hurries out.*]

[SAM *goes to the outer door, leaving it open as he goes through. Voices are heard outside. A pause. Then* JANET ORMUND *enters slowly. She is an attractive sensitive woman about twenty-eight, and is dressed for the country in a simple but expensive style. She enters the room with a slow indifference, then suddenly stiffens, frowns, looks incredulous, then examines it eagerly, without much movement. It is clear that there is some recognition, mixed with incredulity. The clock chimes at her. A sudden uprush of emotion makes her feel almost faint, and she sinks into a chair, exhausted, breathing heavily.*

Now her husband, WALTER ORMUND, *enters. He is a biggish man in his early forties, whose manner alternates between alert, sharp command, on the one hand, and a gloomy brooding, on the other. He is dressed in quiet tweeds, the kind a man might wear at an office before leaving for the country. He carries a much-used dispatch-case. He has no eyes for the room, only for his wife.*]

ORMUND: What's the matter, Janet?

JANET: I felt rather faint.

[*She takes charge of herself. He would like to help but doesn't know how to, so remains large and helpless. She looks about her, then at him.*]

ORMUND: Probably tired.

JANET: No. . . . I'm not . . . really. [*Looks about her again, then at him.*] I had – a sort of feeling – this room – [*Gives it up.*]

ORMUND: We needn't stay here, y'know.

JANET: No.

ORMUND: We can push on. There's plenty of time.

JANET: Yes, of course we can.

ORMUND: I can simply say 'Sorry, not our kind of place,' give them something for their trouble, and off we go.

JANET: Quite simple. And – I think – rather comforting.

ORMUND [*with a touch of burlesque*]: You mean – one of us hasn't been taken ill – the car hasn't suddenly and mysteriously broken down – there isn't a fog or a flood or a landslide – none of those sinister compulsory things – ?

JANET [*with a smile*]: No, not one. [*Then with sudden seriousness*] We're quite free. We can choose. We're not being compelled.

ORMUND: Not in the least. We can go now. Just say the word.

JANET: Why don't you say it?

ORMUND [*marching to the door*]: All right. I'll say it. Let's go.

JANET [*hesitates, then with a slight laugh*]: No. We'll stay.

ORMUND [*with a touch of bitterness*]: Anything for a change, eh?

JANET: Walter – is that one of the remarks you promised not to make?

ORMUND [*rueful*]: Oh – I hope not.

JANET: It sounded like the beginning of one. Remember – you promised. Play fair.

ORMUND [*who would like to play fair*]: I'm trying, Janet. I'm trying hard. Only – I do seem to be in the one situation in the world where it's impossible for a man to be fair. You've no idea what a devil of a job it is.

JANET: I know, Walter.

ORMUND [*not sharply*]: You don't.

JANET: No – that's the trouble, I suppose – I don't. [*Looking at him with a touch of wistfulness and pity.*] But – just to be easy and friendly – for once, no arguments, no reproaches – that'll be something, won't it?

ORMUND: Yes, it'll be – something.

JANET [*half-laughing, half-vexed*]: Oh – Walter! The very way you said that – !

ORMUND: No, no, I didn't mean it that way. I'm really doing my best. You're right. God knows you're right. It'll be something.

JANET: I'll do my very best.

ORMUND: And I'll do better still. You'll see. Nice. Easy. Friendly. All according to plan.

[*He looks about him, whistling softly. She looks at him, and he breaks off and gives her a careful reassuring smile. She returns it, but nevertheless looks troubled.* SALLY *enters, with an obvious sense of the importance of the occasion.*]

SALLY [*rather breathless*]: Good evening, Mr and Mrs Ormund, isn't it?

JANET: Yes.

SALLY: You did say you wanted both rooms, didn't you?

ORMUND [*humorously*]: Yes. I have to have a room to myself because sometimes I waken up in the middle of the night and begin scribbling figures on bits of paper – and then – I have to smoke. Yes, smoke. Are you insured against fire?

SALLY: Yes, we are that.

ORMUND: It's all right then. I shall smoke a lot – and burn holes in your best sheets.

SALLY [*entering into this*]: I'll make you pay for 'em if you do, Mr Ormund. [*To both of them*] I expect you'd like to see your rooms, wouldn't you?

ORMUND: You have a look at 'em, Janet. I must telephone to Sykes. [JANET *and* SALLY *go out.* ORMUND *telephones.*] Trunks. . . . Is that Trunks? . . . This is – Grindle Five. I want Brensham 67. . . . Yes, Brensham 67. . . . All right. . . .

[*Waits, telephone to ear.* SAM *enters.*]

SAM: Your bags are upstairs, sir, and the car's in the garage.

ORMUND: Thanks. Bring me a large whisky-and-soda, will you. MacFarlane's Old Liqueur, if you've got it. [*Telephoning, as* SAM *goes out.*] Hello, Brensham? Oh – that you, Sykes? Walter Ormund here. We're fixed up in a little pub on the moors – the

Black Bull, Grindle Moor. Phone number's Grindle Five. . . .
Yes, get me here any time – shan't be going far. . . . Yes, will you
work out the marketing costs, and I'll do the rest. . . . I've got all
the information here, including Orgenbaum's report. . . . Who?
Pensfield? . . . No, he won't make any trouble. I'll offer him a
seat on the board. That'll keep him quiet. . . . Not he! I know
too much about him. . . .

> [SAM *comes in with large whisky and soda, and as he is passing,*
> ORMUND *reaches out and takes it, to* SAM's *surprise, and has a*
> *long drink while still listening.* SAM *gives him a droll look and*
> *goes out.*]

Yes . . . nothing in that, Sykes. . . . Add two and a half per cent
to the overhead then. . . . I'll ring you up before Monday
morning. . . . Well, work all night then – put a wet towel round
your head and a bottle of whisky on your desk. . . . Nonsense!
Holidays are for boys and girls, not men. . . . I know all
about your children, but they can get on without you. . . . All
right. I'm depending on you. 'Bye.

> [*He puts down the telephone, takes his drink to the table,*
> *and pulling an old envelope out of his pocket, makes a few quick*
> *notes on it. Then he looks at what he has written, so absorbed*
> *that he does not notice the entrance of* JANET, *who comes in*
> *quietly. She watches him take an absent-minded pull at his*
> *drink.*]

JANET: You know, Walter, you'd several whiskies at that place
where we had dinner.

ORMUND: I know. And I'd several before that. And now I'm
having another. And what I say is this. If the only way I can find
dividends for several hundred shareholders and wages for
several thousands of employees is by drinking several whiskies,
then I must drink several whiskies.

JANET: But you're not going to do any work this week-end?

ORMUND [*now sitting with his notes*]: I must. I've just been telephoning Sykes. We've a whole big scheme to work out before
Wednesday.

JANET: This isn't going to be much of a change for you, is it?
More work – more whisky.

ORMUND: A change is too much to hope for. Let me just keep
ticking over – just ticking over – that'll do.

JANET [*at once sorry and protesting*]: I can't blame you for being bitter, Walter, but it isn't going to help us.

ORMUND [*sincerely*]: Bitter! I'm not being bitter, my dear. Not in the least. [*Takes a good drink.*]

JANET [*getting a whiff perhaps as she passes behind him*]: Loathsome stuff! I can't think how you go on and on drinking it.

ORMUND: There's a good reason why the distilleries are working at full blast. They're busy giving us Old Highland Blended Courage by the case. Faith and Hope at twelve-and-six a bottle. Love seven years in bond.

JANET: And in another minute, Walter, you'll be attacking me again.

ORMUND: No, no, I'm not attacking you, I'm defending whisky. It's dependable. It doesn't change its mind, think it's in love with you and then know better. It may have a little more fusel oil in it this year than last, but that's all the difference. That's why people all over the world now are steadily pickling themselves in it.

JANET: If it made you silly-drunk, I don't think I'd object.

ORMUND: My dear Janet, you'd walk straight out on me.

JANET: No. The trouble is, it only makes you gloomy.

ORMUND: No, if I pour enough down into the darkness inside, they begin to floodlight things down there. Beautiful images begin to shine. Venuses rise from the sea of Scotch and soda, glorious smiling kind wenches, all looking rather alike – [*Breaks off suddenly.*] Rooms all right?

JANET [*grateful for this*]: Yes. Queer little windows and a heavenly country smell.

ORMUND: Any spotted china beasts?

JANET: Yes. Dogs with long necks. They've blue spots in my room, red spots in yours.

ORMUND: Good! I haven't seen any of those beasts for years and I'm fond of 'em.

JANET [*hopefully*]: I believe you're going to like it here.

ORMUND [*with sudden change of mood*]: No. [*He finishes his drink.*] I can't help feeling it was a mistake coming here.

JANET [*mildly*]: It was your idea.

ORMUND: A lot of my ideas are bad. This is too small, too quiet. It throws us straight back on to ourselves –

JANET: That's a good thing.

ORMUND: It's a good thing when people are all right with one another. But when they're trying to be easy and friendly and one of 'em has died on the other, as if he were last year's worst hat, then if they've any sense they want to go and stay at some large damn silly place screaming with jazz bands where you can't possibly think. Here you can't help thinking. I've started already. . . .

[FARRANT *enters, and stops short, and he and* JANET *look at one another. Then* ORMUND *looks too, and the clock joins in with its tick and chime, as if it had been expecting this. An odd tenseness for a moment.*]

FARRANT [*with a certain effort*]: We'd better introduce ourselves. My name's Farrant.

ORMUND [*his bewilderment over*]: That's it, of course. You're Oliver Farrant, Head of Lamberton. I'm Walter Ormund. My wife.

FARRANT: I didn't expect to meet one of the school governors here.

ORMUND [*not importantly*]: I've been too busy to go and see the school yet, but I was one of the governors who put you in there. Thought we ought to have a young man.

FARRANT [*smiling*]: You were quite right.

ORMUND: But what are you doing here. Term time, isn't it?

FARRANT: I was told to knock off and have a rest.

ORMUND: Overworking?

FARRANT: That's what they said. I feel rather a fraud – I'm walking miles and miles every day, and eating like a horse –

ORMUND [*looking hard at him*]: Look a bit nervous, though.

JANET: How did you find your way up here?

FARRANT: Mrs Pratt – that's the landlord's daughter – a widow – has a boy, Charlie, who's at Lamberton. He told me about it.

JANET: Mrs Pratt was telling me all about her boy. Is he clever?

FARRANT [*not at his best*]: Yes, he's got brains. He's the kind of boy who makes me feel glad I'm a schoolmaster. Ought to be fairly certain of an Oxford scholarship later on. We've a good many boys of his kind.

JANET: Do you mean – clever ones or from this sort of home?

FARRANT [*rather deliberately*]: I mean – boys with brains from this class. A lot of them have brains, y'know.

JANET [*who does not like his manner*]: Yes, it never occurred to me that they wouldn't have.

FARRANT: And it's part of our policy at Lamberton to encourage them.

ORMUND [*dryly*]: Yes, it was part of *our* policy when we built the school.

FARRANT: Sorry, I was forgetting.

ORMUND: That's all right. Have a drink?

FARRANT: No, thanks. Too soon after supper.

ORMUND: There's a bar in there, isn't there?

FARRANT: Yes. But the talk's not very amusing.

ORMUND [*almost giving him up as a bad job*]: Anybody else staying here?

FARRANT: Yes, a Doctor Görtler.

ORMUND: German?

FARRANT: Yes, professor of mathematics taking refuge over here. Judging by his talk at supper, he seems to have wandered a long way from mathematics now. I don't quite make him out.

JANET: Why?

FARRANT: Oh – he seems to be turning mystical. Probably seen too much trouble. The German intellect doesn't always stand the strain. I'll be down later, if you want to talk about the school. [*Nods and goes up to his room, closing door behind him.*]
    [ORMUND *and* JANET *look at one another.*]

ORMUND [*quietly*]: Without having seen him, purely on his record – *and* against considerable opposition, I had that young man appointed Head of Lamberton.

JANET [*rather grimly*]: My dear, I know you did.

ORMUND: Well?

JANET [*with irony*]: Oh – very nice, friendly, modest sort of young man – not the least little bit conceited and dogmatic – very charming – humph!
    [*She laughs.*]

ORMUND: Yes, most extraordinary thing. Thought I'd take to him. Took to him at once on paper. And he *looks* all right. Ought in fact to be a very attractive fellow. But – well – there you are –
    [*He has risen now and turns to the door leading to the dining-*

room and bar. This brings him face to face with DR GÖRTLER, *who has just entered.* DR GÖRTLER *looks curiously at the* ORMUNDS, *especially at* JANET, *and is then ceremonious.*]

DR GÖRTLER [*with a little bow*]: Doctor Görtler. Mr and Mrs Ormund?

ORMUND: Yes, good evening.

JANET: Good evening.

DR GÖRTLER: And a very beautiful evening.

JANET: Yes, hasn't it been?

ORMUND: Would you like to join me in a drink?

DR GÖRTLER: No, thank you.

ORMUND: Janet?

JANET: No, thank you, Walter.

ORMUND [*gravely*]: Then – I think – I shall try the bar. [*As* JANET *makes a murmur of protest.*] No, no. Shan't be long. [*He goes out.*]

[DR GÖRTLER *settles down and looks in a friendly but very deliberate fashion at* JANET, *who smiles in return.*]

JANET: Have you been up here before, Dr Görtler?

DR GÖRTLER [*watching her*]: No. Have you?

JANET [*frowning a little*]: No – I haven't – really.

DR GÖRTLER: You do not seem very certain.

JANET [*slowly*]: I've been wondering –

DR GÖRTLER [*as she hesitates*]: Yes?

JANET: I was only wondering if I could have been here when I was a very small child. [*She breaks off, and looks at him, and then away from him.*]

[*Pause.*]

DR GÖRTLER: Mrs Ormund, I am a student – a very old one now. Sometimes we students do not seem to have very good manners. I do not wish you to think I am – inquisitive, impertinent.

JANET [*with slight smile*]: It didn't occur to me that you were – or might be.

DR GÖRTLER: Lately I have been enlarging my studies – to include the human mind. So I go about asking questions.

JANET: If this means you want to ask me some questions, you can. But I don't think you'd find me much use. I've always thought the psycho-analysts monstrously exaggerated everything. I can't believe that all the little fears and fancies one has are of any real interest or value.

DR GÖRTLER: Even a few years ago, I would have agreed with you. But now I see that we do not understand ourselves, the nature of our lives. What seems to happen continually just outside the edge of our attention – the little fears and fancies, as you call them – may be all-important because they belong to a profounder reality, like the vague sounds of the city outside that we hear sometimes inside a theatre.

JANET: Oh! [*She stares at him, almost terrified.*]

DR GÖRTLER: What is it?

JANET [*hesitantly and with wonder*]: You see ... suddenly I felt ... I could have sworn ... you'd said all that to me before. ... You and I – sitting, talking, like this ... and then you said 'because they belong ... to a profounder reality ... like the sounds of the city ... we hear sometimes inside a theatre. ...' [*Dismisses the mood, then hastily*] I'm so sorry. I must be tired.

[*A pause.*]

DR GÖRTLER: Mrs Ormund, what made you come here?

JANET: Oh – pure chance. We wanted to spend this week-end somewhere in the country. A man at the hotel we dined at – tonight – not an hour ago – suggested this place. I'd never heard of it before.

DR GÖRTLER: It was all quite dull, ordinary?

JANET: Yes ... until we were driving from Marlingset up here. ...

DR GÖRTLER: Yes?

JANET: I find this – rather difficult – [*She breaks off, and then, with urgency*] Quite suddenly, I began to feel excited. ... About nothing, it seemed. ... My heart was beating terribly. ... We stopped once ... only a moment, to make sure about the way. ... At the roadside there were some white harebells ... just some white harebells. ... Of course they looked lovely there ... white and fragile and perfect, at the edge of the great dark moor. ... It must have been – just that ... anything else – is silly.

DR GÖRTLER [*slowly*]: There has not been in your life so far a moment of crisis that you associate with these flowers?

JANET [*slowly, and staring at him*]: No. But that's exactly the feeling I had about them.

DR GÖRTLER [*prompting her*]: And then – you arrived here?

JANET [*rather slowly*]: Yes.

[*A distinct pause, during which* DR GÖRTLER *rises and goes nearer to her.*]

DR GÖRTLER: You have met Mr Farrant?

JANET: Yes. But only for a few minutes.

DR GÖRTLER: He is very young for such a responsible post.

JANET: Yes.

DR GÖRTLER: But that does not matter, of course. He is fortunate, but he deserves to be. Very clever – and very charming, very good-hearted too, I think – [*Looks at her questioningly.*]

JANET [*rather stiffly*]: I'm sure he must be, Dr Görtler. [*As he stares at her speculatively.*] Why do you stare at me like that?

DR GÖRTLER: I beg your pardon. I was thinking. [*Pause.*] Mr Ormund – does he feel any of these things tonight?

JANET [*with a slight smile*]: I think you'd better ask him that yourself.

DR GÖRTLER: Yes, I will.

JANET [*rather hastily, with a resumption of more social manner*]: You may find him – a little difficult. I mean – you mustn't mind if he seems rather brusque – odd.

DR GÖRTLER: Why should I? I am – brusque and odd – myself.

JANET [*hastily*]: He's really very kind and considerate, when you know him, but he's got the most tremendous responsibilities. I thought he was going to have a rest this week-end but he's brought a lot of work with him. He works far too hard.

DR GÖRTLER [*calmly*]: Yes, I think he is an unhappy man.

JANET [*shocked, reproachful*]: Dr Görtler – ! [*Then dropping social manner*] Why do you say that?

DR GÖRTLER: I have seen enough unhappiness now to recognize it.

[FARRANT *enters from his room, with a rather large book under his arm. He and* JANET *take a quick look at one another.* DR GÖRTLER *watches them both. Then* FARRANT *crosses to the bureau to sit down with his book. You feel the silence.* JANET *obviously does not like it.* DR GÖRTLER *is interested, watchful.*]

JANET [*who must break this horrible silence*]: What are your special subjects, Mr Farrant?

FARRANT [*rather too carefully keeping his place open in book*]: History and economics.

JANET [*doing her best*]: I don't care about economics. It never seems to me to be true. But I wish I knew more history – real history, not the dreary stuff they still taught us when I was at school. I'm always meaning to learn more about it.

FARRANT [*with a suggestion of the schoolmaster*]: Well, it's going on all round you, y'know. It's not something that's dead and done with. We're making it all the time.

JANET: I don't feel I'm making very much.

FARRANT: No, but once you realize you're *in* history, helping to make it, you see the whole thing differently. That's how we try to teach it now. I show them how completely interdependent we are.

DR GÖRTLER [*who has been missing nothing*]: Yes, we are like threads in a pattern.

FARRANT: There's a pretty example of mutual dependence – quite a nice little pattern – here in this pub. Sam and Mrs Pratt are devoted to this boy of hers, Charlie –

DR GÖRTLER: He is at your school. So they depend upon you.

FARRANT: Yes. But the school partly depends on the Ormunds, and especially on your husband, Mrs Ormund –

[*He is interrupted by the entrance of* SALLY, *who is followed after a moment by* ORMUND.]

SALLY: Excuse me, Mrs Ormund. But I just wanted to tell you that we have breakfast at half-past eight, if that's not too early.

JANET: No, I'd like it then, Mrs Pratt.

SALLY: And is that all right for you, Dr Görtler?

DR GÖRTLER: Yes, thank you.

SALLY: And would you like a cup of tea earlier on, Mrs Ormund?

JANET: Not tomorrow morning, thank you. What about you, Walter?

SALLY: Oh – I'm sorry.

ORMUND [*coming forward*]: That's all right. And no tea. And no breakfast either. Just a pot of strong coffee for me – about half past nine.

SALLY: All right, Mr Ormund.

FARRANT [*rather peremptorily*]: I'll be out all day again tomorrow, so can I have some sandwiches in the morning, please?

SALLY: Yes, Mr Farrant.

ORMUND [*to* FARRANT]: Going striding over the moors all day?

FARRANT: I'll be out all day, I don't know about striding.

ORMUND [*to* JANET]: That's what you want, isn't it? Better go along with him.

JANET [*dismayed*]: But what are you going to do?

ORMUND: Oh – I'll do a bit of work – and then slack round. You'd better join up with Farrant here. [*To* FARRANT] She can walk, you know.

FARRANT [*plainly without enthusiasm*]: Well – it might be rather rough going – but of course – if you'd like to come along –

JANET [*furious with both men, shortly*]: No, thank you. I may want some sandwiches, Mrs Pratt. I'll let you know in the morning.

[ORMUND *crosses to outside door and stands looking out.*]

SALLY: Yes, Mrs Ormund. I've a long day tomorrow – Whit Saturday – an' folks wanting lunches and teas – so I thought I'd get to bed in good time tonight.

JANET: Yes, of course.

SALLY [*somewhat embarrassed*]: We're very proud to have you and Mr Ormund here. Nearly all the money father and I have between us – that we saved to help our Charlie later on – is in Ormunds Limited.

JANET: Do you hear that, Walter? You're among shareholders, so be careful.

ORMUND [*half-turning, with mock groan*]: I know, I know.

DR GÖRTLER: There, you see, is more dependence.

SALLY [*distrusting this*]: What's that?

JANET: It sounds like an insult, but it isn't. We've been discovering how much we depend on one another. You're in it because your boy's at Mr Farrant's school.

SALLY: And very lucky he is to be there too – with Mr Farrant looking after him.

JANET: And now you say you've money in Ormunds Limited.

FARRANT: And the school partly depends on Ormunds too. Which brings me in.

JANET: And I'm certainly one of the dependents. Walter, you're the only really great one, the giant Atlas himself. We all depend upon you, but you don't depend upon anybody.

DR GÖRTLER [*quietly, but with startling effect*]: *Nein !* [*They all stare at him.*] Mr Ormund depends very much upon somebody. [*To* JANET] He depends upon you – his wife.

ORMUND [*quietly, with cold anger*]: That's not the kind of remark we appreciate from a stranger in this country, my dear sir.

JANET: Walter!

DR GÖRTLER [*rising*]: I am sorry. I am – as you say – a stranger – in a foreign country.

JANET: It's all right, Dr Görtler.

DR GÖRTLER [*as he moves towards door, to his room*]: Good night.

ORMUND [*crossing to him*]: No, doctor. I shouldn't have spoken like that. Now don't be offended.

DR GÖRTLER: I am not offended. Only tired. So please – no apologies. Good night.

[*The others say good night and watch him go out, closing the door behind him.*]

SALLY [*dropping voice, dubiously*]: I hope it's going to be all right.

JANET: Why, Mrs Pratt, what's wrong?

SALLY: I mean – him being here.

ORMUND: Yes, of course. Why not?

SALLY: Well, Mr Ormund – only that he seems to be upsetting you.

FARRANT [*sharply*]: Now, Mrs Pratt! Just because he's a foreigner.

SALLY: No, it isn't that, Mr Farrant. Though I'll admit I'm not used to foreigners. But what's he doing here?

ORMUND: Well, what are we all doing here?

SALLY: No, that's different, Mr Ormund. Why should he come here looking for you?

ORMUND [*puzzled*]: For me?

SALLY: No, for you three.

[*This linking of the three of them together – for the first time – has its immediate effect, as if it chimed with some deep obscure feeling each of them knew. There is a pause, before SALLY resumes.*]

He comes here – looking about him – and when I tell him we've no room to spare because I'm expecting three visitors – he looks at me and asks if two of 'em are a married couple with the man older than his wife, and the other a younger man. And when I say No, we're expecting three ladies from Manchester, he seems disappointed and says something about it being the wrong year. So off he goes, and then the three ladies say they can't come, and you ring up for rooms, and when he comes back, there's a room for him too, and you're all here, and it's just what he expected.

ORMUND: Oh – he was looking for somebody, and then gave it up.

SALLY: And then upsetting you like that! He makes me feel right uneasy. [*Short pause.*] Nothing more you'll be wanting, Mrs Ormund?

JANET: No, thank you, Mrs Pratt. Good night.

SALLY: Good night.

> [*The two men say good night as she goes.* ORMUND *takes some papers from his dispatch-case, preparing to work.* FARRANT *is going back to his book.*]

JANET [*who has obviously been thinking about it all*]: How could he have been looking for us?

ORMUND [*busy with his papers*]: He couldn't.

FARRANT [*looking up, in light easy tone*]: The arrival of a mysterious foreigner, plus a coincidence, has obviously been too much tonight for poor Mrs Pratt. And Görtler's prophetic manner has only made it worse.

ORMUND: Yes, he rather asks for it.

JANET [*after thinking for a few moments*]: Well, I'm tired, Walter. [*Moving towards door.*] Your room's the far one.

FARRANT [*casually*]: I thought I'd met him before somewhere. [*The clock chimes.*]

JANET [*turning, sharply at door*]: You did! Where?

FARRANT: That's the trouble. Can't remember.

JANET [*tentatively*]: Has it . . . worried you?

FARRANT [*slightly surprised*]: Yes . . . a little. Why?

JANET: I . . . wondered. [*Pause, then coming forward.*] Walter, will you stop working just one minute – ?

ORMUND [*looking up from his work, first at* JANET, *then at* FARRANT, *then back to* JANET, *coolly and humorously*]: You want me to tell you all about it? Quite simple. We're all three a bit off our heads. Farrant says he's been overworking and the doctor sent him away. I've been half-dotty for years. And as for you, Janet, you're just a young woman, always ready to have your fortune told and your horoscope read, always longing for marvels and miracles, not even wanting to be sane.

JANET [*with a smile*]: Yes, that's quite simple – and quite silly. [*Moves.*] Good night.

[*She is now in doorway; the two men stand up and say good night. She looks at them a moment, then nods and goes.* ORMUND *sits down again to resume work, but* FARRANT *remains standing.*]

FARRANT [*after a pause*]: Ormund – I hope – you'll let me talk to you about the school sometime.

ORMUND: Yes, of course. Not now, though, not now.

FARRANT [*after another pause, with touch of nervous diffidence*]: I'm – rather worried – [*Pauses, and* ORMUND *looks at him.*] I feel – I haven't – somehow – created a very good first impression.

ORMUND: On me – or on my wife?

FARRANT: On both of you.

ORMUND: I don't think you have, altogether.

FARRANT: Do you mind – telling me why?

ORMUND: My dear chap, I honestly haven't the least idea. So let's forget it. [*Breaking it off*] What's your book?

FARRANT: *New Pathways in Science.* You might like to look at it afterwards. It answers a lot of questions that have been puzzling me.

ORMUND [*easily, but with an undercurrent of despair*]: Yes, but does it answer the questions that have been puzzling *me*? Who or what are we? What are we supposed to be doing here? What the devil is it all about?

FARRANT: I'm afraid it doesn't.

ORMUND: I thought not. Turning in?

FARRANT [*as he goes*]: Yes, I think so. Good night.

ORMUND [*back at his work*]: Good night.

[ORMUND *tries to settle down to his work but cannot concentrate and looks as if some despairing thought is haunting him. He looks queerly at the wall in front of him, the one he can't see. He rises slowly, and in his distress he snaps the fountain-pen he is holding in two, and as he looks down at the broken pen, the curtain falls.*]

END OF ACT ONE

ACT TWO

Scene as before. Saturday evening. Still daylight, but though the light is still good, it is that of a clear twilight. ORMUND *is discovered sitting at the bureau in the window, smoking and doing some work, making notes and calculations. After a moment or two,* SAM *enters with a tray with bottle of whisky, syphon and glass.* ORMUND *looks up.*

ORMUND: Sam, you have the noble instincts of a good landlord. Thank you.

SAM [*as he puts tray on centre table*]: Well, t'bar's still pretty full and I thought you'd like it handy in here.

ORMUND [*going up to the table*]: Quite right. [*Takes up bottle.*] But not much in this bottle, Sam.

SAM [*with a grin*]: It's one you started on at tea-time, Mr Ormund.

ORMUND: Then I must have had a very good tea.

SAM [*grinning*]: Ay, you didn't do bad.

ORMUND: It looks to me, Sam, as if I drink too much.

SAM: Well, that's not for me to say, Mr Ormund –

ORMUND: Never mind, Sam, say it, say it.

SAM: I haven't seen monny as could shift it better.

ORMUND: Nor carry it better. Admit that, Sam.

SAM: I do, Mr Ormund. There's one or two as comes here – owd Joe Watson, farmer down t'dale, for one – who's got a head on 'em for liquor, but – by gow! – I'd back you, Mr Ormund, against best of 'em. You'd have 'em under table i' no time.

ORMUND: Yes, Sam, and sometimes it's useful to have 'em under table. But it won't do. If I ask for another bottle tonight, remind me that I drink too much. [*He returns to the bureau.*]

SAM: You've had your supper, haven't you, Mr Ormund?

ORMUND: Yes. Had it with Dr Görtler. We got tired of waiting for the other two.

SAM [*going to the door*]: Ay, they're making a long day of it. Let's hope they haven't got lost.

ORMUND: Not much chance of that, is there?

SAM: No, not on these light nights. It's easy enough i' winter, if you stop too long on t'moors. I've known a few daftheads that did. But don't you worry. Mr Farrant's a good head on his shoulders.

ORMUND: I don't think my wife's with Mr Farrant. They went out separately.

SAM: Oh – well – happen she's gone a few mile farther than she thought. But she'll be all right, Mr Ormund.

[DR GÖRTLER *has come in now.* SAM *takes empty tray and goes.*]

ORMUND [*after pause*]: Have a drink, Dr Görtler?

DR GÖRTLER: No, thank you.

ORMUND [*indifferently*]: Don't like too much drinking, eh?

DR GÖRTLER [*coolly, not priggishly*]: It is a kind of escape, and I do not need it. I am not afraid.

ORMUND [*with more attention*]: Not afraid of what?

DR GÖRTLER: I am not afraid of thinking, of reality.

ORMUND [*considering him, after pause*]: I wonder what you think you're doing here.

DR GÖRTLER [*with a smile*]: I am asking questions. [*A pause.*] This drinking, it is an escape – from what?

ORMUND [*really dodging the question*]: Well – as you see – not from responsibility – and work.

DR GÖRTLER: No, I think you work very hard.

ORMUND: I work like hell.

DR GÖRTLER: And that too is a kind of escape.

ORMUND [*not liking this*]: Is it? But don't forget, my dear professor, I've great responsibilities. Even these people here – and their precious boy – would be badly let down if I failed 'em. I have to keep on.

DR GÖRTLER: No, you give yourself these tasks so that you must keep on. You dare not stop.

ORMUND [*with an effort*]: All right. I dare not stop. [*Turns to his notes and looks as if he wanted to be done with this talk, yet cannot bring himself to break it off definitely. A pause.*]

DR GÖRTLER [*with a shade of irony*]: And yet – you are rich.

ORMUND [*turning*]: Have you ever been rich, Dr Görtler, or lived among the rich?

DR GÖRTLER [*who has his own irony*]: No, I have only been poor, and lived among the poor. But that is quite an experience, too.

ORMUND: I've no illusions about that. But being rich isn't simply the opposite of being poor. It's not really worth much – being rich. Half the time there's a thick glass wall between you and most of the fun and friendliness of the world. There's something devilishly dull about most of the rich. Too much money seems to take the taste and colour out of things. It oughtn't to do, but it does – damn it!

DR GÖRTLER: But power – you have that, haven't you?

ORMUND: Yes, and that's a very different thing.

DR GÖRTLER: Ah! – you like power.

ORMUND: Well, you get some fun out of it. I don't mean bullying a lot of poor devils. But putting ideas into action. And not being at the end of somebody else's bit of string.

DR GÖRTLER: And yet that is what you always feel, and that is why you try to escape.

ORMUND [sharply]: What do you mean?

DR GÖRTLER: That you are – as you say – at the end of a bit of string.

ORMUND [as he rises and moves]: Nonsense! Do I look like – a puppet?

DR GÖRTLER [calmly]: No. But I say you feel like one. [Pauses, then with calm force] You are rich. You are successful. You have power. Yet all the time you try to escape, because deep down you feel that your part in this life is settled for you and that it is a tragic one. So all the time you are in despair. [As ORMUND does not reply.] Is that not true?

ORMUND [half-wondering and half-angry as he crosses to the sofa]: Yes – damn your impudence – it is.

DR GÖRTLER [pressing him]: Now please tell me why you – who have so much – should feel this despair.

ORMUND [after a pause, turning, speaking more freely than before]: I suppose – in the last resort – you trust life – or you don't. Well – I don't. There's something malicious . . . corrupt . . . cruel . . . at the heart of it. Nothing's on our side. We don't belong. We're a mistake.

DR GÖRTLER: But you have known – good things?

ORMUND [looking down now at the sitting GÖRTLER]: Yes. When you're young, you snatch at 'em and then find they're bait in a trap. Cheese for the mice. One nibble, you're caught and the wires are boring through your guts. I can feel 'em there.

DR GÖRTLER: No. It is something in yourself, something that hates life.

ORMUND: All right, it's something in me. [*Almost muttering*] Something that's waiting to blot out the whole bloody business. [*Moves restlessly, then finally speaks with more freedom, coming nearer and then sitting at the table across from* DR GÖRTLER.] Görtler – when I was a boy I watched my mother die – of cancer. For two years she was tortured . . . she might as well have been put on the rack and broken on the wheel . . . and when she couldn't suffer any longer . . . when there was nothing left to feel any more devilish bloody torment . . . she was allowed to escape, to die. You see, there wasn't any more fun to be had out of her. Let her go.

DR GÖRTLER: Yes, that was bad. But did she complain?

ORMUND: No, she didn't complain much. She was a very brave woman. I remember – when she could bear it no longer and screamed in the night, she'd apologize next morning. [*With terrible irony*] She was sorry if she'd disturbed us, Görtler, she was sorry if she'd disturbed us. . . . [*Pause.*] No, *she* didn't complain – but – by God! I complain.

DR GÖRTLER: Yes, I understand. [*Pause.*] You feel too much and do not know enough.

ORMUND [*grimly*]: I know too much.

DR GÖRTLER: No. You are like a child who thinks because it rains one morning, he will never play out of doors again. You believe we have only this one existence?

ORMUND: Of course.

DR GÖRTLER [*with irony*]: Of course. We all know that now. It is so obvious. But what a pity – if we are brutes that perish – we have not the dim feelings of brutes that perish. To have this one short existence and to spend it being tortured by cancer – to be given delicate nerves and consciousness only to feel pain – that would be a terrible cruelty. It would be better that nobody should be born at all.

ORMUND: I've thought so many a time.

DR GÖRTLER: Because you do not understand the long drama of the soul. To suffer like that, then to die young, that is not easy nor pleasant, but it is a role, a part – like any other brief appearance here –

ORMUND [*harshly, as he moves away restlessly*]: I'm sorry, Doctor. That may mean something to you. It means nothing to me. Just so many fine useless words.

DR GÖRTLER [*with authority and dignity*]: You will please remember, Mr Ormund, that all my life I have been a man of science, and then a philosopher. I am not a political orator. My fine words mean something. [*Pauses.*] You were in the War?

[SALLY *enters, hears them speaking, goes out quickly.*]

ORMUND [*moving*]: Yes. I went all through it. My brother was killed. And before the lunacy stopped, I'd found half a dozen fellows who were nearly as good as brothers, but they never lasted long. . . . I came out of it to find the whole world limping on one foot and with a hole in its head. . . . Most of us are really half-crazy. I know I am.

DR GÖRTLER: But when you began to forget about the War, things were better, eh?

ORMUND: No. I didn't forget, and things were worse. They were very bad indeed – when – I met my wife, Janet. Then things looked different for a time – [*Breaks off, then resumes in more normal tone*] Well, that's how it's been. Not very cheerful. But I don't suppose *you've* had a rollicking time.

DR GÖRTLER [*quietly and with great dignity*]: I lost my only son in the War – a young boy. I saw all my family and friends ruined by the economic collapse of Germany. I think it was the worry, the shame, of that period which killed my wife. And now I have seen my pupils taken away from me, and have been turned out of my university and out of my country.

ORMUND: I'm sorry, Dr Görtler.

DR GÖRTLER: Yet I do not hate life. I accept it all. Because you see – there is no traitor – here – [*He touches his chest.*]

ORMUND: You think there is – in me?

DR GÖRTLER: I do not know. I can only guess.

ORMUND [*after a pause, more freely*]: Görtler, I'll tell you something I've never told anybody. All my life, I've had a haunted sort of feeling . . . as if, just round the corner, there'd be a sudden blotting out of everything. During the War I thought it meant I was going to be killed, so I didn't give a damn what I did and they thought I was a brave fellow and pinned medals on

me. But when it was all over, I still had the same feeling. It's
getting stronger all the time.

DR GÖRTLER: And then, last night, when you arrived here –

ORMUND: How did you notice that? I didn't know I gave myself away.

DR GÖRTLER: What did you feel?

ORMUND: I felt like a man staring into his grave.

DR GÖRTLER: When you entered this room?

ORMUND: Yes, yes.

DR GÖRTLER: When you saw your bedroom?

ORMUND [*rather impatiently*]: Yes, yes.

DR GÖRTLER: But it was worst in the garage?

ORMUND [*surprised*]: The garage? I haven't been in the garage.
Sam put my car away last night and I haven't looked at it since –
[*Stops, stares at* DR GÖRTLER *suspiciously, then with urgency*] –
how did you know I kept it there?

DR GÖRTLER: Where?

ORMUND: In the car.

DR GÖRTLER: Kept what in the car?

ORMUND: My revolver.

DR GÖRTLER [*significantly*]: So!

ORMUND: I keep a revolver in a side pocket of the car. How did
you know that?

DR GÖRTLER: I did not know.

ORMUND: Then why did you ask me about the garage?

DR GÖRTLER: I wanted to know what you had felt there, that
is all.

ORMUND [*after staring at him a moment, calls*]: Sam. Sam.

DR GÖRTLER: Be careful.

   [SALLY *enters.*]

SALLY: Father's busy in the bar, Mr Ormund. Can I get you
anything?

ORMUND: Is the garage open?

SALLY: Yes, Mr Ormund, straight across the yard.

DR GÖRTLER: Do you want me to come with you?

   [SALLY *gives them a sharp look.* ORMUND *goes out to the yard,
   leaving door ajar.* DR GÖRTLER, *who has risen, looks anxiously
   after him.* SALLY *looks at* DR GÖRTLER, *curiously and
   dubiously.*]

SALLY: Oh – Doctor – er – [*as he turns*] I don't think you said how long you wanted your room, did you?

DR GÖRTLER [*puzzled by this*]: Yes. I said it last night, when I came here.

SALLY [*coldly*]: I don't remember. It wasn't said to me.

DR GÖRTLER: I said I wanted it over the week-end. I could not tell, exactly.

SALLY: Well, folks who come here usually know how long they're staying.

DR GÖRTLER: Yes, but I could not say. I have something to do here.

SALLY [*eyeing him*]: Something to do?

DR GÖRTLER [*still anxious about* ORMUND, *not bothering about her*]: Yes, yes, something very important.

SALLY [*hostile*]: Oh, I see.

DR GÖRTLER [*really attending to her now*]: There is no need to talk to me in this way. I have done you no injury. I am quite a harmless person, even though I am a foreigner – and was once a professor.

SALLY: And so you want to know what's the matter?

DR GÖRTLER: Yes, there is evidently something. What have I done?

SALLY [*sturdily*]: Well – seeing you've asked me, Doctor – er – I'll tell you. You make me feel uneasy in my mind. That wouldn't be so bad, but I've noticed you've a trick of upsetting other people too. And I don't like it.

[*She is about to turn away, when a revolver shot is heard from outside. It is a startling report. She and* DR GÖRTLER *give a cry.*]

DR GÖRTLER [*urgently*]: Ormund! [*He hurries to door and goes out.*]

[SALLY *stands, a hand pressed to her side, breathing rapidly.* SAM *comes in hastily. You feel all these people are unusually nervous tonight.*]

SAM [*hastily*]: What was that, Sally? Who's playing about wi' a gun so near t'house?

SALLY [*breathlessly*]: I don't know. Go and see.

[*As* SAM *begins to cross the room,* ORMUND *enters followed by* DR GÖRTLER. ORMUND *looks pale and shaken but tries to be hearty and genial.*]

ORMUND [*loudly*]: That's all right. Hello, Sam, did it bring you out? Sorry, Mrs Pratt. Silly thing to do – very silly.

SALLY: But whatever happened, Mr Ormund?

ORMUND: Went to the garage to have a look at my car and re-membered I had a revolver in the side pocket. Took it out to see if it was all right, and nearly got to the door when something went scampering past, making me jump.

SAM: A rat, eh?

ORMUND: Yes. Big brute. And I've always hated rats ever since they used to come snuffling over me in the trenches. So I had to have a pop at him.

SAM: Ay. Did you get him, Mr Ormund?

ORMUND: Didn't even get him, Sam. [*He pours himself a good drink.*] Just made a noise and frightened you all. Sorry, Mrs Pratt. Won't occur again.

SAM: Ay, well, I don't know why it should ha' bothered so much – but –

SALLY [*cutting him short*]: All right, Father, they'll be wanting you in the bar.

[*She gets him out.* ORMUND, *no longer bothering to keep up appearances, drops into a chair, takes a huge drink, then rests his head in his hands and rubs his forehead, as if both baffled and depressed.*]

DR GÖRTLER: I am sorry.

ORMUND [*suddenly jumping up, with passion*]: Sorry, sorry! Yes, I went into the garage. Now what do I do next? You must have some more amusing ideas. [*Going close to* DR GÖRTLER.] Who the devil are you to come here and take the lid off my head and stick pins into my guts and say you're sorry?

DR GÖRTLER: I am not amusing myself with you, Mr Ormund.

ORMUND [*laying a hand on him, glaring at him*]: No? Well what *are* you doing here? What's your game?

DR GÖRTLER [*with authority*]: It is not a game. [*He looks steadily at him.* ORMUND *drops his hand, moves away.*] Tell me what happened. [*As* ORMUND *does not reply.*] Please.

ORMUND: What I told them about the rat was true. But of course that wasn't all.

DR GÖRTLER: No, I knew that.

ORMUND: It wasn't so bad until I took out the revolver. And I had to take it out – irresistible impulse. But as soon as I stood there with that gun in my hand, I seemed to be falling into black night, and I felt the only thing left for me to do on earth was to put that revolver to my head. How I struggled to the door I don't know, but then I had to pull the trigger. Luckily there was the rat to fire at. At least I suppose there was a rat. Perhaps not. I'm crazy enough to invent a rat or two. *Was* there a rat ?

DR GÖRTLER: I do not know.

ORMUND [*rather wildly*]: Thank God, there's something you don't know. [*Tries the bottle, which is empty.*] Damn! Look at that. [*Calls*] Sam, Sam. [*Enter* SALLY.] Oh – Mrs Pratt – I want a drink and this bottle's dead and done with.

SALLY [*taking it*]: Bar's quieter now, Mr Ormund, if you'd like to go back there.

ORMUND: I would.

> [*Nods to* DR GÖRTLER *and goes out.* SALLY *remains behind, collecting* ORMUND's *glass and syphon. Then she stands looking at* DR GÖRTLER *in an unfriendly manner, but hesitating to speak. He has been thinking, but now catches her eye.*]

DR GÖRTLER: Is there something you wish to say to me ?

SALLY [*with an effort*]: Yes – there is. There seems to have been a misunderstanding about your room, Dr – er –

DR GÖRTLER [*deliberately*]: Görtler – Gört-ler. And I think the misunderstanding is not about my room, but about me, Mrs Pratt.

SALLY [*heavily*]: I said nothing about you.

DR GÖRTLER: No.

> [*While they are looking at one another, they are interrupted by the entrance of* JANET. *She is dressed for walking and looks tired. She is carrying some wild moorland flowers.*]

SALLY [*glad of this interruption*]: Well you *have* had a long day, Mrs Ormund. But I thought Mr Farrant would be with you.

JANET: No. But he'll be here soon. Oh – I'm tired.

> [*Sits as if almost exhausted.*]

SALLY: I expect you are. Well, I'll see about your suppers.

JANET: I don't want very much, Mrs Pratt.

SALLY: What! after being out all day! That's no way of going on. You want a good meal. [*Nods, smiles, and goes out.*]

DR GÖRTLER [*smiling*]: For once, I think, Mrs Pratt is right. You
   must eat plenty of supper. And it is good too. These people here
   – not like so many of the English now – they still have good
   food.

JANET [*lazily*]: Yes – when I see it – I'll probably be quite greedy.
   But, you know how it is, sometimes when you're feeling tired,
   the idea of enormous platefuls of food ... isn't ... very
   attractive. ...

DR GÖRTLER: You walked a long way?

JANET: Farther than I meant to.

DR GÖRTLER: But it was a good walk?

JANET [*dreamily*]: Heavenly ... across the moors nearly all the
   way.... I found a sort of tiny secret glen ... with a little water-
   fall ... and mossy rocks ... carpets of grass ... harebells. ...
   [*The clock chimes.*]

DR GÖRTLER: White harebells again?

JANET: Yes ... white harebells again. ... You remember things,
   don't you, Dr Görtler?

DR GÖRTLER: Only sometimes. My wife used to say I remembered
   nothing. But that was because I always forgot anniversary
   days or what to take home from shops. [*Pauses, smiles across at*
   JANET.] It was peaceful up there?

JANET: Yes ... no people ... just larks and curlews ... very
   peaceful, very innocent. ... I think there's something – almost
   startling – in the innocence one feels about this sort of country –

DR GÖRTLER: In these high wastelands?

JANET: Yes. You must have felt it, haven't you?

DR GÖRTLER [*with great tenderness*]: Yes. Every summer I used to
   walk on the Thuringian mountains – with my family and my
   friends. Ah! – we did not even know how happy we were, to be
   together and have such summer days – [*His voice drops, he is
   greatly moved.*] I think it would have broken our hearts then to
   know how happy and fortunate we were –

JANET [*moved with him*]: Dr Görtler – I'm so sorry –

DR GÖRTLER [*with an innocent natural pedagogic sense, half
   pathetic and half comic*]: These high places have never been
   settled by men, so they are still innocent. There is not about
   them any accumulation of evil. Where men have lived a long
   time, the very stones are saturated in evil memories. Cruelty

and suffering remain in the world, and I think the earth cries out under its load of evil.

JANET: But the past has gone.

DR GÖRTLER: Gone where? [*Pauses.*] So Mr Farrant was not with you?

JANET: No. . . . I was alone, all day. I was glad to be.

DR GÖRTLER [*smiling*]: To think?

JANET: No . . . you wouldn't call it thinking . . . almost a sort of day-dreaming. . . .

DR GÖRTLER [*after pause*]: You – did not see Mr Farrant today then?

JANET: Yes. . . . I saw him. . . .

DR GÖRTLER: Of course. You told Mrs Pratt he would be here soon.

JANET: Yes. . . . I saw him . . . following . . . behind me.

DR GÖRTLER: And he couldn't catch up to you?

JANET: He didn't catch up to me. . . . I saw him somewhere behind me . . . usually a long way off . . . several times . . . half the day, I suppose. . . .

DR GÖRTLER: You were glad he stayed behind?

JANET: Yes, very. [*Changing to a more normal, social tone*] I suppose Walter – my husband – is in the bar?

DR GÖRTLER: Yes, he has just gone there. Before that we were talking. [*Pauses.*] He is a man of force, of character, such as most women admire, eh?

JANET: Yes, he is.

DR GÖRTLER [*slowly*]: Also, he is a man with deep secret weaknesses, and I think such weaknesses in such a man arouse a woman's pity.

JANET: Yes, I think they might.

DR GÖRTLER [*after pause*]: There is much to love in him.

JANET: Very much.

DR GÖRTLER [*softly*]: Then why, Mrs Ormund, do you love him no longer?

[JANET, *both socially offended and really wounded, rises slowly, obviously giving* DR GÖRTLER *to understand he has been offensive, though she does not say anything. He looks more reproachful than apologetic.*]

You are offended. I am sorry.

[JANET *controls herself, then speaks in a lighter, social tone, itself a rebuke though not a strong one.*]

JANET: Is it true, Dr Görtler, that time is curved? I read some-where the other day that it is.

DR GÖRTLER: Yes, it is. But time is not single and universal. It is only the name we give to higher dimensions of things. In our present state of consciousness, we cannot experience these dimensions spatially, but only successively. That we call time. But there are more times than one –

[SALLY *enters and one might detect a certain pleasure she has in interrupting* DR GÖRTLER.]

SALLY: It's all ready when you are, Mrs Ormund.

JANET: Right, thank you, Mrs Pratt.

[DR GÖRTLER, *rather annoyed at being interrupted and not very comfortable now with* SALLY, *crosses to the outside door, opens it and looks out.* JANET *gives a rather mischievous look at his back, then at* SALLY.]

Dr Görtler is trying to explain to me what time really is.

SALLY: I can tell him what time is. It's a woman's greatest enemy – that's what it is.

JANET: It takes a lot away from us.

SALLY: It does that, and I'm not thinking about the pleasure of looking at yourself in the glass. It can take your man away, turn your baby into a little lad and then into a big lad, off on his own and forgetting you, and soon nothing's the same, except what you go on feeling, right down in your heart. Time doesn't take what you feel right down in your heart, Mrs Ormund. If it did, it'ud be kinder than it is. But it leaves you behind – to suffer.

DR GÖRTLER [*turning*]: No. All that is an illusion. Nothing has really gone, nothing is really lost.

SALLY [*impatiently*]: Isn't it indeed? You wouldn't talk like that if you'd lost as much as I have.

DR GÖRTLER [*with dignity*]: I have lost more than you have. I have lost everything except the love of knowledge – and faith and hope.

[*He turns to go, and almost bumps into* FARRANT, *who enters looking dusty and tired and strained. There is a quite definite sense of strain in his manner.* DR GÖRTLER *smiles at him.*]

So – Mr Farrant, you have had a good walk, eh?

FARRANT: Not bad. [*He passes* DR GÖRTLER *without a smile or a look. The effect is that of a snub.*] Get me a glass of sherry, please, Mrs Pratt.

DR GÖRTLER [*sharply*]: Mr Farrant.

FARRANT [*turning*]: Yes ?

DR GÖRTLER [*rather sadly*]: It does not matter.

    [*He goes out slowly, the other three looking after him.*]

FARRANT: What's wrong with Görtler ?

JANET [*coldly*]: Perhaps he didn't appreciate your very curt manner.

FARRANT [*rather dryly*]: Sorry about that. Didn't mean to offend him.

SALLY [*as she goes*]: Never mind about him, Mr Farrant. [*She goes.*]

    [*There is an awkward silence. Then* JANET *prepares to move.*]

JANET [*with emphasis*]: Thank you for not trying to catch up to me.

FARRANT [*confused by this attack*]: Oh – were you –

JANET [*cutting in as she goes*]: Yes, and you know I was.

    [*He stares after her, and mechanically takes out a cigarette and lights it.* SALLY *enters with a glass of sherry.*]

SALLY: And your supper's all ready, Mr Farrant.

FARRANT: Thanks. I'll come along in a few minutes.

    [*He sips his sherry,* SALLY *looks at him.*]

SALLY: You don't think you're overdoing it a bit, do you, Mr Farrant ? I mean, walking too much.

FARRANT [*off-handedly*]: I'm rather tired today. I slept badly last night.

SALLY: Yes, well you were sent here for a rest, y'know, and you don't want to go and overdo it. You're looking done up tonight, if you don't mind me saying so.

    [*It is now much darker and* SALLY *begins to switch on the lights and draw the curtains and tidy up a little, doing this slowly as she talks and continuing until* SAM *enters.*]

FARRANT: Don't worry, Mrs Pratt. I've always been a lot better than I looked.

SALLY: Well, you mustn't think I'm fussing at you –

FARRANT [*teasing her, nicely*]: Of course you are. And don't pretend you're not.

SALLY: Yes, but I know what it is when folk first comes up here. They do too much. And we can't have you making yourself poorly again, I don't know what our Charlie would say to us. He's depending on you to see him through and so are we. And he thinks the world of you, I'm sure.

FARRANT [*as he goes slowly to the door to his staircase*]: And we'll see him through. We'll have you nearly bursting with pride over him one day. I must wash.

SALLY: Shall I get you some hot water?

FARRANT: No, thanks. [*He goes out.*]

[SALLY *finishes tidying up the room.* SAM *looks in.*]

SAM: Well, lass?

SALLY: What was all that commotion just now in t'bar?

SAM [*grinning, and coming in*]: Oh – that wor only Mr Ormund having a bit of a game wi' owd Watson and Joe.

SALLY [*dropping her voice*]: Is he drunk?

SAM [*dropping his*]: Who? Mr Ormund? Well – amount he's taken tonight he ought to be silly drunk or unconscious – I know I'd be – but you can't say he's more nor a bit wild like. By gow, he can shift it, that chap.

SALLY: And I call it a silly way o' going on. Can't you stop him?

SAM: Course I can't. It's not as if he wor daft with it. He's nobbut a bit wild.

SALLY: Well, I don't like it, Father.

SAM: No, happen not. Still –

SALLY [*continuing, unhappily*]: I'm right sorry now Miss Holmes and her friends couldn't come. I can understand them sort o' folk. I've felt uneasy in my mind ever since last night. And I put most of it down to this Dr Görtler. He's got everybody's back up.

SAM: Nay, it's only 'cos he's a sort of foreigner and a professor and whatnot, and talks so queer. He means no harm, Sally.

SALLY [*with sudden anger*]: Harm or no harm, he leaves here in t'morning. We'll get on better without him. And I'm going to tell him so.

SAM: Now steady on, lass, steady on.

SALLY [*angrily*]: What's use of saying ' steady on' when we're all getting on edge –

[*She is interrupted by* ORMUND *who enters a trifle unsteadily,* a

*glass of whisky in his hand. He has obviously had a lot to drink,
but is not conventionally drunk.*]

ORMUND: Sam, Sam, you're deserting us. And you've not told me
yet what's going to happen to you in the next world.

SALLY [*hastily*]: Mrs Ormund's back, Mr Ormund. She's gone to
get her supper.

ORMUND [*perching himself on table*]: See that she has a beautiful
supper, Mrs Pratt. Including your gooseberry pie. Don't stand
any high-brow nonsense from her on that subject. She must
take her share of gooseberry pie. See to it!

[*Waves at* SALLY, *who nods, smiles faintly, and goes.*]

Now, Sam, what's going to happen to you in the next world?

SAM: Nay, he didn't say t'next world –

[FARRANT *enters from his room. He is tidier than he was, but
still looks pale and strained.*]

ORMUND: Hello, Farrant. Did you show my wife the moors
today?

FARRANT [*rather shortly*]: No.

ORMUND: Weren't you together?

FARRANT: No. I saw her. But we weren't together.

ORMUND: Why didn't you join up?

FARRANT [*rather stiffly*]: I don't know. I suppose we both pre-
ferred our own company.

ORMUND: That's not very complimentary of you.

FARRANT: Sorry. I didn't mean to sound offensive. Actually, I
was feeling – rather dreary, and thought I'd better keep it to
myself.

ORMUND [*pleasantly*]: Well, well. Sam's just going to tell me what
our friend Dr Görtler says will happen to him when he dies.

FARRANT: Well, you know what to expect. I believe Görtler's
turning mystical, like so many Germans when things go wrong.

ORMUND: He's had a packet, you know.

FARRANT: Yes, and I think it's a rotten shame. But even that
doesn't excuse a man of science who's begun to talk bosh.

ORMUND: I suppose it is bosh.

FARRANT: From one or two things he said to me last night, I'm
afraid it will be. Perhaps I'm too impatient with that easy, optimistic half-thinking, but it does seem to me to be poor stuff in
itself and to get in the way of real thought. We shan't get out of

the muddle we're in except by thinking hard and realistically. Don't you agree?

ORMUND: We shan't begin to get out of it until we really *want* to get out. What sort of thinking is going to make us *want* to get out, that's the point.

FARRANT: Well, it won't be Görtler's Teutonic mistiness, will it? I must go and eat. [*Nods and goes.*]

ORMUND [*in a whisper*]: Sam, believe it or not, it was I who voted him into that headmastership at Lamberton. And now having met the young man, I don't like him, and he doesn't like me.

SAM [*stoutly*]: Nay, Mr Ormund, Mr Farrant's a grand young chap when you get to know him. Before you came, he was great company, but this last day or two, he's happen been a bit short and sharp. I fancy he's not so well again.

ORMUND: Perhaps that's it. But now then, Sam, let's hear what's going to happen to you – let's have some bosh.

SAM: Well, it started with me saying last night: 'If I'd my time over again,' which seemed to right tickle Dr Görtler. Because he comes to me this afternoon and tells me I'm going to have my time over again. He started on about time going round i' circles an' spirals, an' i' two minutes, what with his dimensions and eternities and what not, he had me dizzy. He says we all go round and round like dobby-horses.

ORMUND: God forbid!

SAM: Nay, don't say that, Mr Ormund, 'cos I'm all for this arrangement. He says I'm one o' them that'll go on and on wi' t'same life an' nivver change. When I die, I'm born all over again, down at Marlingset, same house, same parents, go to t'same school an' have t'same fights wi' t'other lads, just t'same as before.

ORMUND: But you wouldn't like that, Sam, would you?

SAM: I ask for naught better. It's champion. I wor telling him about day I wor wed. We wor wed early an' then I took her down to Leeds – eh, an' it wor a grand day an' all – Wharfedale shining an' smiling all t'way down – an' Yorkshire wor playing Surrey at Headingley, an' so o' course we went – an' Brown an' Tunnicliffe an' F. S. Jackson knocked them Surrey bowlers silly – an' then we went back to big high tea at Queen's Hotel. Eh, what a day!

ORMUND: Yes, that would be worth having again.

SAM: Well, I says to him, 'Nah is that day coming round again?'
An' he says, 'Yes, it's on its way. Same bright morning,' he says,
'same blushing girl,' he says, 'same sun on t'same fields – everything.' That'll do me, I says.

ORMUND [*half amused, half serious*]: Lucky for you, Sam. But does
he seriously think we all just go on and on with the same life?

SAM: Ay, I think so. That's what he told me.

[DR GÖRTLER *enters. They turn and see him.*]

SAM: Doctor, didn't you tell me we all went on wi' t'same life
round an' round an' round?

DR GÖRTLER: I said you might live the same life over and over
again. But not all.

SAM: Well, what happens to t'others then, Doctor?

DR GÖRTLER: Some people, steadily developing, will exhaust the
possibilities of their circles of time and will finally swing out of
them into new existences. Others – the criminals, madmen,
suicides – live their lives in ever darkening circles of their time.
Fatality begins to haunt them. More and more of their lives are
passed in the shadow of death. They gradually sink –

ORMUND [*passionately*]: For Christ's sake – stop it, can't you!
[*He goes towards* DR GÖRTLER *as if to strike him, then controls
himself and swings away, muttering*] I don't want to hear any
more of that stuff tonight. It's getting on my nerves. [*He goes out
to the bar.*]

[SAM *looks reproachfully at* DR GÖRTLER.]

SAM: You've gone and put your foot in it again, Doctor.

DR GÖRTLER [*staring after* ORMUND *thoughtfully*]: Yes. Perhaps I
was wrong to come here. Or wrong to speak at all of these
things.

[*Enter* SALLY *purposefully.*]

SALLY [*decisively*]: Just a minute, Father.

SAM [*lowering his voice*]: Now, steady on, Sally.

SALLY [*getting rid of him*]: All right, all right.

[SAM *goes.* SALLY *and* DR GÖRTLER *look at one another.*]

DR GÖRTLER: Yes?

SALLY: Dr Görtler, there's been a misunderstanding about your
room. I thought you were just staying last night and tonight and
– well – I promised somebody that room for tomorrow and

Monday – and it's somebody who's stayed here many a time –
so – you see –

DR GÖRTLER: You mean, that you want me to go?

SALLY: I didn't say so. I said we wanted that room.

DR GÖRTLER: Yes, but you have nobody coming for it tomorrow.

SALLY [*sturdily*]: No, but we soon can have. I said that because I
didn't want to hurt your feelings.

DR GÖRTLER: You have already hurt my feelings. But tell me the
real reason why you wish me to leave.

SALLY [*with force*]: Well, if you want to know, it's because I feel
there's something wrong here. I don't know what it is, but I can
feel it all the time. And so can other people.

DR GÖRTLER: Perhaps there *is* something wrong here.

SALLY: Well, there wasn't before you came. And you arrived in a
queer sort of way – asking who was staying here and all that.
And you've got a way of talking and looking at folk that puts
'em on edge. You may not mean it, and then again you may. But
I do know we'd all be a deal more comfortable if you were gone.
And we think a lot o' Mr Farrant and Mr and Mrs Ormund are
folk o' some standing –

DR GÖRTLER [*with sad irony*]: And I am a stranger, a foreigner.

SALLY: Well, if you want to put it like that, you can do. But that's
how it is. We don't expect you to go tonight, y'know.

DR GÖRTLER [*with sudden passion*]: I will go when I please. You
want to be rid of me – that is enough. I will pay you now.

SALLY: Up to tomorrow morning it'll be just two days. We'll call
it a pound.

[*He gives her a pound note and, turning away, goes to the door
and opening it wide stands looking out.*]

SALLY [*uncomfortably*]: I'm sorry – but we only want to do what's
right for everybody –

DR GÖRTLER [*half turning, curtly*]: I am sorry too – for you.

SALLY [*shortly*]: You needn't be sorry for me. [*She goes out.*]

[DR GÖRTLER *looks out of the door a moment longer, then
leaving it wide open, crosses and goes up to his room through the
staircase door. The clock chimes and strikes ten. During the final
strokes,* ORMUND *enters followed by* SAM, *leaving door open
behind them.*]

ORMUND: He's not here.

SAM [*indicating the open door*]: Must ha' gone out. Sally, Sally!
  [SALLY *appears looking a trifle upset.*]

   Has Dr Görtler gone out, 'cos Mr Ormund wants him?

ORMUND: I want to apologize to him.

SALLY [*sulkily*]: He must have gone out. He's off in the morning.

ORMUND: Going? What for?

SALLY [*defiantly*]: Because I asked him to go.

SAM: Nay, Sally, you didn't!

SALLY: Well, you wouldn't. You shuffled out of it. [*She turns to go.*]

ORMUND [*with authority*]: Just a minute, Mrs Pratt. Did you really ask Dr Görtler to leave this inn?

SALLY [*defiantly*]: I did. And I'm not sorry. He's made everybody feel uncomfortable. I heard you complaining and shouting at him yourself, Mr Ormund.

ORMUND: Yes, God help me!

SALLY: So I think I did right.

ORMUND: No, you did wrong.

SALLY: Why did I?

ORMUND: Because he's a stranger, a foreigner, who's had to leave his own country. Even if he says things we don't understand, even if he makes us feel uncomfortable at times, we ought to be courteous. God knows I haven't been. But I was hoping *you* were being considerate to him. My fault probably. I could kick myself.

SAM: Why, Mr Ormund, I can't see it matters much.

ORMUND: It does, Sam, it does. All over this rotten world now, they're slamming doors in the faces of good men. But we've still a door or two open here. We can't bang one of them in the face of this man, who's done none of us any harm. [*Glances at door.*] He can't have gone far. I'm going to tell him I'm sorry and ashamed. [*He goes out hastily, the door closing behind him.*]

  [SAM *looks after him dubiously, then at* SALLY.]

SAM: You shouldn't ha' done it, Sally.

SALLY: Why not? We've got our living to earn – and work hard enough to earn it – and we're the best judge of our own business. It's all right, Mr Ormund talking so grand now. And how much whisky has *he* had?

SAM: I know. But he's far from being nasty-drunk, so I can't interfere. Only one as could is his wife, and it beats me she doesn't.

SALLY [*lowering her voice*]: Happen she's given him up as a bad job.

> [*She does not say any more because* JANET *enters. There is a slight awkward pause.*]

Was your supper all right, Mrs Ormund?

JANET [*who has a strained look*]: Yes, thank you.

SALLY [*motioning* SAM *out*]: You won't be wanting anything else tonight?

JANET: No, thank you.

SAM [*rather awkwardly*]: Mr Ormund's just gone out.

> [JANET *nods and sits down. As* SALLY *and* SAM *are going,* FARRANT *appears.*]

SALLY: You won't be wanting anything else, will you, Mr Farrant?

FARRANT: No, thank you.

SALLY: What about tomorrow? Will you be going out all day again?

FARRANT [*hastily*]: I don't know yet. I haven't made any plans.

> [*They all say* 'Good night' *as* SALLY *and* SAM *go out.* JANET *and* FARRANT *are left silent, not looking at one another. The sense of strain is definitely felt. At last* JANET *can endure it no longer.*]

JANET: Mr Farrant.

FARRANT [*rather startled*]: Yes?

JANET: This afternoon you walked just behind me for several hours. We've just sat through the whole of supper without exchanging a word. I'm sorry, but I can't stand any more of it. If you're going to sit in here, then I'll either go out or up to my room.

FARRANT [*rising*]: Please don't trouble. I'll go.

JANET [*watching him, with a touch of irony*]: Thank you.

> [*As he stands awkwardly, looking doubtfully at her, and not moving.*]

Yes?

FARRANT [*jerkily*]: Would you mind – telling me – how long you're staying up here?

JANET: I really don't see why I should. [*Pause.*] Why do you ask?

FARRANT: Because if you're not leaving, then I must leave.

JANET [*rising*]: I didn't realize you disliked me as much as that.

FARRANT: I don't dislike you. It isn't that. I'd better clear out in the morning.

JANET: But you've no right to talk as if I'm driving you out.

FARRANT: No, I don't mean that, Mrs Ormund.

JANET [*moving a step or two nearer*]: I'm not trying to be difficult. It's simply that I find these long silences intolerable.

FARRANT [*a step nearer to her*]: I know they are. I feel just the same. And I do assure you – it's quite unusual for me. I'm often accused of talking too much. But – you see – last night I never slept at all –

JANET: Neither did I, for that matter. But that doesn't excuse us –

FARRANT: No, no, I know. But then, you see, all today when I was out, of course I felt fagged. You must have done too.

JANET: I did. And when I came back, I felt absolutely worn out. I couldn't possibly make any effort at supper. Still, I think you might have done –

FARRANT: I tried, y'know, tried all the time. I kept – you know how one does – kept forming words –

JANET [*a step forward*]: Yes, I did that too. But couldn't bring them out.

FARRANT: Exactly. And then when I came in here, the silence had gone on so long, it seemed – y'know – absolutely indestructible –

JANET: It was nearly. I had to take a hammer to it.

FARRANT [*moving a step nearer*]: I'm glad you did, because I wanted to explain. You must think me a fool –

JANET [*quicker than before*]: No, of course I felt you disliked me, but then with not sleeping last night and being so tired today, you see –

FARRANT [*eagerly, very quickly*]: Yes, well, probably I'm imagining I'm fitter than I am, y'know –

JANET [*she is quite close to him now*]: You look rather nervously tired –

FARRANT [*looking at her*]: Perhaps we're both – y'know – not quite – our usual selves.

JANET: No.

[*Involuntarily she steps into his arms and he holds her closely to him. The clock chimes. A tremendous inevitability rather than a sudden gust of passion is felt here. They remain in this embrace for a few moments. They only draw their faces away to speak.*]

FARRANT [*dazed*]: I didn't know. . . . I didn't know.

[*After a pause*]

JANET [*whispering*]: What shall we do?

[*He now does definitely hold her close and they kiss. They are quite ecstatic. Then before they have time to separate,* ORMUND *has entered, clearly taking in the situation. They stand a little apart, dumb.*]

ORMUND [*from just inside the door*]: There may be a storm. And it's nearly Whitsunday – the Feast of Pentecost – the Day of the Spirit, they used to call it. And – curiously enough – they didn't mean motor spirit – quick-starting, anti-knock petrol. They didn't know about that. They didn't know anything. We know it all. Farrant knows it all and is passing on our knowledge to our lucky boys –

[*He breaks off, and comes forward, looking at the other two, who are still dumb.*]

And now what?

[*They are silent.*]

Come on then – damn you! – talk, talk, let's hear all about it.

[*They are silent.*]

I suppose you arranged to meet here. No? Then if you've got as far as this in twenty-four hours, I ought to congratulate you. It's wonderful how everything's being speeded up.

[*Another pause; he looks at* FARRANT.]

Come on, Farrant. Good God, aren't you man enough to stand up for what you're doing?

FARRANT: Ormund – I wish I could explain –

ORMUND: I can do that.

JANET: No, Walter, please. We've got to try and understand what's happening –

ORMUND [*bitterly*]: No difficulty about that. In one day, while the pair of you were pretending to dislike each other, you've suddenly decided you're in love – or in want of amusement – and couldn't even wait –

JANET [*with force*]: No, Walter, can't you see it's not like that?

ORMUND: How can I see what it's like?

FARRANT: Ormund, it's – simply – happened, that's all. Beyond that, we can't explain.

[ORMUND *goes away from them, then turns in a quieter mood.*]

ORMUND: All right, all right. You're neither of you in any fit state to talk, and I know I'm in no fit state to listen. You've fallen in love. You don't know why. You can't help it. That it?

FARRANT: Yes.

JANET: Can't you see we're quite bewildered and helpless? [*Pauses, then with more urgency*] You remember what I felt last night when we arrived here, and I didn't want to stay.

ORMUND: You think you felt then that – this – was about to begin?

JANET: Yes.

ORMUND: But you don't know how it's going to end. [*Looking at both of them*] How does it end? We'd better ask Dr Görtler.

JANET [*urgently*]: Why do you say that?

FARRANT [*quickly*]: He's not serious.

ORMUND: I'm in a state of mind when I've stopped considering whether I'm serious or not. Ask Görtler. Ask the devil.

FARRANT: But Görtler doesn't come into this at all.

ORMUND: Don't be too sure, Farrant.

JANET [*as if making a tremendous discovery*]: He knew it had happened before.

FARRANT [*quickly*]: He couldn't have done.

JANET: He came to find us here.

ORMUND [*almost in a whisper*]: My God! – I'd hate to think that.

JANET: Why, what do you mean?

ORMUND: I've had one grim session with him tonight. What *does* Görtler know?

FARRANT [*with quick contempt*]: Nothing about this.

JANET [*suddenly sinking into chair, exhausted, then speaking slowly*]: I believe he knows everything about us all.

　　[*There is a pause.*]

ORMUND [*harshly*]: Well, what do we do now?

JANET [*in a whisper*]: I'm frightened.

　　[*As they look at one another in silence – DR GÖRTLER crosses the stage from the staircase door to the door, to the open air, in a curiously detached, almost mechanical fashion, carrying his bag. He does not look at them, but they watch him in silence, staring in fascination and amazement at him. They only speak when he is nearing the door.*]

JANET [*in a terribly alarmed tone*]: Dr Görtler!

ORMUND [*in alarm and despair*]: Görtler!

[*But he ignores them and walks straight out of door, banging it behind him, and they remain motionless, staring after him, and then slowly turning their eyes to one another, while the curtain rapidly descends.*]

END OF ACT TWO

ACT THREE

Sunday night. The room is empty. Late evening light. Both doors are closed. The clock chimes. After a moment, SALLY *comes in and goes to telephone.*

SALLY: No! I was sure I heard it. [*Over her shoulder to* SAM, *who is following her*] Come in, Father, there's nobody here. Surely they can't be much longer getting that call through. It's past his bedtime now.

SAM: Well, if t'lad's in bed, he's all right.

SALLY [*sharply, she is worried*]: Unless he's poorly. And how do I know he's safe in bed?

SAM: Why shouldn't he be?

SALLY: I've told you before, Father – I don't know. I expect I'm making a fool of myself. But I can't help it.

SAM: All right, lass, I'm not blaming you.

SALLY: I'm sorry, Father, I didn't mean to be short with you. And if it were anybody else but our Charlie, I'd laugh at myself for getting into such a state.

   [*Telephone rings sharply.* SALLY *hastens to answer.*]

Yes, yes. . . . Well, this is Mrs Pratt speaking . . . . [*Eagerly*] Oh is he? Thank you very much, though I didn't mean to get poor lad out o' bed. . . . [*With marked change of tone*] Oh, Charlie, this is your mother. . . . Are you all right, lad? . . . [*With great relief*] Well, I'm glad to hear it. I've been right worried about you. . . . Nay, I don't know. . . . I must be doting. . . . Yes, it's been nice here, except for a bit of a storm late last night. . . . That's good. . . . How many runs did *you* make? . . . Never mind, better luck next time. . . . Yes, well – look after yourself, Charlie. . . . God bless you, lad! [*She puts down the telephone and gives a great sigh.*] He's all right.

SAM: I didn't expect aught else. How many runs *did* he make?

SALLY [*half laughing*]: You're as bad as he is. Three.

SAM: He will try and hit across, instead o' coming forward – left foot. I've told him.

SALLY: I've been worrying and worrying about that lad all day. Well, that's *one* load off my mind.

SAM: One load? How many more have you?

SALLY: Well, I've this.

[*She produces a rather worn, fairly large notebook, bound in dark leather.* SAM *looks at it in astonishment.*]

SAM: Whose is it?

SALLY: That Doctor Görtler's. I found it in his room this morning. It had slipped down inside the arm-chair.

SAM: Well, you'll have to send it to him.

SALLY: How can I when he didn't leave his address? And another thing. I feel bad about sending him away like that.

SAM: I told you.

SALLY: I never thought he'd leave last night, without another word. I meant to tell him this morning to stay on, if he wanted to – after what Mr Ormund said – he'd made me sort o' feel ashamed – and I was right upset when I found he'd gone. I think that started me off.

SAM [*with awkward tenderness*]: Never mind, lass. We all mak' mistakes.

SALLY: But don't think I'm the only one who's feeling upset here. There's some worse than me – yes, here in this house.

SAM: Ay. I've hardly seen 'em today.

SALLY: Neither have I. But I know.

[FARRANT's *and* JANET's *voices are heard.* SAM *looks that way, and picks up notebook.* JANET *and* FARRANT *enter, looking very serious.*]

SAM: Mr Farrant [*showing notebook*], Dr Görtler left this behind. It had got down side of his chair, way my tobacco pouch has done monny a time. I wor just wondering whether it wor of any importance. It's i' German, I reckon.

FARRANT [*taking notebook*]: I'll see.

[*Looks at first page, curiously.*]

JANET [*very curious*]: What does it say?

FARRANT [*puzzling over it*]: *Wiederkehr und Dazwischenkunft.* That's Return or Recurrence and – Interference or Intervention. This notebook, it says, is for problems and instances of Recurrence and Intervention.

[*Flicks the pages carelessly.*]

Yes –

[*Handing it back casually to* SAM]

he's sure to want that back.

JANET [*who's been thinking*]: What could he mean by problems and instances of Recurrence and Intervention?

FARRANT [*shrugging*]: God knows! But as I've told you before, I don't think Görtler had quite retained his mental balance. It often happens when an elderly scholar suddenly has a lot of trouble.

[*Turns, rather sharply, to* SALLY.]

Mrs Pratt, I'm leaving tonight, so can I have my bill, please. And – Sam – would you mind getting my car out?

SAM [*surprised*]: All right, Mr Farrant. [*He goes.*]

FARRANT [*to* JANET]: I'll pack now.

[*He goes to his room.* SALLY *looks after him in astonishment, then looks at* JANET.]

JANET: Do you know where my husband is, Mrs Pratt?

SALLY [*gravely*]: He was up in his room, Mrs Ormund. I went in about quarter of an hour since, and he was there, writing letters. [*She breaks off, then looking hard at* JANET, *moves a step nearer to her.*] Mrs Ormund, are *you* going tonight, as well as Mr Farrant?

JANET: Yes, we're going together.

SALLY: You're leaving your husband?

JANET: Yes.

SALLY: Leaving him for good?

JANET: Yes.

SALLY [*very earnestly*]: But that's a terrible thing to do, Mrs Ormund.

JANET [*steadily*]: I know it's a very serious thing, Mrs Pratt. But it happens to be the only possible – the only fair – thing to do – in the circumstances. You'll have to believe that.

SALLY: But have you thought, Mrs Ormund?

JANET [*with a rather wan smile*]: I've been doing a lot of thinking.

SALLY: Yes, but I mean – have you thought about what'll happen to Mr Ormund? He's your husband. And what will he do, left to himself? He seems such an unhappy sort o' gentleman with all his drinking and what not.

JANET: I'm afraid he is unhappy.

SALLY: You're not leaving him – surely – because he's taken to drinking too much –

JANET [*cutting in*]: No, Mrs Pratt. My husband always has been unhappy. There was a time when I tried very hard to make him happy, but somehow I couldn't. It was my fault, not his, probably. I just couldn't feel what I ought to have felt for him. No, it's no use.

SALLY [*very earnestly*]: But Mr Farrant too! Have you thought what might happen to him – with his school and everything? That's where my Charlie is, you know. And if anything did happen to Mr Farrant!

JANET [*a trifle less sympathetically*]: You can be sure I've thought about that too. We both have.

SALLY: Oh – I knew there was something wrong. Mrs Ormund, please – I've lost my own man, and I've only this lad of mine – and I'm older than you – listen to me a minute. Don't go snatching at what you think might be happiness, when you don't really know. And please – please – don't rush off and do something you might regret all the rest of your life. We haven't just ourselves to consider, y'know, and the older you get, the more you see that. Mrs Ormund – please – give yourself a bit more time – think it over – for all our sakes –

[*She is disturbed by the entrance of* ORMUND. *He is completely sober.* SALLY *gives him one look and then hurries out.* ORMUND *waits until she has gone.*]

JANET [*quietly but not without emotion*]: I've just told Mrs Pratt that Oliver and I are going away.

ORMUND: When?

JANET: We're going tonight.

ORMUND [*hopelessly*]: I see.

JANET: It's the fairest and wisest thing to do, Walter – to make a clean break now, so that none of us has any more of this agony.

ORMUND: I've no doubt you're right.

JANET: We've talked it all out. We've faced the worst that might happen – even lost the school because of possible scandal.

ORMUND: You mean – you've talked about facing the worst that might happen – you haven't actually faced it yet, y'know.

JANET: Well, we've realized all that this might involve. We're not going away with our eyes closed.

ORMUND: I wonder?

JANET: Why do you say that?

ORMUND: Because I wonder how you know what the worst is that
    might happen. When we decided to come here together, I
    thought the worst that could happen would be that we'd have
    another of our rows. But now something much worse has
    happened. I'm losing you altogether. You see, we don't know.

JANET [*rather wearily*]: I realize that, Walter. I only said that we
    tried to face the possible consequences.

ORMUND [*looking curiously at her*]: You're going away. But you're
    not happy, are you, Janet?

JANET [*with great sincerity*]: No, I'm not. I'm miserable – and
    rather frightened. And perhaps it's a good thing I am.

ORMUND: Why?

JANET [*very seriously*]: Because if I were all excited and feeling
    gay, I might be doing something foolish going away like this. As
    it is, I know what I feel for Oliver Farrant is absolutely real –
    now and for ever. I believe it's always existed, always been part
    of me.

ORMUND [*rather wearily*]: Perhaps it has. Who knows? We know
    so little that's worth knowing about ourselves. We're like
    children groping about in the dark.

    [FARRANT *enters from his room carrying a suitcase, raincoat
    and hat. He stands stiffly when he sees* ORMUND.]

All right, Farrant, all right. Only put that damned gear of yours
outside.

FARRANT: My car should be there. [*He crosses to the door, puts his
    things outside, returns immediately*.]

ORMUND: I was asking Janet if she was happy. She says she isn't.

FARRANT [*stiffly*]: I didn't suppose she would be.

ORMUND: What about you?

FARRANT: No, of course I'm not. This is a hateful business. If I'd
    thought my clearing out would settle it, I'd have cleared out.
    But I knew it wouldn't.

JANET: And I knew it wouldn't. We've talked it all out and we've
    agreed on that.

ORMUND [*to* FARRANT]: You're doing the only possible thing,
    you feel –

FARRANT: Yes.

ORMUND: You're both deeply in love. I hope I'm not overstating it.

FARRANT [*curtly*]: You're not.

ORMUND: And yet you're feeling miserable about it. Why?

FARRANT [*shrugging*]: I suppose it's a bad case of conscience.

ORMUND: Conscience? Come, come.

FARRANT: I believe that a man and woman, feeling as Janet and I do, have a perfect right to do what we're doing. But somewhere at the back of my mind, I've still to contend against centuries of belief that what we're doing is wrong. I'm being worried by my ancestors, as we are all the time. That's about all it is.

JANET [*impulsively*]: No, Oliver. I'm sure it isn't that.

FARRANT [*surprised*]: Well, what is it then?

JANET [*struggling with her thought*]: I don't know. I wish I did. But there's something – some sort of influence – behind all that we do and say here – something compelling – and tragic –

FARRANT: No, that's simply being fanciful, Janet.

ORMUND [*with savage irony*]: No – for God's sake – don't let's be fanciful, not when we live in such a nice, simple, straightforward little world as this.

FARRANT [*with force*]: There's no sense in bewildering ourselves with mysteries of our manufacture. People have done that too long. The point is, we're acting rationally and according to our own code, but our so-called consciences were made for us – during childhood – before we could make our own code. Therefore we can know we're doing right and yet still feel, obscurely but quite strongly, that we're doing wrong. And that's what's the matter with us.

ORMUND: And I don't believe that's the half of it, Farrant. It's all too damn simple, like a lot of your explanations.

FARRANT: But perhaps things are really much simpler than you like to think they are.

ORMUND: I suspect they're even more complicated than I think they are. [*Going nearer to* FARRANT *with marked change of tone*] I don't suppose I'll ever see you again, Farrant. Let me give you one last word. Don't be too sure you know it all. Don't think you've got it all worked out. You bright young men, with your outlines of everything, are going to be horribly surprised yet. [*As* FARRANT *begins to protest*] No. Another word and I've finished. Don't think you know it all, and she knows nothing. She knows more about what's going on in this crazy universe than you or I do. She doesn't get it out of books, because it isn't in books. But she can guess right, now and then, and we can't.

FARRANT: But you're not going to blame me for preferring know-ledge and judgement to guesswork ?

ORMUND: No, but I'm not going to have you gassing about know-ledge and judgement when you can't really account for a single thing that's happened to you these last two days. You can give us nice bright simple outlines of everything under the sun, but the minute something really important happens to you, you can't make head or tail of it, and wonder if you're going mad.

JANET [*urgently*]: That's true, at least, Oliver. You know we're all equally bewildered. And there's something more – something that hasn't been accounted for yet – something that perhaps can never be explained – like so many things –

[*She breaks off, and looks across to the doorway.* ORMUND *and* FARRANT *look too. It has rapidly been growing dimmer in the room.* DR GÖRTLER's *figure – he does not wear a hat or carry a bag – stands very dark in the doorway.*]

ORMUND: It's Görtler.

DR GÖRTLER [*at the door*]: Yes. It is dark in here.

[ORMUND *turns on the light.* DR GÖRTLER *comes forward, gives a little bow to the three of them, rather casually.*]

Thank you. But I am not staying –

ORMUND [*gravely*]: Just a minute, Doctor. [*Goes and calls*] Mrs Pratt, Mrs Pratt!

SALLY [*off*]: Just coming, Mr Ormund.

ORMUND [*to* DR GÖRTLER]: You see, you didn't give us a chance last night to say how sorry we were that you – a stranger, an exile in this country – had been treated with such discourtesy. [SALLY *appears.*] Mrs Pratt, I'm apologizing to Dr Görtler.

SALLY [*coming forward humbly and with feeling*]: Yes, Dr Görtler, I want to beg your pardon. I shouldn't have asked you to leave. You'd done nothing wrong. I was blaming you just because you're a foreigner. I'm sorry.

DR GÖRTLER [*rather embarrassed and touched*]: No, please, please. I lost my temper too – that has always been my trouble – a bad temper – and so I behaved foolishly.

SALLY: I hope you'll stay, now you've come back.

DR GÖRTLER: No, I cannot do that. I only came back because I have lost something – something very important – and I am hoping that I may have left it here –

SALLY [*holding up notebook*]: Is this it?

DR GÖRTLER [*taking it eagerly*]: Yes. Thank you. That is all I want.

[*He glances at the notebook, then looks up at* SALLY, *and gives her a smiling nod of dismissal. She looks at him hesitantly, then turns and goes.*]

I would not like to have lost this. There is a great deal of valuable work here. [*Turns, smiling, and makes a move in the direction of the door.*]

ORMUND [*stopping him*]: Görtler! You're not going?

DR GÖRTLER: Yes. Why not?

[*He looks at* ORMUND. ORMUND *looks from him to the other two.*]

JANET [*impulsively*]: Dr Görtler, you know something, don't you? Something that we don't know.

FARRANT [*quietly*]: That's quite impossible, y'know, Janet.

ORMUND: Is it, though? I'm not so sure.

JANET [*to* DR GÖRTLER]: You know, don't you?

FARRANT [*protesting*]: Janet, really it's –

JANET [*cutting him short*]: Please, Oliver! [*To* DR GÖRTLER] You believe that something happened here before, don't you?

DR GÖRTLER: I know it did.

FARRANT: How could it, seeing that not one of us has ever been here before?

DR GÖRTLER: Are you sure you haven't?

FARRANT [*very decidedly*]: Of course I am. I'm quite capable of remembering exactly where I've been.

DR GÖRTLER: Then there is nothing more to be said.

JANET: Yes, there is. Please! What do you know about us?

FARRANT: Wait a minute, Janet. We can't possibly drag Dr Görtler into our private affairs.

DR GÖRTLER: I have no wish to be dragged into them. [*Looks at him with a slight smile.*] Have you and Mrs Ormund planned to leave here tonight together?

FARRANT: How did you guess?

DR GÖRTLER: It is not guessing.

ORMUND: Görtler, I don't blame you for losing your temper. You were badly treated. But we've apologized. And things are serious here now –

DR GÖRTLER [*coolly*]: They always were – *very* serious.

ORMUND: All right then. Now – the truth, as simply as you can state it, please. You had some definite purpose in coming here, hadn't you?

DR GÖRTLER: Yes.

ORMUND: What was it?

DR GÖRTLER: I came to verify an experiment, and, if possible, to make a further experiment.

ORMUND: But you didn't do anything?

DR GÖRTLER: Yes. Everything happened as I thought it would. I verified my experiment. But then, last night, I suddenly lost patience, because I felt I was being badly treated, so I did not try the further experiment. That does not matter very much. I can try that other experiment with some other example.

JANET [*urgently*]: Dr Görtler, you mean it doesn't matter to you or to your theory or whatever it is, but what about us?

FARRANT [*impatiently*]: How *can* it matter to us, Janet?

[DR GÖRTLER *looks at them indifferently. A pause.*]

ORMUND [*very forcefully*]: Dr Görtler, last night you asked me a good many unusual questions – you remember? – and I told you things I had never told anybody else –

DR GÖRTLER: Yes, that is true. You were very helpful, Mr Ormund.

ORMUND: Now I am asking you something. It is your turn to be helpful. Why did you come to this inn? What was this experiment of yours?

DR GÖRTLER [*after short pause*]: Very well. [*Pauses, then begins in the brisk impersonal tone of the scientist.*] In this notebook are some records of very unusual states of mind and feats of memory. Some of them came to me like clear dreams. They are quite vivid little scenes. [*He rapidly turns the pages of the notebook to a place he wants, then glances at it.*] In the best of them, I remember not only what I have seen, but also what has been said. I was fortunate enough to have a very good example about three months ago. I put down all the details here. [*Looks at the notebook a moment, then at his listeners.*] In this memory – this dream if you prefer it – I found myself a year or two older than I am now, but situated as I am now, an exile living in London. I was in rooms – cheap rooms not unlike those I am in now – but here the rooms above mine, very poor rooms, were occupied by two people, a man and his wife, still quite young, but very shabby, very poor, and very unhappy. They had been quarrelling bitterly and I had heard them, and because I was sorry, I went up to see what I could do. Then, I learned their history. [*He stops.* JANET *stirs and draws a sharp breath.*] This was not the woman's first husband. She had been the wife of a rich man, older than herself, with whom she had fallen out of love. But they had gone on a little holiday together, at Whitsuntide, to a small inn, which they described. There she had instantly fallen in love with a younger man – the one now her husband – and they had run away. [*He pauses again.*]

[JANET *draws a sharp breath again and looks at* FARRANT. *He shakes his head impatiently.*]

JANET: Dr Görtler –

DR GÖRTLER: Then there came, out of this, as they now realized, the ruin of many innocent lives. A great business collapsed, and many people, simple people – like this landlord and his daughter here – lost their money. Not only that, but there had been a great scandal, so that this young man had been driven out of his profession, and both of them had to endure poverty and loneliness. But what made them so bitter was that though their love for one another had compelled them to take this course, had made them poor and lonely and neglected, it had given them nothing in return. This love of theirs, it had died.

JANET [*very sharply, painfully*]: No, it couldn't have done that.

DR GÖRTLER: Yes. They admitted that. There were too many shadows between them, too many reproachful faces. They could no longer be happy together, yet they could not be indifferent to one another, having suffered so much, so now they were quarrelsome, bitter –

JANET [*with a heart-broken cry*]: Oh – God – no – not that –

FARRANT [*angrily*]: But – Janet –

JANET: It was us he saw, Oliver, of course it was us.

FARRANT [*angrily*]: It's only some fantastic dream of his.

JANET: No. You recognized us here, didn't you?

DR GÖRTLER: Yes. At once.

JANET [*to* FARRANT]: You see, I knew all the time, there was something –

FARRANT [*almost savagely*]: Wait a minute. [*Turning on* DR GÖRTLER] How did you induce these dreams of yours?

DR GÖRTLER: They weren't dreams. They were actual memories.

FARRANT: Memories of what?

DR GÖRTLER: Of past cycles of my own life.

FARRANT: You're contradicting yourself – on your own ridiculous theory. You said you were then as you are now, an exile living in London.

DR GÖRTLER: Why not? I have been an exile in London in past cycles of my life. We repeat our lives, with some differences, over and over again.

FARRANT: You can't expect us to believe that.

DR GÖRTLER: My friend, I do not care whether you believe it or not. You asked me to explain and I am explaining.

FARRANT: Yes, but you're not merely airing a fantastic theory now, you're interfering in our affairs. How did you induce these states of mind?

DR GÖRTLER: By a certain method I have developed. We have to change the focus of attention, which we have trained ourselves to concentrate on the present. My problem was to drift away from the present – as we do in dreams – and yet be attentive, noticing everything –

FARRANT [*with savage intensity*]: Yes, yes, but how did you do it? By going without food, I suppose?

DR GÖRTLER: Yes, to some extent.

FARRANT: I thought so. And did you use drugs?

DR GÖRTLER: A German colleague found a certain narcotic for me –

FARRANT [*triumphantly to* JANET]: I knew it. You see. I suspected that all along. He's starved himself and drugged himself and let himself be hag-ridden by a completely illogical fantastic theory of life, and then comes here with a story of some ridiculous dream he had –

ORMUND [*cutting in, quietly but sharply*]: Then what are we all doing, playing such convincing parts in it?

[*There is silence.* ORMUND *moves nearer the door.*]

DR GÖRTLER [*quietly*]: I expected this. But it was you who asked me to explain. I have given you my explanation.

JANET [*with a sort of quiet despair*]: I believe it's true.

FARRANT [*angry and resentful*]: Janet, you can't.

JANET: Yes. It accounts for so many things. [*To* DR GÖRTLER] But afterwards – when you had made your notes – ?

DR GÖRTLER: That was three months ago. I soon found that these things had not yet happened in this cycle of your lives – because I discovered at once that Mr Oliver Farrant was still the head-master of Lamberton School –

JANET: You had our *names*?

DR GÖRTLER: Yes, of course.

FARRANT: What proof have we of that?

DR GÖRTLER: I think you read German? My handwriting is not good, but you can read enough, I hope, to convince you. [*He hands over the notebook, open, to* FARRANT, *who takes it and stares at it in amazement.* ORMUND, *after watching* FARRANT'*s face a moment, slips out quietly by door to dining-room.*] You will see I had not the actual name of the inn – only an idea of the sort of place it was and its situation among these hills.

FARRANT [*handing back the notebook*]: I don't understand this. Must be some sort of clairvoyance, clairaudience. I believe there are instances –

[DR GÖRTLER *shakes his head, with a little smile.*]

DR GÖRTLER: So I came here for this Whitsuntide holiday. At first, when two of you were not even expected here, I thought I had chosen the wrong year. But no. I was fortunate.

JANET: That's why – you asked those questions – ?

DR GÖRTLER: Yes. I also found that you were all closely inter-dependent. And I saw also that two of you were so instantly and fatally attracted that you were superficially resentful of one another. It was like watching a performance of a play that one has first read carefully.

JANET [*wildly*]: You're talking as if we were marionettes, with no minds and wills of our own.

FARRANT [*resentfully*]: Going round and round. It's a monstrous, hellish theory.

DR GÖRTLER: Yet – what have you felt these last two days ? Have you felt you had minds and wills of your own ?

JANET: No. [*Then with a sort of despairing energy*] But – Dr Görtler – we're not really like that. I know – I *know* we're not. We *can* make our own lives, can't we ?

DR GÖRTLER: Once we know, yes. It is knowledge alone that gives us freedom. I believe that the very grooves in which our lives run are created by our feeling, imagination and will. If we know and then make the effort, we can change our lives. We are not going round and round in hell. And we can help each other.

JANET: How ?

DR GÖRTLER: If I have more knowledge than you, then I can intervene, like a man who stops you on a journey to tell you that the road ahead is flooded. That was the further experiment I had hoped to make. To intervene.

JANET [*pointing to the notebook*]: Recurrence and Intervention.

DR GÖRTLER: Yes. That seemed possible, too. I discovered some things I did not know before. Two of you, troubled by memories, were instantly attracted to each other. That I expected. But the third –

JANET: You mean Walter ?

DR GÖRTLER: Yes. The one I had not met before, I soon discovered that he was a man who felt he had a tragic destiny and was moving nearer and nearer to self-destruction –

JANET [*startled*]: Suicide!

DR GÖRTLER: Yes, that was why the great business collapsed, why so many were ruined, why everybody knew the story. You told me when you left him, ran away, your husband went into the garage here and shot himself –

JANET [*looking round*]: Walter! [*Sees he is not there.*] Where did he go ?

FARRANT [*pointing to main door*]: Not that way.

JANET [*urgently*]: Dr Görtler, he keeps a revolver in one of the pockets of his car. Will you go and get it for me, please ?

DR GÖRTLER [*gravely*]: Yes, that would be better. [*Moves towards door, and then turns.*] That is one thing to do, but there are others, more important.

JANET [*quietly*]: Yes, I understand.

[DR GÖRTLER *goes out.* FARRANT *turns eagerly to* JANET.]

FARRANT [*with passion*]: Janet – you're not going to let that fantastic stuff of his make any difference to us?

JANET [*urgently*]: But – you see, Oliver, I believe it. It explains so
many things I couldn't understand before. It explains *us* – why
it's all happened so quickly between us. And it explains why I've
never felt happy about it, why there's been a great shadow over it
all. [*Pauses, then announces quietly*] So you must go. But I must
stay.

FARRANT: Janet, if you'd told me to go last night, I'd have gone
without a word. But after what we've said to one another today,
I can't go without you, I *can't*.

JANET: You must, Oliver.

FARRANT [*pleading*]: But nothing's been really changed. We're
exactly the same people that we were an hour ago. If it was impossible for you to stay here with Ormund then, it's impossible
now. We still feel the same about each other. Can't you see,
Janet, everything's just the same?

JANET [*distressed*]: No it isn't, because now we know more.

FARRANT: We know nothing. My God, Janet, you're not going
back on everything we've said, everything we've planned,
because of this old German's mystical rubbish?

JANET: Oh – my dear – I must. I feel it's true – here – [*Putting a
hand over her heart.*] Just as I feel the truth of my love and yours.

FARRANT: But now it means tearing our lives in two.

JANET: But it's better to do that than tear so many other people's
lives in two – only to find in the end we'd lost one another. And
this can't be for ever, you know.

FARRANT [*bitterly*]: It can for me. I happen to know I've only one
life, not dozens of 'em like the rest of you. Only one, and now it's
in bits – [*Almost breaking down.*] Oh – Janet – and you'll do
nothing to mend it –

[*This is almost inaudible, as she is now trying to comfort him,
with great tenderness.*]

JANET [*very quietly*]: No, my dear, if this wasn't the beginning,
then this can't be the end of it all. There must be somewhere –
our own place, our own time. [*Taking his face between her hands.*]
Let me look at you.

FARRANT [*almost mumbling*]: Why? What does it matter now?

JANET: I'm trying to make myself remember every single line of your face. And I know I shan't. Very soon I shall try to see it again, and there'll be nothing but a blur while hundreds of faces that mean nothing will come between us. It's a hard world for love, Oliver. Even the memory of its face won't stay to comfort us.

[*Enter* DR GÖRTLER. JANET *and* OLIVER *are now apart again.*]

DR GÖRTLER: The revolver is not there now. And it was there yesterday.

JANET [*hurriedly*]: Will you please find my husband – tell him I am saying good-bye to Oliver – and stay with him until I come in again ? Oliver –

[*He watches* OLIVER *go with* JANET *through door. Before* JANET *has closed the door behind them,* DR GÖRTLER *moves towards door to the dining-room and calls.*]

DR GÖRTLER: Ormund. Ormund.

[ORMUND *enters looking rather wild.*]

ORMUND: Where are they ?

DR GÖRTLER: Out there – but they are saying good-bye.

ORMUND: Good-bye ?

DR GÖRTLER: He is going. She will stay with you. [*Pauses.*] She sent me to find your revolver, but it was not there.

ORMUND: No, because it's here.

[*Pulls it out of his pocket.*]

DR GÖRTLER: It would be better to give that to me.

ORMUND: If I'd any sense I'd use it. No more questions that can't be answered, twisting like knives in your guts. Sleep, a good sleep, the only good sleep.

DR GÖRTLER: I am afraid you will be disappointed. It will be a sleep full of dreams – like this. And the questions will be still there. You cannot blow them to bits with a pistol. But why should you want to try now ? It is all different.

ORMUND: I don't see any difference.

DR GÖRTLER: Your wife will not leave you now. And perhaps she will be changed a little – with a new kindness.

ORMUND: I don't want her kindness. Let her go.

DR GÖRTLER: But now she does not want to go.

ORMUND: Yes, she does. But she's afraid to. And I've lost her, whether she goes or stays, so there's no difference. She can't keep me alive simply by staying by my side.

DR GÖRTLER: No one can keep you alive but yourself.

ORMUND: And I don't want to go on living.

DR GÖRTLER [*dryly*]: I am not going to cry over you, my friend.

ORMUND [*angrily*]: Who the devil asked you to?

DR GÖRTLER: But I must remind you – there's no escape.

ORMUND: No? I suppose because you believe that if I take the jump into the dark, I'll find myself back again on the old tread-mill. Well, I don't believe it. I can find peace.

DR GÖRTLER: You can't. Peace is not somewhere just waiting for you.

ORMUND: Where is it then?

DR GÖRTLER: You have to create it.

ORMUND: How could I? You've some idea of what's gone on in my head these last twenty years. Where's the peace coming from?

DR GÖRTLER [*sternly*]: If you must talk and act like a child, then at least be as humble as a child. If you cannot create your own peace, then pray for it. Go down on your knees and ask for it. If you have no knowledge, then have faith.

ORMUND: Faith in what? Fairy tales?

DR GÖRTLER [*with authority and passion*]: Yes, my friend – if you will – in fairy tales.

ORMUND: I've lived too long – and thought too much – to begin now –

DR GÖRTLER: I have lived longer than you. I have thought more, and I have suffered more. And I tell you there is more truth to the fundamental nature of things in the most foolish fairy tales than there is in any of your complaints against life.

ORMUND: Rubbish! Why?

DR GÖRTLER: Because all events are shaped in the end by magic –

ORMUND [*scornfully*]: Yes, I thought we'd come to that. Magic!

DR GÖRTLER: Yes. The creative magic of our feeling, imagination and will. These are the realities – our feeling, imagination, and will – and all our histories are their dreams.

ORMUND: All very easy!

DR GÖRTLER [*with passion*]: It is not easy. Life is not easy. It provides no short cuts, no effortless escapes. Peace and ecstasy are not laid on like hot and cold water.

ORMUND [*with savage irony*]: You needn't tell me that. I know it.

DR GÖRTLER: Yes, but you do not know – you will not understand
– that life is penetrated through and through by our feeling,
imagination and will. In the end the whole universe must
respond to every real effort we make. We each live a fairy tale
created by ourselves.

ORMUND: What – by going round and round the same damned
dreary circle of existence, as you believe?

DR GÖRTLER: We do not go round a circle. That is an illusion, just
as the circling of the planets and stars is an illusion. We move
along a spiral track. It is not quite the same journey from the
cradle to the grave each time. Sometimes the differences are
small, sometimes they are very important. We must set out each
time on the same road but along that road we have a choice of
adventures.

ORMUND: I wish I could believe that, Görtler.

DR GÖRTLER: What has happened before – many times perhaps –
will probably happen again. That is why some people can
prophesy what is to happen. They do not see the future, as they
think, but the past, what has happened before. But something
new may happen. You may have brought your wife here for this
holiday over and over again. She may have met Farrant here
over and over again. But you and I have not talked here before.
This is new. This may be one of those great moments of our
lives.

ORMUND: And which are they?

DR GÖRTLER [impressively]: When a soul can make a fateful
decision. I see this as such a moment for you, Ormund. You
can return to the old dark circle of existence, dying endless
deaths, or you can break the spell and swing out into new
life.

ORMUND [after a pause, staring at DR GÖRTLER, then with a certain
breadth and nobility of manner]: New life! I wish I could believe
that. They've never told me yet about a God so generous and
noble and wise that he won't allow a few decisions that we make
in our ignorance, haste and bewilderment to settle our fate for
ever. Why should this poor improvisation be our whole existence? Why should this great theatre of suns and moons and
starlight have been created for the first pitiful charade we can
contrive?

DR GÖRTLER: It was not. We must play our parts until the drama
is perfect.

ORMUND [*very slowly*]: I think what I've resented most is that the
only wisdom we have is wisdom after the event. We learn, but
always too late. When I was no longer a boy, I knew at last what
sort of boy I ought to have been. By the time we are forty, we
know how to behave at twenty. Always too late. So that the little
wisdom we get is useless to us.

DR GÖRTLER [*very quietly*]: In your world. Not in mine.

[ORMUND *stands erect, but with his head bowed for a moment.*
DR GÖRTLER *watches him in silence, without moving. Finally*
ORMUND *slips the revolver into his pocket and looks up, ob-*
viously having arrived at a decision.]

Well?

ORMUND [*very quietly*]: At least we can improve on this Whitsuntide drama of yours. I'll live. [*Pauses.*] But on nobody's self-
sacrifice. Ask my wife to come in here for a moment. I can't talk
to her out there with Farrant. And please tell Farrant to stop out
there.

[DR GÖRTLER *nods and goes.* ORMUND *takes out the revolver*
and begins unloading it, then pockets it again as JANET *slowly*
enters, and looks anxiously at him.]

JANET [*quietly*]: I was just saying good-bye to Oliver.

ORMUND: Yes.

JANET: You understand – I'm not leaving you now.

ORMUND: You love him. He loves you. You are certain of
that.

JANET: Yes, absolutely certain.

[*He looks at her gravely for a moment, turns away restlessly, then*
swings round almost savagely.]

ORMUND: Go on then. Go with him.

JANET [*suddenly lighting up with great hope*]: Walter! [*Then she*
realizes it could not work, and the eagerness and light go.] I
couldn't – you see – not now when I know –

ORMUND [*harshly*]: You don't know. How could you?

JANET: Dr Görtler said –

ORMUND [*cutting in sharply*]: These are our lives, not his. Go, I
tell you. There'll be no suicide, no scandal, no disasters. Everything'll go on. You can depend on me.

JANET [*with growing excitement and eagerness*]: Oh – Walter – are
   you sure ? If only I could –
ORMUND [*with a touch of impatience*]: I tell you it's all right.
   Farrant's only got to take you away now for a little time, perhaps
   abroad, and then go quietly back to his work. And whatever
   happens, I'll see he's not howled out of his school.
JANET [*she is radiant now, and speaks confusedly*]: Walter – I can't –
   is it really true ? – oh, I can't talk – I'm too happy –
ORMUND [*with a touch of bitterness*]: Yes, I never remember seeing
   you so happy before.
JANET [*eagerly*]: It's not just for myself – or even for Oliver – but
   for you too, Walter. You've changed everything now.
ORMUND [*with a slight effort*]: All right, keep on being happy then,
   Janet. You were meant to be happy, to be radiant. I always
   wanted you to be – but somehow it didn't work. Now – it seems
   – it's working.
JANET [*looking at him, slowly, with great affection*]: Walter –
   something tremendous has happened to you –
ORMUND: I wonder. [*Looks at her, then slowly smiles.*]
JANET: Yes. You're suddenly quite different. And yet – as you
   always ought to have been. I know now – you're bigger than I
   am – bigger than Oliver. I think – now – you'll be a great man,
   Walter.
ORMUND: Not a chance. I'll never be a great man. There aren't
   many of them, and you have to stand a long way off to see their
   true size. Perhaps I'm at last – a man – a real man – and not a
   mere bundle of fears and self-indulgences.
JANET: That's not how I shall think of you. What will you do
   now ?
ORMUND: Stay here tonight, probably tomorrow night, too. And
   try and think. I've never done much real thinking. I've always
   been afraid to.
      [SALLY *enters, hesitantly and anxiously.* ORMUND *turns and
      sees her.*]
   Oh – Mrs Pratt – ask Sam to put Mrs Ormund's things in the
   car outside.
SALLY: Your car ?
ORMUND: No, Mr Farrant's. [*As she stops and looks troubled and
   anxious, he adds gently*] Everything will be all right, Mrs Pratt.

And stop worrying about that boy of yours. He'll have his chance. Nobody's going to let you down.

SALLY: Thank you, Mr Ormund. [*She goes out.*]

ORMUND [*quietly*]: I'll say good-bye now, Janet. I won't come out.

JANET: There seem to be a thousand things I want to say now, Walter.

ORMUND: Then don't forget them. Because some day, soon, I want to hear them. [DR GÖRTLER *appears at door.*] Good-bye, Janet. Keep on being happy.

[*He holds out a hand, but as she takes it she moves forward and kisses him.*]

JANET [*whispering*]: Dear Walter – good-bye – God bless you!

[*She hurries out,* DR GÖRTLER *holding the door open for her.* ORMUND *watches her go. There is a slight pause after she has gone.*]

ORMUND [*very quietly*]: Close that door, Doctor.

DR GÖRTLER [*after closing door*]: I too must be going now.

ORMUND [*with a slight smile*]: Having concluded the experiment. [*Pause.*] I am still wondering whether I believe a word of it.

DR GÖRTLER: It is very difficult at first, like all new knowledge. [*He is staring curiously at* ORMUND.]

ORMUND: You look at me as a doctor looks at his patient.

DR GÖRTLER [*calmly*]: Yes, because if my theory is correct, you are now in the unusual and interesting position of a man who is moving out on a new time track, like a man who is suddenly born into a strange new world –

ORMUND [*raising his hand as the sound of* FARRANT's *car going off is heard*]: Just a minute, Doctor. [*They listen a moment until sound of car dies away,* ORMUND *listening with a painful intensity.*] Like a man who's suddenly born into a strange new world, eh? Well, that's not altogether fanciful, Görtler. I feel rather like a new-born creature. Rather cold, small, lonely. [*He shivers a little.*]

DR GÖRTLER [*with a little smile*]: Yes, it may be hard at first. But it will pass. There are a million suns waiting to keep you warm and to light your way. [*He goes towards door.* ORMUND *follows him slowly.*] Perhaps we shall meet again. So I will say *Auf Wiedersehn.*

ORMUND: Yes, we'll meet again. Good-bye.

[*They shake hands.* DR GÖRTLER *goes and* ORMUND *stands at door looking out into the night, which faintly lights him with moonlight. As he stands there, he mechanically brings out his pipe and pouch and begins to fill the pipe.* SAM *enters hesitantly – pipe in hand – from the bar, and looks doubtfully and sympathetically across at* ORMUND. *As he clears his throat,* ORMUND *turns and sees him, and comes into the room, closing door behind him.*]

Well, Sam ?

SAM [*with awkward kindness*]: I just wondered – like – Mr Ormund – whether there might be aught I could do for you – like –

ORMUND: Well, you can sit down and smoke your pipe, Sam.

SAM: Ay. [*Both men sit, they light their pipes, and smoke slowly.*] I hear them shepherds t'other side o' Grindle Top's been having a bit o' bother.

ORMUND [*slowly*]: Yes, I heard something about that, Sam.

SAM [*slowly, philosophically*]: Folks thinks shepherds has a quiet life, but they have their bits o' bother, them chaps, like onnybody else.

ORMUND: Yes, I suppose they do, Sam.

[*They are smoking away companionably, in silence, as the curtain slowly falls.*]

END OF PLAY

An Inspector Calls

A PLAY IN THREE ACTS

TO MICHAEL MACOWAN

CHARACTERS

ARTHUR BIRLING
SYBIL BIRLING
SHEILA BIRLING
ERIC BIRLING
GERALD CROFT
EDNA
INSPECTOR GOOLE

Acts

All three Acts, which are continuous, take place in the dining-room of the Birlings' house in Brumley, an industrial city in the North Midlands. It is an evening in spring, 1912.

'An Inspector Calls' was first produced at the New Theatre in October 1946, with the following cast:

ARTHUR BIRLING	Julien Mitchell
GERALD CROFT	Harry Andrews
SHEILA BIRLING	Margaret Leighton
SYBIL BIRLING	Marian Spencer
EDNA	Marjorie Dunkels
ERIC BIRLING	Alec Guinness
INSPECTOR GOOLE	Ralph Richardson

Produced by Basil Dean

ACT ONE

The dining-room of a fairly large suburban house, belonging to a prosperous manufacturer. It has good solid furniture of the period. The general effect is substantial and heavily comfortable, but not cosy and homelike. (If a realistic set is used, then it should be swung back, as it was in the Old Vic production at the New Theatre. By doing this, you can have the dining-table centre downstage during Act One, when it is needed there, and then, swinging back, can reveal the fireplace for Act Two, and then for Act Three can show a small table with telephone on it, downstage of fireplace; and by this time the dining-table and its chairs have moved well upstage. Producers who wish to avoid this tricky business, which involves two re-settings of the scene and some very accurate adjustments of the extra flats necessary, would be well advised to dispense with an ordinary realistic set, if only because the dining-table becomes a nuisance. The lighting should be pink and intimate until the INSPECTOR arrives, and then it should be brighter and harder.)

At rise of curtain, the four BIRLINGS and GERALD are seated at the table, with ARTHUR BIRLING at one end, his wife at the other, ERIC downstage, and SHEILA and GERALD seated upstage. EDNA, the parlour-maid, is just clearing the table, which has no cloth, of dessert plates and champagne glasses, etc., and then replacing them with decanter of port, cigar box and cigarettes. Port glasses are already on the table. All five are in evening dress of the period, the men in tails and white ties, not dinner-jackets. ARTHUR BIRLING is a heavy-looking, rather portentous man in his middle fifties with fairly easy manners but rather provincial in his speech. His wife is about fifty, a rather cold woman and her husband's social superior. SHEILA is a pretty girl in her early twenties, very pleased with life and rather excited. GERALD CROFT is an attractive chap about thirty, rather too manly to be a dandy but very much the easy well-bred young man-about-town. ERIC is in his early twenties, not quite at ease, half shy, half assertive. At the moment they have all had a good dinner, are celebrating a special occasion, and are pleased with themselves.

BIRLING: Giving us the port, Edna? That's right. [*He pushes it towards* ERIC.] You ought to like this port, Gerald. As a matter of fact, Finchley told me it's exactly the same port your father gets from him.

GERALD: Then it'll be all right. The governor prides himself on being a good judge of port. I don't pretend to know much about it.

SHEILA [*gaily, possessively*]: I should jolly well think not, Gerald. I'd hate you to know all about port – like one of these purple-faced old men.

BIRLING: Here, I'm not a purple-faced old man.

SHEILA: No, not yet. But then you don't know all about port – do you?

BIRLING [*noticing that his wife has not taken any*]: Now then, Sybil, you must take a little tonight. Special occasion, y'know, eh?

SHEILA: Yes, go on, Mummy. You must drink our health.

MRS BIRLING [*smiling*]: Very well, then. Just a little, thank you. [*To* EDNA, *who is about to go, with tray*] All right, Edna. I'll ring from the drawing-room when we want coffee. Probably in about half an hour.

EDNA [*going*]: Yes, ma'am.

[EDNA *goes out. They now have all the glasses filled.* BIRLING *beams at them and clearly relaxes.*]

BIRLING: Well, well – this is very nice. Very nice. Good dinner too, Sybil. Tell cook from me.

GERALD [*politely*]: Absolutely first-class.

MRS BIRLING [*reproachfully*]: Arthur, you're not supposed to say such things –

BIRLING: Oh – come, come – I'm treating Gerald like one of the family. And I'm sure he won't object.

SHEILA [*with mock aggressiveness*]: Go on, Gerald – just you object!

GERALD [*smiling*]: Wouldn't dream of it. In fact, I insist upon being one of the family now. I've been trying long enough, haven't I? [*As she does not reply, with more insistence*] Haven't I? You know I have.

MRS BIRLING [*smiling*]: Of course she does.

SHEILA [*half serious, half playful*]: Yes – except for all last summer, when you never came near me, and I wondered what had happened to you.

GERALD: And I've told you – I was awfully busy at the works all that time.

SHEILA [*same tone as before*]: Yes, that's what *you* say.

MRS BIRLING: Now, Sheila, don't tease him. When you're married you'll realize that men with important work to do sometimes have to spend nearly all their time and energy on their business. You'll have to get used to that, just as I had.

SHEILA: I don't believe I will. [*Half playful, half serious, to* GERALD] So you be careful.

GERALD: Oh – I will, I will.

[ERIC *suddenly guffaws. His parents look at him.*]

SHEILA [*severely*]: Now – what's the joke?

ERIC: I don't know – really. Suddenly I felt I just had to laugh.

SHEILA: You're squiffy.

ERIC: I'm not.

MRS BIRLING: What an expression, Sheila! Really, the things you girls pick up these days!

ERIC: If you think that's the best she can do –

SHEILA: Don't be an ass, Eric.

MRS BIRLING: Now stop it, you two. Arthur, what about this famous toast of yours?

BIRLING: Yes, of course. [*Clears his throat.*] Well, Gerald, I know you agreed that we should only have this quiet little family party. It's a pity Sir George and – er – Lady Croft can't be with us, but they're abroad and so it can't be helped. As I told you, they sent me a very nice cable – couldn't be nicer. I'm not sorry that we're celebrating quietly like this –

MRS BIRLING: Much nicer really.

GERALD: I agree.

BIRLING: So do I, but it makes speech-making more difficult –

ERIC [*not too rudely*]: Well, don't do any. We'll drink their health and have done with it.

BIRLING: No, we won't. It's one of the happiest nights of my life. And one day, I hope, Eric, when you've a daughter of your own, you'll understand why. Gerald, I'm going to tell you frankly, without any pretences, that your engagement to Sheila means a tremendous lot to me. She'll make you happy, and I'm sure you'll make her happy. You're just the kind of son-in-law I always wanted. Your father and I have been friendly rivals in business for some time now – though Crofts Limited are both older and bigger than Birling and Company – and now you've brought us together, and perhaps we may look forward to the time when Crofts and Birlings are no longer competing but are working together – for lower costs and higher prices.

GERALD: Hear, hear! And I think my father would agree to that.

MRS BIRLING: Now, Arthur, I don't think you ought to talk business on an occasion like this.

SHEILA: Neither do I. All wrong.

BIRLING: Quite so, I agree with you. I only mentioned it in passing. What I did want to say was – that Sheila's a lucky girl – and I think you're a pretty fortunate young man too, Gerald.

GERALD: I know I am – this once anyhow.

BIRLING [*raising his glass*]: So here's wishing the pair of you – the very best that life can bring. Gerald and Sheila.

MRS BIRLING [*raising her glass, smiling*]: Yes, Gerald. Yes, Sheila darling. Our congratulations and very best wishes!

GERALD: Thank you.

MRS BIRLING: Eric!

ERIC [*rather noisily*]: All the best! She's got a nasty temper sometimes – but she's not bad really. Good old Sheila!

SHEILA: Chump! I can't drink to this, can I? When do I drink?

GERALD: You can drink to me.

SHEILA [*quiet and serious now*]: All right then. I drink to you, Gerald.

[*For a moment they look at each other.*]

GERALD [*quietly*]: Thank you. And I drink to you – and hope I can make you as happy as you deserve to be.

SHEILA [*trying to be light and easy*]: You be careful – or I'll start weeping.

GERALD [*smiling*]: Well, perhaps this will help to stop it. [*He produces a ring case.*]

SHEILA [*excited*]: Oh – Gerald – you've got it – is it the one you wanted me to have?

GERALD [*giving the case to her*]: Yes – the very one.

SHEILA [*taking out the ring*]: Oh – it's wonderful! Look – Mummy – isn't it a beauty? Oh – darling – [*She kisses* GERALD *hastily.*]

ERIC: Steady the Buffs!

SHEILA [*who has put ring on, admiringly*]: I think it's perfect. Now I really feel engaged.

MRS BIRLING: So you ought, darling. It's a lovely ring. Be careful with it.

SHEILA: Careful! I'll never let it go out of my sight for an instant.

MRS BIRLING [*smiling*]: Well, it came just at the right moment. That was clever of you, Gerald. Now, Arthur, if you've no more to say, I think Sheila and I had better go into the drawing-room and leave you men –

BIRLING [*rather heavily*]: I just want to say this. [*Noticing that* SHEILA *is still admiring her ring*] Are you listening, Sheila ? This concerns you too. And after all I don't often make speeches at you –

SHEILA: I'm sorry, Daddy. Actually I was listening.

[*She looks attentive, as they all do. He holds them for a moment before continuing.*]

BIRLING: I'm delighted about this engagement and I hope it won't be too long before you're married. And I want to say this. There's a good deal of silly talk about these days – *but* – and I speak as a hard-headed business man, who has to take risks and know what he's about – I say, you can ignore all this silly pessimistic talk. When you marry, you'll be marrying at a very good time. Yes, a very good time – and soon it'll be an even better time. Last month, just because the miners came out on strike, there's a lot of wild talk about possible labour trouble in the near future. Don't worry. We've passed the worst of it. We employers at last are coming together to see that our interests – and the interests of Capital – are properly protected. And we're in for a time of steadily increasing prosperity.

GERALD: I believe you're right, sir.

ERIC: What about war ?

BIRLING: Glad you mentioned it, Eric. I'm coming to that. Just because the Kaiser makes a speech or two, or a few German officers have too much to drink and begin talking nonsense, you'll hear some people say that war's inevitable. And to that I say – fiddlesticks! The Germans don't want war. Nobody wants war, except some half-civilized folks in the Balkans. And why ? There's too much at stake these days. Everything to lose and nothing to gain by war.

ERIC: Yes, I know – but still –

BIRLING: Just let me finish, Eric. You've a lot to learn yet. And I'm talking as a hard-headed, practical man of business. And I say there isn't a chance of war. The world's developing so fast that it'll make war impossible. Look at the progress we're making. In a year or two we'll have aeroplanes that will be able to go anywhere. And look at the way the automobile's making headway – bigger and faster all the time. And then ships. Why, a friend of mine went over this new liner last week – the *Titanic* – she sails next week – forty-six thousand eight hundred tons – forty-six thousand eight hundred tons – New York in five days – and every luxury – and unsinkable, absolutely unsinkable. That's what you've got to keep your eye on, facts like that, progress like that – and not a few German officers talking nonsense and a few scaremongers here making a fuss about nothing. Now you three young people, just listen to this – and remember what I'm telling you now. In twenty or thirty years' time – let's say, in 1940 – you may be giving a little party like this – your son or daughter might be getting engaged – and I tell you by that time you'll be living in a world that'll have forgotten all these Capital versus Labour agitations and all these silly little war scares. There'll be peace and prosperity and rapid progress everywhere – except of course in Russia, which will always be behindhand, naturally.

MRS BIRLING: Arthur!

[*As* MRS BIRLING *shows signs of interrupting*]

BIRLING: Yes, my dear, I know – I'm talking too much. But you youngsters just remember what I said. We can't let these Bernard Shaws and H. G. Wellses do all the talking. We hard-headed practical business men must say something sometime. And we don't guess – we've had experience – and we *know*.

MRS BIRLING [*rising. The others rise*]: Yes, of course, dear. Well – don't keep Gerald in here too long. Eric – I want you a minute.

[*She and* SHEILA *and* ERIC *go out*. BIRLING *and* GERALD *sit down again*.]

BIRLING: Cigar?

GERALD: No, thanks. Can't really enjoy them.

BIRLING [*taking one himself*]: Ah, you don't know what you're missing. I like a good cigar. [*Indicating decanter*] Help yourself.

GERALD: Thank you.

[BIRLING *lights his cigar and* GERALD, *who has lit a cigarette, helps himself to port then pushes decanter to* BIRLING.]

BIRLING: Thanks. [*Confidentially*] By the way, there's something I'd like to mention – in strict confidence – while we're by ourselves. I have an idea that your mother – Lady Croft – while she doesn't object to my girl – feels you might have done better for yourself socially –

[GERALD, *rather embarrassed, begins to murmur some dissent, but* BIRLING *checks him*.]

No, Gerald, that's all right. Don't blame her. She comes from an old county family – landed people and so forth – and so it's only natural. But what I wanted to say is – there's a fair chance that I might find my way into the next Honours List. Just a knighthood, of course.

GERALD: Oh – I say – congratulations!

BIRLING: Thanks. But it's a bit too early for that. So don't say anything. But I've had a hint or two. You see, I was Lord Mayor here two years ago when Royalty visited us. And I've always been regarded as a sound useful party man. So – well – I gather there's a very good chance of a knighthood – so long as we behave ourselves, don't get into the police court or start a scandal – eh?

[*Laughs complacently*.]

GERALD [*laughs*]: You seem to be a nice well-behaved family –

BIRLING: We think we are –

GERALD: So if that's the only obstacle, sir, I think you might as well accept my congratulations now.

BIRLING: No, no, I couldn't do that. And don't say anything yet.

GERALD: Not even to my mother? I know she'd be delighted.

BIRLING: Well, when she comes back, you might drop a hint to her. And you can promise her that we'll try to keep out of trouble during the next few months.

[*They both laugh.* ERIC *enters*.]

ERIC: What's the joke? Started telling stories?

BIRLING: No. Want another glass of port?

ERIC [*sitting down*]: Yes, please. [*Takes decanter and helps himself*.] Mother says we mustn't stay too long. But I don't think it matters. I left 'em talking about clothes again. You'd think a girl never had any clothes before she gets married. Women are potty about 'em.

BIRLING: Yes, but you've got to remember, my boy, that clothes mean something quite different to a woman. Not just something to wear – and not only something to make 'em look prettier – but – well, a sort of sign or token of their self-respect.

GERALD: That's true.

ERIC [*eagerly*]: Yes, I remember – [*but he checks himself.*]

BIRLING: Well, what do you remember?

ERIC [*confused*]: Nothing.

BIRLING: Nothing?

GERALD [*amused*]: Sounds a bit fishy to me.

BIRLING [*taking it in same manner*]: Yes, you don't know what some of these boys get up to nowadays. More money to spend and time to spare than I had when I was Eric's age. They worked us hard in those days and kept us short of cash. Though even then – we broke out and had a bit of fun sometimes.

GERALD: I'll bet you did.

BIRLING [*solemnly*]: But this is the point. I don't want to lecture you two young fellows again. But what so many of you don't seem to understand now, when things are so much easier, is that a man has to make his own way – has to look after himself – and his family too, of course, when he has one – and so long as he does that he won't come to much harm. But the way some of these cranks talk and write now, you'd think everybody has to look after everybody else, as if we were all mixed up together like bees in a hive – community and all that nonsense. But take my word for it, you youngsters – and I've learnt in the good hard school of experience – that a man has to mind his own business and look after himself and his own – and –

[*We hear the sharp ring of a front door bell.* BIRLING *stops to listen.*]

ERIC: Somebody at the front door.

BIRLING: Edna'll answer it. Well, have another glass of port, Gerald – and then we'll join the ladies. That'll stop me giving you good advice.

ERIC: Yes, you've piled it on a bit tonight, Father.

BIRLING: Special occasion. And feeling contented, for once, I wanted you to have the benefit of my experience.

[EDNA *enters*.]

EDNA: Please, sir, an inspector's called.

BIRLING: An inspector? What kind of inspector?

EDNA: A police inspector. He says his name's Inspector Goole.

BIRLING: Don't know him. Does he want to see me?

EDNA: Yes, sir. He says it's important.

BIRLING: All right, Edna. Show him in here. Give us some more light.

[EDNA *does, then goes out*.]

I'm still on the Bench. It may be something about a warrant.

GERALD [*lightly*]: Sure to be. Unless Eric's been up to something. [*Nodding confidentially to* BIRLING] And that would be awkward, wouldn't it?

BIRLING [*humorously*]: Very.

ERIC [*who is uneasy, sharply*]: Here, what do you mean?

GERALD [*lightly*]: Only something we were talking about when you were out. A joke really.

ERIC [*still uneasy*]: Well, I don't think it's very funny.

BIRLING [*sharply, staring at him*]: What's the matter with *you*?

ERIC [*defiantly*]: Nothing.

EDNA [*opening door, and announcing*]: Inspector Goole.

[*The* INSPECTOR *enters, and* EDNA *goes, closing door after her. The* INSPECTOR *need not be a big man but he creates at once an impression of massiveness, solidity and purposefulness. He is a man in his fifties, dressed in a plain darkish suit of the period. He speaks carefully, weightily, and has a disconcerting habit of looking hard at the person he addresses before actually speaking*.]

INSPECTOR: Mr Birling?

BIRLING: Yes. Sit down, Inspector.

INSPECTOR [*sitting*]: Thank you, sir.

BIRLING: Have a glass of port – or a little whisky?

INSPECTOR: No, thank you, Mr Birling. I'm on duty.

BIRLING: You're new, aren't you?

INSPECTOR: Yes, sir. Only recently transferred.

BIRLING: I thought you must be. I was an alderman for years – and Lord Mayor two years ago – and I'm still on the Bench – so I know the Brumley police officers pretty well – and I thought I'd never seen you before.

INSPECTOR: Quite so.

BIRLING: Well, what can I do for you? Some trouble about a warrant?

INSPECTOR: No, Mr Birling.

BIRLING [*after a pause, with a touch of impatience*]: Well, what is it then?

INSPECTOR: I'd like some information, if you don't mind, Mr Birling. Two hours ago a young woman died in the Infirmary. She'd been taken there this afternoon because she'd swallowed a lot of strong disinfectant. Burnt her inside out, of course.

ERIC [*involuntarily*]: My God!

INSPECTOR: Yes, she was in great agony. They did everything they could for her at the Infirmary, but she died. Suicide of course.

BIRLING [*rather impatiently*]: Yes, yes. Horrible business. But I don't understand why you should come here, Inspector –

INSPECTOR [*cutting through, massively*]: I've been round to the room she had, and she'd left a letter there and a sort of diary. Like a lot of these young women who get into various kinds of trouble, she'd used more than one name. But her original name – her real name – was Eva Smith.

BIRLING [*thoughtfully*]: Eva Smith?

INSPECTOR: Do you remember her, Mr Birling?

BIRLING [*slowly*]: No – I seem to remember hearing that name – Eva Smith – somewhere. But it doesn't convey anything to me. And I don't see where I come into this.

INSPECTOR: She was employed in your works at one time.

BIRLING: Oh – that's it, is it? Well, we've several hundred young women there, y'know, and they keep changing.

INSPECTOR: This young woman, Eva Smith, was a bit out of the ordinary. I found a photograph of her in her lodgings. Perhaps you'd remember her from that.

[INSPECTOR *takes a photograph, about postcard size, out of his pocket and goes to* BIRLING. *Both* GERALD *and* ERIC *rise to have a look at the photograph, but the* INSPECTOR *interposes himself between them and the photograph. They are surprised and rather annoyed.* BIRLING *stares hard, and with recognition, at the photograph, which the* INSPECTOR *then replaces in his pocket.*]

GERALD [*showing annoyance*]: Any particular reason why I shouldn't see this girl's photograph, Inspector?

INSPECTOR [*coolly, looking hard at him*]: There might be.

ERIC: And the same applies to me, I suppose?

INSPECTOR: Yes.

GERALD: I can't imagine what it could be.

ERIC: Neither can I.

BIRLING: And I must say, I agree with them, Inspector.

INSPECTOR: It's the way I like to go to work. One person and one line of inquiry at a time. Otherwise, there's a muddle.

BIRLING: I see. Sensible really. [*Moves restlessly, then turns.*] You've had enough of that port, Eric.

[*The* INSPECTOR *is watching* BIRLING *and now* BIRLING *notices him.*]

INSPECTOR: I think you remember Eva Smith now, don't you, Mr Birling?

BIRLING: Yes, I do. She was one of my employees and then I discharged her.

ERIC: Is that why she committed suicide? When was this, Father?

BIRLING: Just keep quiet, Eric, and don't get excited. This girl left us nearly two years ago. Let me see – it must have been in the early autumn of nineteen-ten.

INSPECTOR: Yes. End of September, nineteen-ten.

BIRLING: That's right.

GERALD: Look here, sir. Wouldn't you rather I was out of this?

BIRLING: I don't mind your being here, Gerald. And I'm sure you've no objection, have you, Inspector? Perhaps I ought to explain first that this is Mr Gerald Croft – the son of Sir George Croft – you know, Crofts Limited.

INSPECTOR: Mr Gerald Croft, eh?

BIRLING: Yes. Incidentally we've been modestly celebrating his engagement to my daughter, Sheila.

INSPECTOR: I see. Mr Croft is going to marry Miss Sheila Birling?

GERALD [*smiling*]: I hope so.

INSPECTOR [*gravely*]: Then I'd prefer you to stay.

GERALD [*surprised*]: Oh – all right.

BIRLING [*somewhat impatiently*]: Look – there's nothing mysterious – or scandalous – about this business – at least not so far as I'm concerned. It's a perfectly straightforward case, and as it happened more than eighteen months ago – nearly two years ago – obviously it has nothing whatever to do with the wretched girl's suicide. Eh, Inspector?

INSPECTOR: No, sir. I can't agree with you there.

BIRLING: Why not?

INSPECTOR: Because what happened to her then may have determined what happened to her afterwards, and what happened to her afterwards may have driven her to suicide. A chain of events.

BIRLING: Oh well – put like that, there's something in what you say. Still, I can't accept any responsibility. If we were all responsible for everything that happened to everybody we'd had anything to do with, it would be very awkward, wouldn't it?

INSPECTOR: Very awkward.

BIRLING: We'd all be in an impossible position, wouldn't we?

ERIC: By Jove, yes. And as you were saying, Dad, a man has to look after himself –

BIRLING: Yes, well, we needn't go into all that.

INSPECTOR: Go into what?

BIRLING: Oh – just before you came – I'd been giving these young men a little good advice. Now – about this girl, Eva Smith. I remember her quite well now. She was a lively good-looking girl – country-bred, I fancy – and she'd been working in one of our machine shops for over a year. A good worker too. In fact, the foreman there told me he was ready to promote her into what we call a leading operator – head of a small group of girls. But after they came back from their holidays that August, they were all rather restless, and they suddenly decided to ask for more money. They were averaging about twenty-two and six, which was neither more nor less than is paid generally in our industry. They wanted the rates raised so that they could average about twenty-five shillings a week. I refused, of course.

INSPECTOR: Why?

BIRLING [surprised]: Did you say 'Why?'?

INSPECTOR: Yes. Why did you refuse?

BIRLING: Well, Inspector, I don't see that it's any concern of yours how I choose to run my business. Is it now?

INSPECTOR: It might be, you know.

BIRLING: I don't like the tone.

INSPECTOR: I'm sorry. But you asked me a question.

BIRLING: And you asked me a question before that, a quite unnecessary question too.

INSPECTOR: It's my duty to ask questions.

BIRLING: Well, it's my duty to keep labour costs down, and if I'd agreed to this demand for a new rate we'd have added about twelve per cent to our labour costs. Does that satisfy you ? So I refused. Said I couldn't consider it. We were paying the usual rates and if they didn't like those rates, they could go and work somewhere else. It's a free country, I told them.

ERIC: It isn't if you can't go and work somewhere else.

INSPECTOR: Quite so.

BIRLING [to ERIC]: Look – just you keep out of this. You hadn't even started in the works when this happened. So they went on strike. That didn't last long, of course.

GERALD: Not if it was just after the holidays. They'd be all broke – if I know them.

BIRLING: Right, Gerald. They mostly were. And so was the strike, after a week or two. Pitiful affair. Well, we let them all come back – at the old rates – except the four or five ringleaders, who'd started the trouble. I went down myself and told them to clear out. And this girl, Eva Smith, was one of them. She'd had a lot to say – far too much – so she had to go.

GERALD: You couldn't have done anything else.

ERIC: He could. He could have kept her on instead of throwing her out. I call it tough luck.

BIRLING: Rubbish! If you don't come down sharply on some of these people, they'd soon be asking for the earth.

GERALD: I should say so!

INSPECTOR: They might. But after all it's better to ask for the earth than to take it.

BIRLING [staring at the INSPECTOR]: What did you say your name was, Inspector ?

INSPECTOR: Goole. G – double O – L – E.

BIRLING: How do you get on with our Chief Constable, Colonel Roberts ?

INSPECTOR: I don't see much of him.

BIRLING: Perhaps I ought to warn you that he's an old friend of mine, and that I see him fairly frequently. We play golf together sometimes up at the West Brumley.

INSPECTOR [*dryly*]: I don't play golf.

BIRLING: I didn't suppose you did.

ERIC [*bursting out*]: Well, I think it's a dam' shame.

INSPECTOR: No, I've never wanted to play.

ERIC: No. I mean about this girl – Eva Smith. Why shouldn't they try for higher wages ? We try for the highest possible prices. And I don't see why she should have been sacked just because she'd a bit more spirit than the others. You said yourself she was a good worker. I'd have let her stay.

BIRLING [*rather angrily*]: Unless you brighten your ideas, you'll never be in a position to let anybody stay or to tell anybody to go. It's about time you learnt to face a few responsibilities. That's something this public-school-and-Varsity life you've had doesn't seem to teach you.

ERIC [*sulkily*]: Well, we don't need to tell the Inspector all about that, do we ?

BIRLING: I don't see we need to tell the Inspector anything more. In fact, there's nothing I can tell him. I told the girl to clear out, and she went. That's the last I heard of her. Have you any idea what happened to her after that ? Get into trouble ? Go on the streets ?

INSPECTOR [*rather slowly*]: No, she didn't exactly go on the streets.

[SHEILA *has now entered.*]

SHEILA [*gaily*]: What's this about streets ? [*Noticing the* IN-SPECTOR.] Oh – sorry. I didn't know. Mummy sent me in to ask you why you didn't come along to the drawing-room.

BIRLING: We shall be along in a minute now. Just finishing.

INSPECTOR: I'm afraid not.

BIRLING [*abruptly*]: There's nothing else, y'know. I've just told you that.

SHEILA: What's all this about ?

BIRLING: Nothing to do with you, Sheila. Run along.

INSPECTOR: No, wait a minute, Miss Birling.

BIRLING [*angrily*]: Look here, Inspector, I consider this uncalled-for and officious. I've half a mind to report you. I've told you all I know – and it doesn't seem to me very important – and now there isn't the slightest reason why my daughter should be dragged into this unpleasant business.

SHEILA [*coming farther in*]: What business? What's happening?

INSPECTOR [*impressively*]: I'm a police inspector, Miss Birling. This afternoon a young woman drank some disinfectant, and died, after several hours of agony, tonight in the Infirmary.

SHEILA: Oh – how horrible! Was it an accident?

INSPECTOR: No. She wanted to end her life. She felt she couldn't go on any longer.

BIRLING: Well, don't tell me that's because I discharged her from my employment nearly two years ago.

ERIC: That might have started it.

SHEILA: Did you, Dad?

BIRLING: Yes. The girl had been causing trouble in the works. I was quite justified.

GERALD: Yes, I think you were. I know we'd have done the same thing. Don't look like that, Sheila.

SHEILA [*rather distressed*]: Sorry! It's just that I can't help thinking about this girl – destroying herself so horribly – and I've been so happy tonight. Oh I wish you hadn't told me. What was she like? Quite young?

INSPECTOR: Yes. Twenty-four.

SHEILA: Pretty?

INSPECTOR: She wasn't pretty when I saw her today, but she had been pretty – very pretty.

BIRLING: That's enough of that.

GERALD: And I don't really see that this inquiry gets you anywhere, Inspector. It's what happened to her since she left Mr Birling's works that is important.

BIRLING: Obviously. I suggested that some time ago.

GERALD: And we can't help you there because we don't know.

INSPECTOR [*slowly*]: Are you sure you don't know? [*He looks at* GERALD, *then at* ERIC, *then at* SHEILA.]

BIRLING: And are you suggesting now that one of them knows something about this girl?

INSPECTOR: Yes.

BIRLING: You didn't come here just to see me then?

INSPECTOR: No.

[*The other four exchange bewildered and perturbed glances.*]

BIRLING [*with marked change of tone*]: Well, of course, if I'd known that earlier, I wouldn't have called you officious and talked about reporting you. You understand that, don't you, Inspector ? I thought that – for some reason best known to yourself – you were making the most of this tiny bit of information I could give you. I'm sorry. This makes a difference. You sure of your facts ?

INSPECTOR: Some of them – yes.

BIRLING: I can't think they can be of any great consequence.

INSPECTOR: The girl's dead though.

SHEILA: What do you mean by saying that ? You talk as if we were responsible –

BIRLING [cutting in]: Just a minute, Sheila. Now, Inspector, perhaps you and I had better go and talk this over quietly in a corner –

SHEILA [cutting in]: Why should you ? He's finished with you. He says it's one of us now.

BIRLING: Yes, and I'm trying to settle it sensibly for you.

GERALD: Well, there's nothing to settle as far as I'm concerned. I've never known an Eva Smith.

ERIC: Neither have I.

SHEILA: Was that her name ? Eva Smith ?

GERALD: Yes.

SHEILA: Never heard it before.

GERALD: So where are you now, Inspector ?

INSPECTOR: Where I was before, Mr Croft. I told you – that like a lot of these young women, she'd used more than one name. She was still Eva Smith when Mr Birling sacked her – for wanting twenty-five shillings a week instead of twenty-two and six. But after that she stopped being Eva Smith. Perhaps she'd had enough of it.

ERIC: Can't blame her.

SHEILA [to BIRLING]: I think it was a mean thing to do. Perhaps that spoilt everything for her.

BIRLING: Rubbish! [To INSPECTOR] Do you know what happened to this girl after she left my works ?

INSPECTOR: Yes. She was out of work for the next two months. Both her parents were dead, so that she'd no home to go back to. And she hadn't been able to save much out of what Birling and Company had paid her. So that after two months, with no work, no money coming in, and living in lodgings, with no relatives to help her, few friends, lonely, half-starved, she was feeling desperate.

SHEILA [*warmly*]: I should think so. It's a rotten shame.

INSPECTOR: There are a lot of young women living that sort of existence in every city and big town in this country, Miss Birling. If there weren't, the factories and warehouses wouldn't know where to look for cheap labour. Ask your father.

SHEILA: But these girls aren't cheap labour – they're *people*.

INSPECTOR [*dryly*]: I've had that notion myself from time to time. In fact, I've thought that it would do us all a bit of good if sometimes we tried to put ourselves in the place of these young women counting their pennies in their dingy little back bedrooms.

SHEILA: Yes, I expect it would. But what happened to her then?

INSPECTOR: She had what seemed to her a wonderful stroke of luck. She was taken on in a shop – and a good shop too – Milwards.

SHEILA: Milwards! We go there – in fact, I was there this afternoon – [*archly to* GERALD] for *your* benefit.

GERALD [*smiling*]: Good!

SHEILA: Yes, she was lucky to get taken on at Milwards.

INSPECTOR: That's what she thought. And it happened that at the beginning of December that year – nineteen-ten – there was a good deal of influenza about, and Milwards suddenly found themselves short-handed. So that gave her her chance. It seems she liked working there. It was a nice change from a factory. She enjoyed being among pretty clothes, I've no doubt. And now she felt she was making a good fresh start. You can imagine how she felt.

SHEILA: Yes, of course.

BIRLING: And then she got herself into trouble there, I suppose?

INSPECTOR: After about a couple of months, just when she felt she was settling down nicely, they told her she'd have to go.

BIRLING: Not doing her work properly?

INSPECTOR: There was nothing wrong with the way she was doing her work. They admitted that.

BIRLING: There must have been something wrong.

INSPECTOR: All she knew was – that a customer complained about her – and so she had to go.

SHEILA [*staring at him, agitated*]: When was this?

INSPECTOR [*impressively*]: At the end of January – last year.

SHEILA: What – what did this girl look like?

INSPECTOR: If you'll come over here, I'll show you.

> [*He moves nearer a light – perhaps standard lamp – and she crosses to him. He produces the photograph. She looks at it closely, recognizes it with a little cry, gives a half-stifled sob, and then runs out. The* INSPECTOR *puts the photograph back into his pocket and stares speculatively after her. The other three stare in amazement for a moment.*]

BIRLING: What's the matter with her?

ERIC: She recognized her from the photograph, didn't she?

INSPECTOR: Yes.

BIRLING [*angrily*]: Why the devil do you want to go upsetting the child like that?

INSPECTOR: I didn't do it. She's upsetting herself.

BIRLING: Well – why – why?

INSPECTOR: I don't know – yet. That's something I have to find out.

BIRLING [*still angrily*]: Well – if you don't mind – I'll find out first.

GERALD: Shall I go to her?

BIRLING [*moving*]: No, leave this to me. I must also have a word with my wife – tell her what's happening. [*Turns at door, staring at* INSPECTOR *angrily.*] We were having a nice little family celebration tonight. And a nasty mess you've made of it now, haven't you?

INSPECTOR [*steadily*]: That's more or less what I was thinking earlier tonight, when I was in the Infirmary looking at what was left of Eva Smith. A nice little promising life there, I thought, and a nasty mess somebody's made of it.

> [BIRLING *looks as if about to make some retort, then thinks better of it, and goes out, closing door sharply behind him.* GERALD *and* ERIC *exchange uneasy glances. The* INSPECTOR *ignores them.*]

GERALD: I'd like to have a look at that photograph now, Inspector.

INSPECTOR: All in good time.

GERALD: I don't see why –

INSPECTOR [*cutting in, massively*]: You heard what I said before, Mr Croft. One line of inquiry at a time. Otherwise we'll all be talking at once and won't know where we are. If you've anything to tell me, you'll have an opportunity of doing it soon.

GERALD [*rather uneasily*]: Well, I don't suppose I have –

ERIC [*suddenly bursting out*]: Look here, I've had enough of this.

INSPECTOR [*dryly*]: I dare say.

ERIC [*uneasily*]: I'm sorry – but you see – we were having a little party – and I've had a few drinks, including rather a lot of champagne – and I've got a headache – and as I'm only in the way here – I think I'd better turn in.

INSPECTOR: And I think you'd better stay here.

ERIC: Why should I?

INSPECTOR: It might be less trouble. If you turn in, you might have to turn out again soon.

GERALD: Getting a bit heavy-handed, aren't you, Inspector?

INSPECTOR: Possibly. But if you're easy with me, I'm easy with you.

GERALD: After all, y'know, we're respectable citizens and not criminals.

INSPECTOR: Sometimes there isn't as much difference as you think. Often, if it was left to me, I wouldn't know where to draw the line.

GERALD: Fortunately, it isn't left to you, is it?

INSPECTOR: No, it isn't. But some things are left to me. Inquiries of this sort, for instance.

   [*Enter* SHEILA, *who looks as if she's been crying.*]
   Well, Miss Birling?

SHEILA [*coming in, closing door*]: You knew it was me all the time, didn't you?

INSPECTOR: I had an idea it might be – from something the girl herself wrote.

SHEILA: I've told my father – he didn't seem to think it amounted to much – but I felt rotten about it at the time and now I feel a lot worse. Did it make much difference to her?

INSPECTOR: Yes, I'm afraid it did. It was the last real steady job she had. When she lost it – for no reason that she could discover – she decided she might as well try another kind of life.

SHEILA [*miserably*]: So I'm really responsible?

INSPECTOR: No, not entirely. A good deal happened to her after that. But you're partly to blame. Just as your father is.

ERIC: But what did Sheila do?

SHEILA [*distressed*]: I went to the manager at Milwards and I told him that if they didn't get rid of that girl, I'd never go near the place again and I'd persuade mother to close our account with them.

INSPECTOR: And why did you do that?

SHEILA: Because I was in a furious temper.

INSPECTOR: And what had this girl done to make you lose your temper?

SHEILA: When I was looking at myself in the mirror I caught sight of her smiling at the assistant, and I was furious with her. I'd been in a bad temper anyhow.

INSPECTOR: And was it the girl's fault?

SHEILA: No, not really. It was my own fault. [*Suddenly, to* GERALD] All right, Gerald, you needn't look at me like that. At least, I'm trying to tell the truth. I expect you've done things you're ashamed of too.

GERALD [*surprised*]: Well, I never said I hadn't. I don't see why –

INSPECTOR [*cutting in*]: Never mind about that. You can settle that between you afterwards. [*To* SHEILA] What happened?

SHEILA: I'd gone in to try something on. It was an idea of my own – mother had been against it, and so had the assistant – but I insisted. As soon as I tried it on, I knew they'd been right. It just didn't suit me at all. I looked silly in the thing. Well, this girl had brought the dress up from the workroom, and when the assistant – Miss Francis – had asked her something about it, this girl, to show us what she meant, had held the dress up, as if she was wearing it. And it just suited her. She was the right type for it, just as I was the wrong type. She was a very pretty girl too – with big dark eyes – and that didn't make it any better. Well, when I tried the thing on and looked at myself and knew that it was all wrong, I caught sight of this girl smiling at Miss Francis – as if to say: 'Doesn't she look awful' – and I was absolutely furious. I was very rude to both of them, and then I went to the manager and told him that this girl had been very impertinent – and – and – [*She almost breaks down, but just controls herself.*] How could I know what would happen afterwards? If she'd been some miserable plain little creature, I don't suppose I'd have done it. But she was very pretty and looked as if she could take care of herself. I couldn't be sorry for her.

INSPECTOR: In fact, in a kind of way, you might be said to have been jealous of her.

SHEILA: Yes, I suppose so.

INSPECTOR: And so you used the power you had, as a daughter of a good customer and also of a man well-known in the town, to punish the girl just because she made you feel like that?

SHEILA: Yes, but it didn't seem to be anything very terrible at the time. Don't you understand? And if I could help her now, I would –

INSPECTOR [*harshly*]: Yes, but you can't. It's too late. She's dead.

ERIC: My God, it's a bit thick, when you come to think of it –

SHEILA [*stormily*]: Oh shut up, Eric. I know, I know. It's the only time I've ever done anything like that, and I'll never, never do it again to anybody. I've noticed them giving me a sort of look sometimes at Milwards – I noticed it even this afternoon – and I suppose some of them remember. I feel now I can never go there again. Oh – why had this to happen?

INSPECTOR [*sternly*]: That's what I asked myself tonight when I was looking at that dead girl. And then I said to myself: 'Well, we'll try to understand why it had to happen.' And that's why I'm here, and why I'm not going until I know *all* that happened. Eva Smith lost her job with Birling and Company because the strike failed and they were determined not to have another one. At last she found another job – under what name I don't know – in a big shop, and had to leave there because you were annoyed with yourself and passed the annoyance on to her. Now she had to try something else. So first she changed her name to Daisy Renton –

GERALD [*startled*]: What?

INSPECTOR [*steadily*]: I said she changed her name to Daisy Renton.

GERALD [*pulling himself together*]: D'you mind if I give myself a drink, Sheila?

[SHEILA *merely nods, still staring at him, and he goes across to the tantalus on the sideboard for a whisky.*]

INSPECTOR: Where is your father, Miss Birling?

SHEILA: He went into the drawing-room, to tell my mother what was happening here. Eric, take the Inspector along to the drawing-room. [*As* ERIC *moves, the* INSPECTOR *looks from* SHEILA *to* GERALD, *then goes out with* ERIC.] Well, Gerald?

GERALD [*trying to smile*]: Well what, Sheila?

SHEILA: How did you come to know this girl – Eva Smith?

GERALD: I didn't.

SHEILA: Daisy Renton then – it's the same thing.

GERALD: Why should I have known her?

SHEILA: Oh don't be stupid. We haven't much time. You gave yourself away as soon as he mentioned her other name.

GERALD: All right. I knew her. Let's leave it at that.

SHEILA: We can't leave it at that.

GERALD [*approaching her*]: Now listen, darling –

SHEILA: No, that's no use. You not only knew her but you knew her very well. Otherwise, you wouldn't look so guilty about it. When did you first get to know her? [*He does not reply.*] Was it after she left Milwards? When she changed her name, as he said, and began to lead a different sort of life? Were you seeing her last spring and summer, during that time when you hardly came near me and said you were so busy? Were you? [*He does not reply but looks at her.*] Yes, of course you were.

GERALD: I'm sorry, Sheila. But it was all over and done with, last summer. I hadn't set eyes on the girl for at least six months. I don't come into this suicide business.

SHEILA: I thought I didn't, half an hour ago.

GERALD: You don't. Neither of us does. So – for God's sake – don't say anything to the Inspector.

SHEILA: About you and this girl?

GERALD: Yes. We can keep it from him.

SHEILA [*laughs rather hysterically*]: Why – you fool – *he knows.* Of course he knows. And I hate to think how much he knows that we don't know yet. You'll see. You'll see. [*She looks at him almost in triumph.*]

    [*He looks crushed. The door slowly opens and the* INSPECTOR *appears, looking steadily and searchingly at them.*]

INSPECTOR: Well?

END OF ACT ONE

ACT TWO

At rise, scene and situation are exactly as they were at end of Act One.

[*The* INSPECTOR *remains at the door for a few moments looking at* SHEILA *and* GERALD. *Then he comes forward, leaving door open behind him.*]

INSPECTOR [*to* GERALD]: Well?

SHEILA [*with hysterical laugh, to* GERALD]: You see? What did I tell you?

INSPECTOR: What did you tell him?

GERALD [*with an effort*]: Inspector, I think Miss Birling ought to be excused any more of this questioning. She's nothing more to tell you. She's had a long, exciting and tiring day – we were celebrating our engagement, you know – and now she's obviously had about as much as she can stand. You heard her.

SHEILA: He means that I'm getting hysterical now.

INSPECTOR: And are you?

SHEILA: Probably.

INSPECTOR: Well, I don't want to keep you here. I've no more questions to ask you.

SHEILA: No, but you haven't finished asking questions – have you?

INSPECTOR: No.

SHEILA [*to* GERALD]: You see? [*To* INSPECTOR] Then I'm staying.

GERALD: Why should you? It's bound to be unpleasant and disturbing.

INSPECTOR: And you think young women ought to be protected against unpleasant and disturbing things?

GERALD: If possible – yes.

INSPECTOR: Well, we know one young woman who wasn't, don't we?

GERALD: I suppose I asked for that.

SHEILA: Be careful you don't ask for any more, Gerald.

GERALD: I only meant to say to you – Why stay when you'll hate it?

SHEILA: It can't be any worse for me than it has been. And it might be better.

GERALD [*bitterly*]: I see.

SHEILA: What do you see?

GERALD: You've been through it – and now you want to see somebody else put through it.

SHEILA [*bitterly*]: So that's what you think I'm really like. I'm glad I realized it in time, Gerald.

GERALD: No, no, I didn't mean –

SHEILA [*cutting in*]: Yes, you did. And if you'd really loved me, you couldn't have said that. You listened to that nice story about me. I got that girl sacked from Milwards. And now you've made up your mind I must obviously be a selfish, vindictive creature.

GERALD: I neither said that nor even suggested it.

SHEILA: Then why say I want to see somebody else put through it? That's not what I meant at all.

GERALD: All right then, I'm sorry.

SHEILA: Yes, but you don't believe me. And this is just the wrong time not to believe me.

INSPECTOR [*massively taking charge*]: Allow me, Miss Birling. [*To* GERALD] I can tell you why Miss Birling wants to stay on and why she says it might be better for her if she did. A girl died tonight. A pretty, lively sort of girl, who never did anybody no harm. But she died in misery and agony – hating life –

SHEILA [*distressed*]: Don't please – I know, I know – and I can't stop thinking about it –

INSPECTOR [*ignoring this*]: Now Miss Birling has just been made to understand what she did to this girl. She feels responsible. And if she leaves us now, and doesn't hear any more, then she'll feel she's entirely to blame, she'll be alone with her responsibility, the rest of tonight, all tomorrow, all the next night –

SHEILA [*eagerly*]: Yes, that's it. And I know I'm to blame – and I'm desperately sorry – but I can't believe – I won't believe – it's simply my fault that in the end she – she committed suicide. That would be too horrible –

INSPECTOR [*sternly to them both*]: You see, we have to share something. If there's nothing else, we'll have to share our guilt.

SHEILA [*staring at him*]: Yes. That's true. You know. [*She goes closer to him, wonderingly.*] I don't understand about you.

INSPECTOR [*calmly*]: There's no reason why you should.

[*He regards her calmly while she stares at him wonderingly and dubiously. Now* MRS BIRLING *enters, briskly and self-confidently, quite out of key with the little scene that has just passed.* SHEILA *feels this at once.*]

MRS BIRLING [*smiling, social*]: Good evening, Inspector.

INSPECTOR: Good evening, madam.

MRS BIRLING [*same easy tone*]: I'm Mrs Birling, y'know. My husband has just explained why you're here, and while we'll be glad to tell you anything you want to know, I don't think we can help you much.

SHEILA: No, Mother – please!

MRS BIRLING [*affecting great surprise*]: What's the matter, Sheila?

SHEILA [*hesitantly*]: I know it sounds silly –

MRS BIRLING: What does?

SHEILA: You see, I feel you're beginning all wrong. And I'm afraid you'll say something or do something that you'll be sorry for afterwards.

MRS BIRLING: I don't know what you're talking about, Sheila.

SHEILA: We all started like that – so confident, so pleased with ourselves until he began asking us questions.

[MRS BIRLING *looks from* SHEILA *to the* INSPECTOR.]

MRS BIRLING: You seem to have made a great impression on this child, Inspector.

INSPECTOR [*coolly*]: We often do on the young ones. They're more impressionable.

[*He and* MRS BIRLING *look at each other for a moment. Then* MRS BIRLING *turns to* SHEILA *again.*]

MRS BIRLING: You're looking tired, dear. I think you ought to go to bed – and forget about this absurd business. You'll feel better in the morning.

SHEILA: Mother, I couldn't possibly go. Nothing could be worse for me. We've settled all that. I'm staying here until I know why that girl killed herself.

MRS BIRLING: Nothing but morbid curiosity.

SHEILA: No it isn't.

MRS BIRLING: Please don't contradict me like that. And in any case I don't suppose for a moment that we can understand why the girl committed suicide. Girls of that class –

SHEILA [*urgently, cutting in*]: Mother, don't – please don't. For your own sake, as well as ours, you mustn't –

MRS BIRLING [*annoyed*]: Mustn't – what? Really, Sheila!

SHEILA [*slowly, carefully now*]: You mustn't try to build up a kind of wall between us and that girl. If you do, then the Inspector will just break it down. And it'll be all the worse when he does.

MRS BIRLING: I don't understand you. [*To* INSPECTOR] Do you?

INSPECTOR: Yes. And she's right.

MRS BIRLING [*haughtily*]: I beg your pardon!

INSPECTOR [*very plainly*]: I said Yes – I do understand her. And she's right.

MRS BIRLING: That – I consider – is a trifle impertinent, Inspector. [SHEILA *gives short hysterical laugh.*] Now, what is it, Sheila?

SHEILA: I don't know. Perhaps it's because *impertinent* is such a silly word.

MRS BIRLING: In any case . . .

SHEILA: But, Mother, do stop before it's too late.

MRS BIRLING: If you mean that the Inspector will take offence –

INSPECTOR [*cutting in, calmly*]: No, no. I never take offence.

MRS BIRLING: I'm glad to hear it. Though I must add that it seems to me that we have more reason for taking offence.

INSPECTOR: Let's leave *offence* out of it, shall we?

GERALD: I think we'd better.

SHEILA: So do I.

MRS BIRLING [*rebuking them*]: *I'm* talking to the Inspector now, if you don't mind. [*To* INSPECTOR, *rather grandly*] I realize that you may have to conduct some sort of inquiry, but I must say that so far you seem to be conducting it in a rather peculiar and offensive manner. You know of course that my husband was Lord Mayor only two years ago and that he's still a magistrate –

GERALD [*cutting in, rather impatiently*]: Mrs Birling, the Inspector knows all that. And I don't think it's a very good idea to remind him –

SHEILA [*cutting in*]: It's crazy. Stop it, please, Mother.

INSPECTOR [*imperturbable*]: Yes. Now what about Mr Birling?

MRS BIRLING: He's coming back in a moment. He's just talking to my son, Eric, who seems to be in an excitable silly mood.

INSPECTOR: What's the matter with him?

MRS BIRLING: Eric? Oh – I'm afraid he may have had rather too much to drink tonight. We were having a little celebration here –

INSPECTOR [cutting in]: Isn't he used to drinking?

MRS BIRLING: No, of course not. He's only a boy.

INSPECTOR: No, he's a young man. And some young men drink far too much.

SHEILA: And Eric's one of them.

MRS BIRLING [very sharply]: Sheila!

SHEILA [urgently]: I don't want to get poor Eric into trouble. He's probably in enough trouble already. But we really must stop these silly pretences. This isn't the time to pretend that Eric isn't used to drink. He's been steadily drinking too much for the last two years.

MRS BIRLING [staggered]: It isn't true. You know him, Gerald – and you're a man – you must know it isn't true.

INSPECTOR [as GERALD hesitates]: Well, Mr Croft?

GERALD [apologetically, to MRS BIRLING]: I'm afraid it is, y'know. Actually I've never seen much of him outside this house – but – well, I have gathered that he does drink pretty hard.

MRS BIRLING [bitterly]: And this is the time you choose to tell me.

SHEILA: Yes, of course it is. That's what I meant when I talked about building up a wall that's sure to be knocked flat. It makes it all the harder to bear.

MRS BIRLING: But it's you – and not the Inspector here – who's doing it –

SHEILA: Yes, but don't you see? *He hasn't started on you yet.*

MRS BIRLING [after pause, recovering herself]: If necessary I shall be glad to answer any questions the Inspector wishes to ask me. Though naturally I don't know anything about this girl.

INSPECTOR [gravely]: We'll see, Mrs Birling.

[Enter BIRLING, who closes door behind him.]

BIRLING [rather hot, bothered]: I've been trying to persuade Eric to go to bed, but he won't. Now he says you told him to stay up. Did you?

INSPECTOR: Yes, I did.

BIRLING: Why?

INSPECTOR: Because I shall want to talk to him, Mr Birling.

BIRLING: I can't see why you should, but if you must, then I suggest you do it now. Have him in and get it over, then let the lad go.

INSPECTOR: No, I can't do that yet. I'm sorry, but he'll have to wait.

BIRLING: Now look here, Inspector –

INSPECTOR [cutting in, with authority]: He must wait his turn.

SHEILA [to MRS BIRLING]: You see?

MRS BIRLING: No, I don't. And please be quiet, Sheila.

BIRLING [angrily]: Inspector, I've told you before, I don't like your tone nor the way you're handling this inquiry. And I don't propose to give you much more rope.

INSPECTOR: You needn't give me any rope.

SHEILA [rather wildly, with laugh]: No, he's giving us rope – so that we'll hang ourselves.

BIRLING [to MRS BIRLING]: What's the matter with that child?

MRS BIRLING: Over-excited. And she refused to go. [With sudden anger, to INSPECTOR] Well, come along – what is it you want to know?

INSPECTOR [coolly]: At the end of January, last year, this girl Eva Smith had to leave Milwards, because Miss Birling compelled them to discharge her, and then she stopped being Eva Smith, looking for a job, and became Daisy Renton, with other ideas. [Sharply turning on him] Mr Croft, when did you first get to know her?

[An exclamation of surprise from BIRLING and MRS BIRLING.]

GERALD: Where did you get the idea that I did know her?

SHEILA: It's no use, Gerald. You're wasting time.

INSPECTOR: As soon as I mentioned the name Daisy Renton, it was obvious you'd known her. You gave yourself away at once.

SHEILA [bitterly]: Of course he did.

INSPECTOR: And anyhow I knew already. When and where did you first meet her?

GERALD: All right, if you must have it. I met her first, some time in March last year, in the stalls bar at the Palace. I mean the Palace music hall here in Brumley –

SHEILA: Well, we didn't think you meant Buckingham Palace.

GERALD [to SHEILA]: Thanks. You're going to be a great help, I can see. You've said your piece, and you're obviously going to hate this, so why on earth don't you leave us to it?

SHEILA: Nothing would induce me. I want to understand exactly what happens when a man says he's so busy at the works that he can hardly ever find time to come and see the girl he's supposed to be in love with. I wouldn't miss it for worlds –

INSPECTOR [*with authority*]: Yes, Mr Croft – in the stalls bar at the Palace Variety Theatre . . .

GERALD: I happened to look in, one night, after a rather long dull day, and as the show wasn't very bright, I went down into the bar for a drink. It's a favourite haunt of women of the town –

MRS BIRLING: Women of the town?

BIRLING: Yes, yes. But I see no point in mentioning the subject – especially – [*indicating* SHEILA.]

MRS BIRLING: It would be much better if Sheila didn't listen to this story at all.

SHEILA: But you're forgetting I'm supposed to be engaged to the hero of it. Go on, Gerald. You went down into the bar, which is a favourite haunt of women of the town.

GERALD: I'm glad I amuse you –

INSPECTOR [*sharply*]: Come along, Mr Croft. What happened?

GERALD: I didn't propose to stay long down there. I hate those hard-eyed dough-faced women. But then I noticed a girl who looked quite different. She was very pretty – soft brown hair and big dark eyes – [*breaks off.*] My God!

INSPECTOR: What's the matter?

GERALD [*distressed*]: Sorry – I – well, I've suddenly realized – taken it in properly – that she's dead –

INSPECTOR [*harshly*]: Yes, she's dead.

SHEILA: And probably between us we killed her.

MRS BIRLING [*sharply*]: Sheila, don't talk nonsense.

SHEILA: You wait, Mother.

INSPECTOR [*to* GERALD]: Go on.

GERALD: She looked young and fresh and charming and altogether out of place down there. And obviously she wasn't enjoying herself. Old Joe Meggarty, half-drunk and goggle-eyed, had wedged her into a corner with that obscene fat carcase of his –

MRS BIRLING [*cutting in*]: There's no need to be disgusting. And surely you don't mean Alderman Meggarty?

GERALD: Of course I do. He's a notorious womanizer as well as being one of the worst sots and rogues in Brumley –

INSPECTOR: Quite right.

MRS BIRLING [*staggered*]: Well, really! Alderman Meggarty! I must say, we *are* learning something tonight.

SHEILA [*coolly*]: Of course we are. But everybody knows about that horrible old Meggarty. A girl I know had to see him at the Town Hall one afternoon and she only escaped with a torn blouse –

BIRLING [*sharply, shocked*]: Sheila!

INSPECTOR [*to* GERALD]: Go on, please.

GERALD: The girl saw me looking at her and then gave me a glance that was nothing less than a cry for help. So I went across and told Joe Meggarty some nonsense – that the manager had a message for him or something like that – got him out of the way – and then told the girl that if she didn't want any more of that sort of thing, she'd better let me take her out of there. She agreed at once.

INSPECTOR: Where did you go?

GERALD: We went along to the County Hotel, which I knew would be quiet at that time of night, and we had a drink or two and talked.

INSPECTOR: Did she drink much at that time?

GERALD: No. She only had a port and lemonade – or some such concoction. All she wanted was to talk – a little friendliness – and I gathered that Joe Meggarty's advances had left her rather shaken – as well they might –

INSPECTOR: She talked about herself?

GERALD: Yes. I asked her questions about herself. She told me her name was Daisy Renton, that she'd lost both parents, that she came originally from somewhere outside Brumley. She also told me she'd had a job in one of the works here and had had to leave after a strike. She said something about the shop too, but wouldn't say which it was, and she was deliberately vague about what happened. I couldn't get any exact details from her about her past life. She wanted to talk about herself – just because she felt I was interested and friendly – but at the same time she wanted to be Daisy Renton – and not Eva Smith. In fact, I heard that name for the first time tonight. What she did let slip – though she didn't mean to – was that she was desperately hard up and at that moment was actually hungry. I made the people at the County find some food for her.

INSPECTOR: And then you decided to keep her – as your mistress?

MRS BIRLING: What?

SHEILA: Of course, Mother. It was obvious from the start. Go on, Gerald. Don't mind Mother.

GERALD [*steadily*]: I discovered, not that night but two nights later, when we met again – not accidentally this time of course – that in fact she hadn't a penny and was going to be turned out of the miserable back room she had. It happened that a friend of mine, Charlie Brunswick, had gone off to Canada for six months and had let me have the key of a nice little set of rooms he had – in Morgan Terrace – and had asked me to keep an eye on them for him and use them if I wanted to. So I insisted on Daisy moving into those rooms and I made her take some money to keep her going there. [*Carefully, to the* INSPECTOR] I want you to understand that I didn't install her there so that I could make love to her. I made her go to Morgan Terrace because I was sorry for her, and didn't like the idea of her going back to the Palace bar. I didn't ask for anything in return.

INSPECTOR: I see.

SHEILA: Yes, but why are you saying that to him? You ought to be saying it to me.

GERALD: I suppose I ought really. I'm sorry, Sheila. Somehow I –

SHEILA [*cutting in, as he hesitates*]: I know. Somehow he makes you.

INSPECTOR: But she became your mistress?

GERALD: Yes. I suppose it was inevitable. She was young and pretty and warm-hearted – and intensely grateful. I became at once the most important person in her life – you understand?

INSPECTOR: Yes. She was a woman. She was lonely. Were you in love with her?

SHEILA: Just what I was going to ask!

BIRLING [*angrily*]: I really must protest –

INSPECTOR [*turning on him sharply*]: Why should you do any protesting? It was you who turned the girl out in the first place.

BIRLING [*rather taken aback*]: Well, I only did what any employer might have done. And what I was going to say was that I protest against the way in which my daughter, a young unmarried girl, is being dragged into this –

INSPECTOR [*sharply*]: Your daughter isn't living on the moon. She's here in Brumley too.

SHEILA: Yes, and it was I who had the girl turned out of her job at Milwards. *And* I'm supposed to be engaged to Gerald. And I'm not a child, don't forget. I've a right to know. *Were* you in love with her, Gerald?

GERALD [*hesitantly*]: It's hard to say. I didn't feel about her as she felt about me.

SHEILA [*with sharp sarcasm*]: Of course not. You were the wonderful Fairy Prince. You must have adored it, Gerald.

GERALD: All right – I did for a time. Nearly any man would have done.

SHEILA: That's probably about the best thing you've said tonight. At least it's honest. Did you go and see her every night?

GERALD: No. I wasn't telling you a complete lie when I said I'd been very busy at the works all that time. We were very busy. But of course I did see a good deal of her.

MRS BIRLING: I don't think we want any further details of this disgusting affair –

SHEILA [*cutting in*]: I do. And, anyhow, we haven't had any details yet.

GERALD: And you're not going to have any. [*To* MRS BIRLING] You know, it wasn't disgusting.

MRS BIRLING: It's disgusting to me.

SHEILA: Yes, but after all, you didn't come into this, did you, Mother?

GERALD: Is there anything else you want to know – that you ought to know?

INSPECTOR: Yes. When did this affair end?

GERALD: I can tell you exactly. In the first week of September. I had to go away for several weeks then – on business – and by that time Daisy knew it was coming to an end. So I broke it off definitely before I went.

INSPECTOR: How did she take it?

GERALD: Better than I'd hoped. She was – very gallant – about it.

SHEILA [*with irony*]: That was nice for you.

GERALD: No, it wasn't. [*He waits a moment, then in low, troubled tone*] She told me she'd been happier than she'd ever been before – but that she knew it couldn't last – hadn't expected it to last. She didn't blame me at all. I wish to God she had now. Perhaps I'd feel better about it.

INSPECTOR: She had to move out of those rooms?

GERALD: Yes, we'd agreed about that. She'd saved a little money during the summer – she'd lived very economically on what I'd allowed her – and didn't want to take any more from me, but I insisted on a parting gift of enough money – though it wasn't so very much – to see her through to the end of the year.

INSPECTOR: Did she tell you what she proposed to do after you'd left her?

GERALD: No. She refused to talk about that. I got the idea once or twice from what she said, that she thought of leaving Brumley. Whether she did or not – I don't know. Did she?

INSPECTOR: Yes. She went away for about two months. To some seaside place.

GERALD: By herself?

INSPECTOR: Yes. I think she went away – to be alone, to be quiet, to remember all that had happened between you.

GERALD: How do you know that?

INSPECTOR: She kept a rough sort of diary. And she said there that she had to go away and be quiet and remember 'just to make it last longer'. She felt there'd never be anything as good again for her – so she had to make it last longer.

GERALD [*gravely*]: I see. Well, I never saw her again, and that's all I can tell you.

INSPECTOR: It's all I want to know from you.

GERALD: In that case – as I'm rather more – upset – by this business than I probably appear to be – and – well, I'd like to be alone for a little while – I'd be glad if you'd let me go.

INSPECTOR: Go where? Home?

GERALD: No. I'll just go out – walk about – for a while, if you don't mind. I'll come back.

INSPECTOR: All right, Mr Croft.

SHEILA: But just in case you forget – or decide not to come back, Gerald, I think you'd better take this with you. [*She hands him the ring.*]

GERALD: I see. Well, I was expecting this.

SHEILA: I don't dislike you as I did half an hour ago, Gerald. In fact, in some odd way, I rather respect you more than I've ever done before. I knew anyhow you were lying about those months last year when you hardly came near me. I knew there was something fishy about that time. And now at least you've been honest. And I believe what you told us about the way you helped her at first. Just out of pity. And it was my fault really that she was so desperate when you first met her. But this has made a difference. You and I aren't the same people who sat down to dinner here. We'd have to start all over again, getting to know each other –

BIRLING: Now, Sheila, I'm not defending him. But you must understand that a lot of young men –

SHEILA: Don't interfere, please, Father. Gerald knows what I mean, and you apparently don't.

GERALD: Yes, I know what you mean. But I'm coming back – if I may.

SHEILA: All right.

MRS BIRLING: Well, really, I don't know. I think we've just about come to an end of this wretched business –

GERALD: I don't think so. Excuse me.

[*He goes out. They watch him go in silence. We hear the front door slam.*]

SHEILA [*to* INSPECTOR]: You know, you never showed him that photograph of her.

INSPECTOR: No. It wasn't necessary. And I thought it better not to.

MRS BIRLING: You have a photograph of this girl?

INSPECTOR: Yes. I think you'd better look at it.

MRS BIRLING: I don't see any particular reason why I should –

INSPECTOR: Probably not. But you'd better look at it.

MRS BIRLING: Very well.

[*He produces the photograph and she looks hard at it.*]

INSPECTOR [*taking back the photograph*]: You recognize her?

MRS BIRLING: No. Why should I?

INSPECTOR: Of course she might have changed lately, but I can't believe she could have changed so much.

MRS BIRLING: I don't understand you, Inspector.

INSPECTOR: You mean you don't choose to do, Mrs Birling.

MRS BIRLING [*angrily*]: I meant what I said.

INSPECTOR: You're not telling me the truth.

MRS BIRLING: I beg your pardon!

BIRLING [angrily, to INSPECTOR]: Look here, I'm not going to have this, Inspector. You'll apologize at once.

INSPECTOR: Apologize for what – doing my duty?

BIRLING: No, for being so offensive about it. I'm a public man –

INSPECTOR [massively]: Public men, Mr Birling, have responsibilities as well as privileges.

BIRLING: Possibly. But you weren't asked to come here to talk to me about my responsibilities.

SHEILA: Let's hope not. Though I'm beginning to wonder.

MRS BIRLING: Does that mean anything, Sheila?

SHEILA: It means that we've no excuse now for putting on airs and that if we've any sense we won't try. Father threw this girl out because she asked for decent wages. I went and pushed her farther out, right into the street, just because I was angry and she was pretty. Gerald set her up as his mistress and then dropped her when it suited him. And now you're pretending you don't recognize her from that photograph. I admit I don't know why you should, but I know jolly well you did in fact recognize her, from the way you looked. And if you're not telling the truth, why should the Inspector apologize? And can't you see, both of you, you're making it worse? [She turns away.]

[We hear the front door slam again.]

BIRLING: That was the door again.

MRS BIRLING: Gerald must have come back.

INSPECTOR: Unless your son has just gone out.

BIRLING: I'll see. [He goes out quickly.]

[INSPECTOR turns to MRS BIRLING.]

INSPECTOR: Mrs Birling, you're a member – a prominent member – of the Brumley Women's Charity Organization, aren't you?

[MRS BIRLING does not reply.]

SHEILA: Go on, Mother. You might as well admit it. [To INSPECTOR] Yes, she is. Why?

INSPECTOR [calmly]: It's an organization to which women in distress can appeal for help in various forms. Isn't that so?

MRS BIRLING [with dignity]: Yes. We've done a great deal of useful work in helping deserving cases.

INSPECTOR: There was a meeting of the interviewing committee two weeks ago?

MRS BIRLING: I dare say there was.

INSPECTOR: You know very well there was, Mrs Birling. You were in the chair.

MRS BIRLING: And if I was, what business is it of yours?

INSPECTOR [*severely*]: Do you want me to tell you – in plain words?

[*Enter* BIRLING, *looking rather agitated.*]

BIRLING: That must have been Eric.

MRS BIRLING [*alarmed*]: Have you been up to his room?

BIRLING: Yes. And I called out on both landings. It must have been Eric we heard go out then.

MRS BIRLING: Silly boy! Where can he have gone to?

BIRLING: I can't imagine. But he was in one of his excitable queer moods, and even though we don't need him here –

INSPECTOR [*cutting in, sharply*]: We do need him here. And if he's not back soon, I shall have to go and find him.

[BIRLING *and* MRS BIRLING *exchange bewildered and rather frightened glances.*]

SHEILA: He's probably just gone to cool off. He'll be back soon.

INSPECTOR [*severely*]: I hope so.

MRS BIRLING: And why should you hope so?

INSPECTOR: I'll explain why when you've answered my questions, Mrs Birling.

BIRLING: Is there any reason why my wife should answer questions from you, Inspector?

INSPECTOR: Yes, a very good reason. You'll remember that Mr Croft told us – quite truthfully, I believe – that he hadn't spoken to or seen Eva Smith since last September. But Mrs Birling spoke to and saw her only two weeks ago.

SHEILA [*astonished*]: Mother!

BIRLING: Is this true?

MRS BIRLING [*after a pause*]: Yes, quite true.

INSPECTOR: She appealed to your organization for help?

MRS BIRLING: Yes.

INSPECTOR: Not as Eva Smith?

MRS BIRLING: No. Nor as Daisy Renton.

INSPECTOR: As what then?

MRS BIRLING: First, she called herself Mrs Birling –

BIRLING [*astounded*]: *Mrs Birling !*

MRS BIRLING: Yes. I think it was simply a piece of gross impertinence – quite deliberate – and naturally that was one of the things that prejudiced me against her case.

BIRLING: And I should think so! Damned impudence!

INSPECTOR: You admit being prejudiced against her case ?

MRS BIRLING: Yes.

SHEILA: Mother, she's just died a horrible death – don't forget.

MRS BIRLING: I'm very sorry. But I think she had only herself to blame.

INSPECTOR: Was it owing to your influence, as the most prominent member of the committee, that help was refused the girl ?

MRS BIRLING: Possibly.

INSPECTOR: Was it or was it not your influence ?

MRS BIRLING [*stung*]: Yes, it was. I didn't like her manner. She'd impertinently made use of our name, though she pretended afterwards it just happened to be the first she thought of. She had to admit, after I began questioning her, that she had no claim to the name, that she wasn't married, and that the story she told at first – about a husband who'd deserted her – was quite false. It didn't take me long to get the truth – or some of the truth – out of her.

INSPECTOR: Why did she want help ?

MRS BIRLING: You know very well why she wanted help.

INSPECTOR: No, I don't. I know why she *needed* help. But as I wasn't there, I don't know what she asked from your committee.

MRS BIRLING: I don't think we need discuss it.

INSPECTOR: You have no hope of *not* discussing it, Mrs Birling.

MRS BIRLING: If you think you can bring any pressure to bear upon me, Inspector, you're quite mistaken. Unlike the other three, I did nothing I'm ashamed of or that won't bear investigation. The girl asked for assistance. We are asked to look carefully into the claims made upon us. I wasn't satisfied with this girl's claim – she seemed to me to be not a good case – and so I used my influence to have it refused. And in spite of what's happened to the girl since, I consider I did my duty. So if I prefer not to discuss it any farther, you have no power to make me change my mind.

INSPECTOR: Yes I have.

MRS BIRLING: No you haven't. Simply because I've done nothing wrong – and you know it.

INSPECTOR [*very deliberately*]: I think you did something terribly wrong – and that you're going to spend the rest of your life regretting it. I wish you'd been with me tonight in the Infirmary. You'd have seen –

SHEILA [*bursting in*]: No, no, please! Not that again. I've imagined it enough already.

INSPECTOR [*very deliberately*]: Then the next time you imagine it, just remember that this girl was going to have a child.

SHEILA [*horrified*]: No! Oh – horrible – horrible! How could she have wanted to kill herself?

INSPECTOR: Because she'd been turned out and turned down too many times. This was the end.

SHEILA: Mother, you must have known.

INSPECTOR: It was because she was going to have a child that she went for assistance to your mother's committee.

BIRLING: Look here, this wasn't Gerald Croft –

INSPECTOR [*cutting in, sharply*]: No, no. Nothing to do with him.

SHEILA: Thank goodness for that! Though I don't know why I should care now.

INSPECTOR [*to* MRS BIRLING]: And you've nothing further to tell me, eh?

MRS BIRLING: I'll tell you what I told her. Go and look for the father of the child. It's his responsibility.

INSPECTOR: That doesn't make it any the less yours. She came to you for help, at a time when no woman could have needed it more. And you not only refused it yourself but saw to it that the others refused it too. She was here alone, friendless, almost penniless, desperate. She needed not only money, but advice, sympathy, friendliness. You've had children. You must have known what she was feeling. And you slammed the door in her face.

SHEILA [*with feeling*]: Mother, I think it was cruel and vile.

BIRLING [*dubiously*]: I must say, Sybil, that when this comes out at the inquest, it isn't going to do us much good. The Press might easily take it up –

MRS BIRLING [*agitated now*]: Oh, stop it, both of you. And please remember before you start accusing me of anything again that it wasn't I who had her turned out of her employment – which probably began it all. [*Turning to* INSPECTOR] In the circumstances I think I was justified. The girl had begun by telling us a pack of lies. Afterwards, when I got at the truth, I discovered that she knew who the father was, she was quite certain about that, and so I told her it was her business to make him responsible. If he refused to marry her – and in my opinion he ought to be compelled to – then he must at least support her.

INSPECTOR: And what did she reply to that?

MRS BIRLING: Oh – a lot of silly nonsense!

INSPECTOR: What was it?

MRS BIRLING: Whatever it was, I know it made me finally lose all patience with her. She was giving herself ridiculous airs. She was claiming elaborate fine feelings and scruples that were simply absurd in a girl in her position.

INSPECTOR [*very sternly*]: Her position now is that she lies with a burnt-out inside on a slab. [*As* BIRLING *tries to protest, turns on him.*] Don't stammer and yammer at me again, man. I'm losing all patience with you people. *What did she say?*

MRS BIRLING [*rather cowed*]: She said that the father was only a youngster – silly and wild and drinking too much. There couldn't be any question of marrying him – it would be wrong for them both. He had given her money but she didn't want to take any more money from him.

INSPECTOR: Why didn't she want to take any more money from him?

MRS BIRLING: All a lot of nonsense – I didn't believe a word of it.

INSPECTOR: I'm not asking you if you believed it. I want to know what she said. Why didn't she want to take any more money from this boy?

MRS BIRLING: Oh – she had some fancy reason. As if a girl of that sort would ever refuse money!

INSPECTOR [*sternly*]: I warn you, you're making it worse for yourself. What reason did she give for not taking any more money?

MRS BIRLING: Her story was – that he'd said something one night, when he was drunk, that gave her the idea that it wasn't his money.

INSPECTOR: Where had he got it from then?

MRS BIRLING: He'd stolen it.

INSPECTOR: So she'd come to you for assistance because she didn't want to take stolen money?

MRS BIRLING: That's the story she finally told, after I'd refused to believe her original story – that she was a married woman who'd been deserted by her husband. I didn't see any reason to believe that one story should be any truer than the other. Therefore, you're quite wrong to suppose I shall regret what I did.

INSPECTOR: But if her story was true, if this boy had been giving her stolen money, then she came to you for help because she wanted to keep this youngster out of any more trouble – isn't that so?

MRS BIRLING: Possibly. But it sounded ridiculous to me. So I was perfectly justified in advising my committee not to allow her claim for assistance.

INSPECTOR: You're not even sorry now, when you know what happened to the girl?

MRS BIRLING: I'm sorry she should have come to such a horrible end. But I accept no blame for it at all.

INSPECTOR: Who is to blame then?

MRS BIRLING: First, the girl herself.

SHEILA [bitterly]: For letting Father and me have her chucked out of her jobs!

MRS BIRLING: Secondly, I blame the young man who was the father of the child she was going to have. If, as she said, he didn't belong to her class, and was some drunken young idler, then that's all the more reason why he shouldn't escape. He should be made an example of. If the girl's death is due to anybody, then it's due to him.

INSPECTOR: And if her story is true – that he was stealing money –

MRS BIRLING [rather agitated now]: There's no point in assuming that –

INSPECTOR: But suppose we do, what then?

MRS BIRLING: Then he'd be entirely responsible – because the girl wouldn't have come to us, and have been refused assistance, if it hadn't been for him –

INSPECTOR: So he's the chief culprit anyhow.

MRS BIRLING: Certainly. And he ought to be dealt with very severely –

SHEILA [*with sudden alarm*]: Mother – stop – stop!

BIRLING: Be quiet, Sheila!

SHEILA: But don't you see –

MRS BIRLING [*severely*]: You're behaving like an hysterical child tonight. [SHEILA *begins crying quietly.* MRS BIRLING *turns to* INSPECTOR.] And if you'd take some steps to find this young man and then make sure that he's compelled to confess in public his responsibility – instead of staying here asking quite unnecessary questions – then you really would be doing your duty.

INSPECTOR [*grimly*]: Don't worry, Mrs Birling. I shall do my duty. [*He looks at his watch.*]

MRS BIRLING [*triumphantly*]: I'm glad to hear it.

INSPECTOR: No hushing up, eh? Make an example of the young man, eh? Public confession of responsibility – um?

MRS BIRLING: Certainly. I consider it your duty. And now no doubt you'd like to say good night.

INSPECTOR: Not yet. I'm waiting.

MRS BIRLING: Waiting for what?

INSPECTOR: To do my duty.

SHEILA [*distressed*]: Now, Mother – don't you see?

MRS BIRLING [*understanding now*]: But surely . . . I mean . . . it's ridiculous . . . [*She stops, and exchanges a frightened glance with her husband.*]

BIRLING [*terrified now*]: Look, Inspector, you're not trying to tell us that – that my boy – is mixed up in this – ?

INSPECTOR [*sternly*]: If he is, then we know what to do, don't we? Mrs Birling has just told us.

BIRLING [*thunderstruck*]: My God! But – look here –

MRS BIRLING [*agitated*]: I don't believe it. I *won't* believe it . . .

SHEILA: Mother – I begged you and begged you to stop –

[INSPECTOR *holds up a hand. We hear the front door. They wait, looking towards door.* ERIC *enters, looking extremely pale and distressed. He meets their inquiring stares.*

Curtain falls quickly.]

END OF ACT TWO

ACT THREE

Exactly as at the end of Act Two. ERIC *is standing just inside the room and the others are staring at him.*

ERIC: You know, don't you?

INSPECTOR [*as before*]: Yes, we know.

[ERIC *shuts the door and comes farther in.*]

MRS BIRLING [*distressed*]: Eric, I can't believe it. There must be some mistake. You don't know what we've been saying.

SHEILA: It's a good job for him he doesn't, isn't it?

ERIC: Why?

SHEILA: Because Mother's been busy blaming everything on the young man who got this girl into trouble, and saying he shouldn't escape and should be made an example of –

BIRLING: That's enough, Sheila.

ERIC [*bitterly*]: You haven't made it any easier for me, have you, Mother?

MRS BIRLING: But I didn't know it was *you* – I never dreamt. Besides, you're not that type – you don't get drunk –

SHEILA: Of course he does. I told you he did.

ERIC: *You* told her. Why, you little sneak!

SHEILA: No, that's not fair, Eric. I could have told her months ago, but of course I didn't. I only told her tonight because I knew everything was coming out – it was simply bound to come out tonight – so I thought she might as well know in advance. Don't forget – I've already been through it.

MRS BIRLING: Sheila, I simply don't understand your attitude.

BIRLING: Neither do I. If you'd had any sense of loyalty –

INSPECTOR [*cutting in, smoothly*]: Just a minute, Mrs Birling. There'll be plenty of time, when I've gone, for you all to adjust your family relationships. But now I must hear what your son has to tell me. [*Sternly, to the three of them*] And I'll be obliged if you'll let us get on without any further interruptions. [*Turning to* ERIC] Now then.

ERIC [*miserably*]: Could I have a drink first?

BIRLING [*explosively*]: No.

INSPECTOR [*firmly*]: Yes. [*As* BIRLING *looks like interrupting explosively*] I know – he's your son and this is your house – but look at him. He needs a drink now just to see him through.

BIRLING [*to* ERIC]: All right. Go on.

[ERIC *goes for a whisky. His whole manner of handling the decanter and then the drink shows his familiarity with quick heavy drinking. The others watch him narrowly.*]

[*Bitterly*] I understand a lot of things now I didn't understand before.

INSPECTOR: Don't start on that. I want to get on. [*To* ERIC] When did you first meet this girl?

ERIC: One night last November.

INSPECTOR: Where did you meet her?

ERIC: In the Palace bar. I'd been there an hour or so with two or three chaps. I was a bit squiffy.

INSPECTOR: What happened then?

ERIC: I began talking to her, and stood her a few drinks. I was rather far gone by the time we had to go.

INSPECTOR: Was she drunk too?

ERIC: She told me afterwards that she was a bit, chiefly because she'd not had much to eat that day.

INSPECTOR: Why had she gone there – ?

ERIC: She wasn't the usual sort. But – well, I suppose she didn't know what to do. There was some woman who wanted her to go there. I never quite understood about that.

INSPECTOR: You went with her to her lodgings that night?

ERIC: Yes, I insisted – it seems. I'm not very clear about it, but afterwards she told me she didn't want me to go in but that – well, I was in that state when a chap easily turns nasty – and I threatened to make a row.

INSPECTOR: So she let you in?

ERIC: And that's when it happened. And I didn't even remember – that's the hellish thing. Oh – my God! – how stupid it all is!

MRS BIRLING [*with a cry*]: Oh – Eric – how could you?

BIRLING [*sharply*]: Sheila, take your mother along to the drawing-room –

SHEILA [*protesting*]: But – I want to –

BIRLING [*very sharply*]: You heard what I said. [*Gentler*] Go on, Sybil.

[*He goes to open the door while* SHEILA *takes her mother out. Then he closes it and comes in.*]

INSPECTOR: When did you meet her again?

ERIC: About a fortnight afterwards.

INSPECTOR: By appointment?

ERIC: No. And I couldn't remember her name or where she lived. It was all very vague. But I happened to see her again in the Palace bar.

INSPECTOR: More drinks?

ERIC: Yes, though that time I wasn't so bad.

INSPECTOR: But you took her home again?

ERIC: Yes. And this time we talked a bit. She told me something about herself and I talked too. Told her my name and what I did.

INSPECTOR: And you made love again?

ERIC: Yes. I wasn't in love with her or anything – but I liked her – she was pretty and a good sport –

BIRLING [*harshly*]: So you had to go to bed with her?

ERIC: Well, I'm old enough to be married, aren't I, and I'm not married, and I hate these fat old tarts round the town – the ones I see some of your respectable friends with –

BIRLING [*angrily*]: I don't want any of that talk from you –

INSPECTOR [*very sharply*]: I don't want any of it from either of you. Settle it afterwards. [*To* ERIC] Did you arrange to see each other after that?

ERIC: Yes. And the next time – or the time after that – she told me she thought she was going to have a baby. She wasn't quite sure. And then she was.

INSPECTOR: And of course she was very worried about it?

ERIC: Yes, and so was I. I was in a hell of a state about it.

INSPECTOR: Did she suggest that you ought to marry her?

ERIC: No. She didn't want me to marry her. Said I didn't love her – and all that. In a way, she treated me – as if I were a kid. Though I was nearly as old as she was.

INSPECTOR: So what did you propose to do?

ERIC: Well, she hadn't a job – and didn't feel like trying again for one – and she'd no money left – so I insisted on giving her enough money to keep her going – until she refused to take any more –

INSPECTOR: How much did you give her altogether?

ERIC: I suppose – about fifty pounds all told.

BIRLING: Fifty pounds – on top of drinking and going round the town! Where did you get fifty pounds from?

[*As* ERIC *does not reply*]

INSPECTOR: That's my question too.

ERIC [*miserably*]: I got it – from the office –

BIRLING: *My* office?

ERIC: Yes.

INSPECTOR: You mean – you stole the money?

ERIC: Not really.

BIRLING [*angrily*]: What do you mean – *not really?*

[ERIC *does not reply because now* MRS BIRLING *and* SHEILA *come back.*]

SHEILA: This isn't my fault.

MRS BIRLING [*to* BIRLING]: I'm sorry, Arthur, but I simply couldn't stay in there. I had to know what's happening.

BIRLING [*savagely*]: Well, I can tell you what's happening. He's admitted he was responsible for the girl's condition, and now he's telling us he supplied her with money he stole from the office.

MRS BIRLING [*shocked*]: Eric! You stole money?

ERIC: No, not really. I intended to pay it back.

BIRLING: We've heard that story before. How could you have paid it back?

ERIC: I'd have managed somehow. I had to have some money –

BIRLING: I don't understand how you could take as much as that out of the office without somebody knowing.

ERIC: There were some small accounts to collect, and I asked for cash –

BIRLING: Gave the firm's receipt and then kept the money, eh?

ERIC: Yes.

BIRLING: You must give me a list of those accounts. I've got to cover this up as soon as I can. You damned fool – why didn't you come to me when you found yourself in this mess?

ERIC: Because you're not the kind of father a chap could go to when he's in trouble – that's why.

BIRLING [*angrily*]: Don't talk to me like that. Your trouble is – you've been spoilt –

INSPECTOR [*cutting in*]: And my trouble is – that I haven't much time. You'll be able to divide the responsibility between you when I've gone. [*To* ERIC] Just one last question, that's all. The girl discovered that this money you were giving her was stolen, didn't she?

ERIC [*miserably*]: Yes. That was the worst of all. She wouldn't take any more, and she didn't want to see me again. [*Sudden startled tone*] Here, but how did you know that? Did she tell you?

INSPECTOR: No. She told me nothing. I never spoke to her.

SHEILA: She told Mother.

MRS BIRLING [*alarmed*]: Sheila!

SHEILA: Well, he has to know.

ERIC [*to* MRS BIRLING]: She told you? Did she come here – but then she couldn't have done, she didn't even know I lived here. What happened? [MRS BIRLING, *distressed, shakes her head but does not reply*.] Come on, don't just look like that. Tell me – tell me – what happened?

INSPECTOR [*with calm authority*]: I'll tell you. She went to your mother's committee for help, after she'd done with you. Your mother refused that help.

ERIC [*nearly at breaking point*]: Then – you killed her. She came to you to protect me – and you turned her away – yes, and you killed her – and the child she'd have had too – my child – your own grandchild – you killed them both – damn you, damn you –

MRS BIRLING [*very distressed now*]: No – Eric – please – I didn't know – I didn't understand –

ERIC [*almost threatening her*]: You don't understand anything. You never did. You never even tried – you –

SHEILA [*frightened*]: Eric, don't – don't –

BIRLING [*furious, intervening*]: Why, you hysterical young fool – get back – or I'll –

INSPECTOR [*taking charge, masterfully*]: Stop! [*They are suddenly quiet, staring at him*.] And be quiet for a moment and listen to me. I don't need to know any more. Neither do you. This girl killed herself – and died a horrible death. But each of you helped to kill her. Remember that. Never forget it. [*He looks from one to the other of them carefully*.] But then I don't think you ever will. Remember what you did, Mrs Birling. You turned her away when she most needed help. You refused her even the pitiable little bit of organized charity you had in your power to grant her. Remember what you did –

ERIC [*unhappily*]: My God – I'm not likely to forget.

INSPECTOR: Just used her for the end of a stupid drunken evening, as if she was an animal, a thing, not a person. No, you won't
forget. [*He looks at* SHEILA.]

SHEILA [*bitterly*]: I know. I had her turned out of a job. I started
it.

INSPECTOR: You helped – but didn't start it. [*Rather savagely, to*
BIRLING] You started it. She wanted twenty-five shillings a week
instead of twenty-two and sixpence. You made her pay a heavy
price for that. And now she'll make you pay a heavier price still.

BIRLING [*unhappily*]: Look, Inspector – I'd give thousands – yes,
thousands –

INSPECTOR: You're offering the money at the wrong time, Mr
Birling. [*He makes a move as if concluding the session, possibly
shutting up notebook, etc. Then surveys them sardonically.*] No, I
don't think any of you will forget. Nor that young man, Croft,
though he at least had some affection for her and made her
happy for a time. Well, Eva Smith's gone. You can't do her any
more harm. And you can't do her any good now, either. You
can't even say 'I'm sorry, Eva Smith.'

SHEILA [*who is crying quietly*]: That's the worst of it.

INSPECTOR: But just remember this. One Eva Smith has gone –
but there are millions and millions and millions of Eva Smiths
and John Smiths still left with us, with their lives, their hopes
and fears, their suffering, and chance of happiness, all intertwined with our lives, with what we think and say and do. We
don't live alone. We are members of one body. We are responsible for each other. And I tell you that the time will soon
come when, if men will not learn that lesson, then they will be
taught it in fire and blood and anguish. Good night.

[*He walks straight out, leaving them staring, subdued and
wondering.* SHEILA *is still quietly crying.* MRS BIRLING *has
collapsed into a chair.* ERIC *is brooding desperately.* BIRLING,
*the only active one, hears the front door slam, moves hesitatingly
towards the door, stops, looks gloomily at the other three, then
pours himself out a drink, which he hastily swallows.*]

BIRLING [*angrily to* ERIC]: You're the one I blame for this.

ERIC: I'll bet I am.

BIRLING [*angrily*]: Yes, and you don't realize yet all you've done.

Most of this is bound to come out. There'll be a public scandal.

ERIC: Well, I don't care now.

BIRLING: You! You don't seem to care about anything. But I care. I was almost certain for a knighthood in the next Honours List –

[ERIC *laughs rather hysterically, pointing at him.*]

ERIC [*laughing*]: Oh – for God's sake! What does it matter now whether they give you a knighthood or not?

BIRLING [*stormily*]: It doesn't matter to you. Apparently nothing matters to you. But it may interest you to know that until every penny of that money you stole is repaid, you'll work for nothing. And there's going to be no more of this drinking round the town – and picking up women in the Palace bar –

MRS BIRLING [*coming to life*]: I should think not. Eric, I'm absolutely ashamed of you.

ERIC: Well, I don't blame you. But don't forget I'm ashamed of you as well – yes, both of you.

BIRLING [*angrily*]: Drop that. There's every excuse for what both your mother and I did – it turned out unfortunately, that's all –

SHEILA [*scornfully*]: *That's all.*

BIRLING: Well, what have you to say?

SHEILA: I don't know where to begin.

BIRLING: Then don't begin. Nobody wants you to.

SHEILA: I behaved badly too. I know I did. I'm ashamed of it. But now you're beginning all over again to pretend that nothing much has happened –

BIRLING: Nothing much has happened! Haven't I already said there'll be a public scandal – unless we're lucky – and who here will suffer from that more than I will?

SHEILA: But that's not what I'm talking about. I don't care about that. The point is, you don't seem to have learnt anything.

BIRLING: Don't I? Well, you're quite wrong there. I've learnt plenty tonight. And you don't want me to tell you what I've learnt, I hope. When I look back on tonight – when I think of what I was feeling when the five of us sat down to dinner at that table –

ERIC [*cutting in*]: Yes, and do you remember what you said to Gerald and me after dinner, when you were feeling so pleased with yourself? You told us that a man has to make his own way, look after himself and mind his own business, and that we weren't to take any notice of these cranks who tell us that everybody has to look after everybody else, as if we were all mixed up together. Do you remember? Yes – and then one of those cranks walked in – the Inspector. [*Laughs bitterly.*] I didn't notice you told him that it's every man for himself.

SHEILA [*sharply attentive*]: Is that when the Inspector came, just after Father had said that?

ERIC: Yes. What of it?

MRS BIRLING: Now what's the matter, Sheila?

SHEILA [*slowly*]: It's queer – very queer – [*she looks at them reflectively.*]

MRS BIRLING [*with some excitement*]: I know what you're going to say. Because I've been wondering myself.

SHEILA: It doesn't much matter now, of course – but *was* he really a police inspector?

BIRLING: Well, if he wasn't, it matters a devil of a lot. Makes all the difference.

SHEILA: No, it doesn't.

BIRLING: Don't talk rubbish. Of course it does.

SHEILA: Well, it doesn't to me. And it oughtn't to you, either.

MRS BIRLING: Don't be childish, Sheila.

SHEILA [*flaring up*]: I'm not being. If you want to know, it's you two who are being childish – trying not to face the facts.

BIRLING: I won't have that sort of talk. Any more of that and you leave this room.

ERIC: That'll be terrible for her, won't it?

SHEILA: I'm going anyhow in a minute or two. But don't you see, if all that's come out tonight is true, then it doesn't much matter who it was who made us confess. And it *was* true, wasn't it? You turned the girl out of one job, and I had her turned out of another. Gerald kept her – at a time when he was supposed to be too busy to see me. Eric – well, we know what Eric did. And Mother hardened her heart and gave her the final push that finished her. That's what's important – and not whether a man is a police inspector or not.

ERIC: He was our police inspector all right.

SHEILA: That's what I mean, Eric. But if it's any comfort to you –

and it isn't to me – I have an idea – and I had it all along vaguely – that there was something curious about him. He never seemed like an ordinary police inspector –

BIRLING [*rather excited*]: You're right. I felt it too. [*To* MRS BIRLING] Didn't you?

MRS BIRLING: Well, I must say his manner was quite extraordinary; so – so rude – and assertive –

BIRLING: Then look at the way he talked to me. Telling me to shut up – and so on. He must have known I was an ex-Lord Mayor and a magistrate and so forth. Besides – the way he talked – you remember. I mean, they don't *talk* like that. I've had dealings with dozens of them.

SHEILA: All right. But it doesn't make any real difference, y'know.

MRS BIRLING: Of course it does.

ERIC: No, Sheila's right. It doesn't.

BIRLING [*angrily*]: That's comic, that is, coming from you. You're the one it makes *most* difference to. You've confessed to theft, and now he knows all about it, and he can bring it out at the inquest, and then if necessary carry it to court. He can't do anything to your mother and Sheila and me – except perhaps make us look a bit ashamed of ourselves in public – but as for you, he can ruin you. You know.

SHEILA [*slowly*]: We hardly ever told him anything he didn't know. Did you notice that?

BIRLING: That's nothing. He had a bit of information, left by the girl, and made a few smart guesses – but the fact remains that if we hadn't talked so much, he'd have had little to go on. [*Looks angrily at them*] And really, when I come to think of it, why you all had to go letting everything come out like that, beats me.

SHEILA: It's all right talking like that now. But he made us confess.

MRS BIRLING: He certainly didn't make me *confess* – as you call it. I told him quite plainly that I thought I had done no more than my duty.

SHEILA: Oh – Mother!

BIRLING: The fact is, you allowed yourselves to be bluffed. Yes – bluffed.

MRS BIRLING [*protesting*]: Now really – Arthur.

BIRLING: No, not you, my dear. But these two. That fellow ob-

viously didn't like us. He was prejudiced from the start.
Probably a Socialist or some sort of crank – he talked like one.
And then, instead of standing up to him, you let him bluff you
into talking about your private affairs. You ought to have stood
up to him.

ERIC [*sulkily*]: Well, I didn't notice you standing up to him.

BIRLING: No, because by that time you'd admitted you'd been
taking money. What chance had I after that? I was a fool not to
have insisted upon seeing him alone.

ERIC: That wouldn't have worked.

SHEILA: Of course it wouldn't.

MRS BIRLING: Really, from the way you children talk, you might
be wanting to help him instead of us. Now just be quiet so that
your father can decide what we ought to do. [*Looks expectantly
at* BIRLING.]

BIRLING [*dubiously*]: Yes – well. We'll have to do something – and
get to work quickly too. [*As he hesitates there is a ring at the front
door. They look at each other in alarm.*] Now who's this? Had I
better go?

MRS BIRLING: No. Edna'll go. I asked her to wait up to make us
some tea.

SHEILA: It might be Gerald coming back.

BIRLING [*relieved*]: Yes, of course. I'd forgotten about him.
       [EDNA *appears.*]

EDNA: It's Mr Croft.
       [GERALD *appears, and* EDNA *withdraws.*]

GERALD: I hope you don't mind my coming back?

MRS BIRLING: No, of course not, Gerald.

GERALD: I had a special reason for coming. When did that
Inspector go?

SHEILA: Only a few minutes ago. He put us all through it –

MRS BIRLING [*warningly*]: Sheila!

SHEILA: Gerald might as well know.

BIRLING [*hastily*]: Now – now – we needn't bother him with all
that stuff.

SHEILA: All right. [*To* GERALD] But we're all in it – up to the
neck. It got worse after you left.

GERALD: How did he behave?

SHEILA: He was – frightening.

BIRLING: If you ask me, he behaved in a very peculiar and suspicious manner.

MRS BIRLING: The rude way he spoke to Mr Birling and me – it was quite extraordinary!

GERALD: Hm – hm!

[*They all look inquiringly at* GERALD.]

BIRLING [*excitedly*]: You know something. What is it?

GERALD [*slowly*]: That man wasn't a police officer.

BIRLING [*astounded*]: What?

MRS BIRLING: Are you certain?

GERALD: I'm almost certain. That's what I came back to tell you.

BIRLING [*excitedly*]: Good lad! You asked about him, eh?

GERALD: Yes. I met a police sergeant I know down the road. I asked him about this Inspector Goole and described the chap carefully to him. He swore there wasn't any Inspector Goole or anybody like him on the force here.

BIRLING: You didn't tell him –

GERALD [*cutting in*]: No, no. I passed it off by saying I'd been having an argument with somebody. But the point is – this sergeant was dead certain they hadn't any inspector at all like the chap who came here.

BIRLING [*excitedly*]: By Jingo! A fake!

MRS BIRLING [*triumphantly*]: Didn't I tell you? Didn't I say I couldn't imagine a real police inspector talking like that to us?

GERALD: Well, you were right. There isn't any such inspector. We've been had.

BIRLING [*beginning to move*]: I'm going to make certain of this.

MRS BIRLING: What are you going to do?

BIRLING: Ring up the Chief Constable – Colonel Roberts.

MRS BIRLING: Careful what you say, dear.

BIRLING [*now at telephone*]: Of course. [*At telephone*] Brumley eight seven five two. [*To others as he waits*] I was going to do this anyhow. I've had my suspicions all along. [*At telephone*] Colonel Roberts, please. Mr Arthur Birling here. ... Oh, Roberts – Birling here. Sorry to ring you up so late, but can you tell me if an Inspector Goole has joined your staff lately ... Goole. G-O-O-L-E ... a new man ... tall, clean-shaven. [*Here he can describe the appearance of the actor playing the* INSPECTOR.] I see ... yes ... well, that settles it. ... No, just a little argument we were having here. .... Good night. [*He puts down the telephone and looks at the others.*] There's no Inspector Goole on the police. That man definitely wasn't a police inspector at all. As Gerald says – we've been had.

MRS BIRLING: I felt it all the time. He never talked like one. He never even looked like one.

BIRLING: This makes a difference, y'know. In fact, it makes *all* the difference.

GERALD: Of course!

SHEILA [*bitterly*]: I suppose we're all nice people now.

BIRLING: If you've nothing more sensible than that to say, Sheila, you'd better keep quiet.

ERIC: She's right, though.

BIRLING [*angrily*]: And *you*'d better keep quiet anyhow. If that *had* been a police inspector and he'd heard you confess –

MRS BIRLING [*warningly*]: Arthur – careful!

BIRLING [*hastily*]: Yes, yes.

SHEILA: You see, Gerald, you haven't to know the rest of our crimes and idiocies.

GERALD: That's all right, I don't want to. [*To* BIRLING] What do you make of this business now? Was it a hoax?

BIRLING: Of course. Somebody put that fellow up to coming here and hoaxing us. There are people in this town who dislike me enough to do that. We ought to have seen through it from the first. In the ordinary way, I believe I would have done. But coming like that, bang on top of our little celebration, just when we were all feeling so pleased with ourselves, naturally it took me by surprise.

MRS BIRLING: I wish I'd been here when that man first arrived. I'd have asked *him* a few questions before I allowed him to ask us any.

SHEILA: It's all right saying that now.

MRS BIRLING: I was the only one of you who didn't give in to him. And now I say we must discuss this business quietly and sensibly and decide if there's anything to be done about it.

BIRLING [*with hearty approval*]: You're absolutely right, my dear. Already we've discovered one important fact – that that fellow was a fraud and we've been hoaxed – and that may not be the end of it by any means.

GERALD: I'm sure it isn't.

BIRLING [*keenly interested*]: You are, eh ? Good! [*To* ERIC, *who is restless*] Eric, sit down.

ERIC [*sulkily*]: I'm all right.

BIRLING: All right? You're anything but all right. And you needn't stand there – as if – as if –

ERIC: As if – what ?

BIRLING: As if you'd nothing to do with us. Just remember your own position, young man. If anybody's up to the neck in this business, you are, so you'd better take some interest in it.

ERIC: I do take some interest in it. I take too much, that's my trouble.

SHEILA: It's mine too.

BIRLING: Now listen, you two. If you're still feeling on edge, then the least you can do is to keep quiet. Leave this to us. I'll admit that fellow's antics rattled us a bit. But we've found him out – and all we have to do is to keep our heads. Now it's our turn.

SHEILA: Our turn to do – what ?

MRS BIRLING [*sharply*]: To behave sensibly, Sheila – which is more than you're doing.

ERIC [*bursting out*]: What's the use of talking about behaving sensibly ? You're beginning to pretend now that nothing's really happened at all. And I can't see it like that. This girl's still dead, isn't she ? Nobody's brought her to life, have they ?

SHEILA [*eagerly*]: That's just what I feel, Eric. And it's what they don't seem to understand.

ERIC: Whoever that chap was, the fact remains that I did what I did. And Mother did what she did. And the rest of you did what you did to her. It's still the same rotten story whether it's been told to a police inspector or to somebody else. According to you, I ought to feel a lot better – [*To* GERALD] I stole some money, Gerald, you might as well know – [*As* BIRLING *tries to interrupt*] I don't care, let him know. The money's not the important thing. It's what happened to the girl and what we all did to her that matters. And I still feel the same about it, and that's why I don't feel like sitting down and having a nice cosy talk.

SHEILA: And Eric's absolutely right. And it's the best thing any one of us has said tonight and it makes me feel a bit less ashamed of us. You're just beginning to pretend all over again.

BIRLING: Look – for God's sake!

MRS BIRLING [*protesting*]: Arthur!

BIRLING: Well, my dear, they're so damned exasperating. They just won't try to understand our position or to see the difference between a lot of stuff like this coming out in private and a downright public scandal.

ERIC [*shouting*]: And I say the girl's dead and we all helped to kill her – and that's what matters –

BIRLING [*also shouting, threatening* ERIC]: And I say – either stop shouting or get out. [*Glaring at him but in quiet tone*] Some fathers I know would have kicked you out of the house anyhow by this time. So hold your tongue if you want to stay here.

ERIC [*quietly, bitterly*]: I don't give a damn now whether I stay here or not.

BIRLING: You'll stay here long enough to give me an account of that money you stole – yes, and to pay it back too.

SHEILA: But that won't bring Eva Smith back to life, will it?

ERIC: And it doesn't alter the fact that we all helped to kill her.

GERALD: But is it a fact?

ERIC: Of course it is. You don't know the whole story yet.

SHEILA: I suppose you're going to prove now you didn't spend last summer keeping this girl instead of seeing me, eh?

GERALD: I did keep a girl last summer. I've admitted it. And I'm sorry, Sheila.

SHEILA: Well, I must admit you came out of it better than the rest of us. The Inspector said that.

BIRLING [*angrily*]: He wasn't an Inspector.

SHEILA [*flaring up*]: Well, he inspected us all right. And don't let's start dodging and pretending now. Between us we drove that girl to commit suicide.

GERALD: Did we? Who says so? Because I say – there's no more real evidence we did than there was that that chap was a police inspector.

SHEILA: Of course there is.

GERALD: No, there isn't. Look at it. A man comes here pretending to be a police officer. It's a hoax of some kind. Now what does he do? Very artfully, working on bits of information he's picked up here and there, he bluffs us into confessing that we've all been mixed up in this girl's life in one way or another.

ERIC: And so we have.

GERALD: *But how do you know it's the same girl?*

BIRLING [*eagerly*]: Now wait a minute! Let's see how that would work. Now – [*hesitates*] no, it wouldn't.

ERIC: We all admitted it.

GERALD: All right, you all admitted something to do with a girl. But how do you know it's the same girl?

[*He looks round triumphantly at them. As they puzzle this out, he turns to* BIRLING, *after a pause.*]

Look here, Mr Birling. You sack a girl called Eva Smith. You've forgotten, but he shows you a photograph of her and then you remember. Right?

BIRLING: Yes, that part's straightforward enough. But what then?

GERALD: Well, then he happens to know that Sheila once had a girl sacked from Milwards shop. He tells us that it's this same Eva Smith. And he shows her a photograph that she recognizes.

SHEILA: Yes. The same photograph.

GERALD: How do you know it's the same photograph? Did you see the one your father looked at?

SHEILA: No, I didn't.

GERALD: And did your father see the one he showed you?

SHEILA: No, he didn't. And I see what you mean now.

GERALD: We've no proof it was the same photograph and therefore no proof it was the same girl. Now take me. I never saw a photograph, remember. He caught me out by suddenly announcing that this girl changed her name to Daisy Renton. I gave myself away at once because I'd known a Daisy Renton.

BIRLING [*eagerly*]: And there wasn't the slightest proof that this Daisy Renton was really Eva Smith. We've only his word for it, and we'd his word for it that he was a police inspector, and we know now he was lying. So he could have been lying all the time.

GERALD: Of course he could. Probably was. Now what happened after I left?

MRS BIRLING: I was upset because Eric had left the house, and this man said that if Eric didn't come back, he'd have to go and find him. Well, that made me feel worse still. And his manner was so severe and he seemed so confident. Then quite suddenly he said I'd seen Eva Smith only two weeks ago.

BIRLING: Those were his exact words.

MRS BIRLING: And like a fool I said Yes I had.

BIRLING: I don't see now why you did that. She didn't call herself Eva Smith when she came to see you at the committee, did she?

MRS BIRLING: No, of course she didn't. But, feeling so worried, when he suddenly turned on me with those questions, I answered more or less as he wanted me to answer.

SHEILA: But, Mother, don't forget that he showed you a photograph of the girl before that, and you obviously recognized it.

GERALD: Did anybody else see it?

MRS BIRLING: No, he showed it only to me.

GERALD: Then, don't you see, there's still no proof it was really the same girl. He might have showed you the photograph of any girl who applied to the committee. And how do we know she was really Eva Smith or Daisy Renton?

BIRLING: Gerald's dead right. He could have used a different photograph each time and we'd be none the wiser. We may all have been recognizing different girls.

GERALD: Exactly. Did he ask you to identify a photograph, Eric?

ERIC: No. He didn't need a photograph by the time he'd got round to me. But obviously it must have been the girl I knew who went round to see Mother.

GERALD: Why must it?

ERIC: She said she had to have help because she wouldn't take any more stolen money. And the girl I knew had told me that already.

GERALD: Even then, that may have been all nonsense.

ERIC: I don't see much nonsense about it when a girl goes and kills herself. You lot may be letting yourselves out nicely, but I can't. Nor can Mother. We did her in all right.

BIRLING [eagerly]: Wait a minute, wait a minute! Don't be in such a hurry to put yourself into court. That interview with your mother could have been just as much a put-up job, like all this police inspector business. The whole damned thing can have been a piece of bluff.

ERIC [angrily]: How can it? The girl's dead, isn't she?

GERALD: What girl? There were probably four or five different girls.

ERIC: That doesn't matter to me. The one I knew is dead.

BIRLING: Is she ? *How do we know she is ?*

GERALD: That's right. You've got it. How do we know any girl killed herself today ?

BIRLING [*looking at them all, triumphantly*]: Now answer that one. Let's look at it from this fellow's point of view. We're having a little celebration here and feeling rather pleased with ourselves. Now he has to work a trick on us. Well, the first thing he has to do is to give us such a shock that after that he can bluff us all the time. So he starts right off. A girl has just died in the Infirmary. She drank some strong disinfectant. Died in agony –

ERIC: All right, don't pile it on.

BIRLING [*triumphantly*]: There you are, you see. Just repeating it shakes you a bit. And that's what he had to do. Shake us at once – and then start questioning us – until we didn't know where we were. Oh – let's admit that. He had the laugh of us all right.

ERIC: He could laugh his head off – if I knew it really was all a hoax.

BIRLING: I'm convinced it is. No police inquiry. No one girl that all this happens to. No scandal –

SHEILA: And no suicide ?

GERALD [*decisively*]: We can settle that at once.

SHEILA: How ?

GERALD: By ringing up the Infirmary. Either there's a dead girl there or there isn't.

BIRLING [*uneasily*]: It will look a bit queer, won't it – ringing up at this time of night –

GERALD: I don't mind doing it.

MRS BIRLING [*emphatically*]: And if there isn't –

GERALD: Anyway we'll see. [*He goes to telephone and looks up number. The others watch tensely.*] Brumley eight nine eight six. . . . Is that the Infirmary ? This is Mr Gerald Croft – of Crofts Limited. . . . Yes. . . . We're rather worried about one of our employees. Have you had a girl brought in this afternoon who committed suicide by drinking disinfectant – or any like suicide ? Yes, I'll wait.

[*As he waits, the others show their nervous tension.* BIRLING *wipes his brow,* SHEILA *shivers,* ERIC *clasps and unclasps his hands, etc.*]

Yes? . . . You're certain of that. . . . I see. Well, thank you very
much. . . . Good night. [*He puts down telephone and looks at
them.*] No girl has died in there today. Nobody's been brought
in after drinking disinfectant. They haven't had a suicide for
months.

BIRLING [*triumphantly*]: There you are! Proof positive. The
whole story's just a lot of moonshine. Nothing but an elaborate
sell! [*He produces a huge sigh of relief.*] Nobody likes to be sold as
badly as that – but – for all that – [*he smiles at them all*] Gerald,
have a drink.

GERALD [*smiling*]: Thanks, I think I could just do with one now.

BIRLING [*going to sideboard*]: So could I.

MRS BIRLING [*smiling*]: And I must say, Gerald, you've argued
this very cleverly, and I'm most grateful.

GERALD [*going for his drink*]: Well, you see, while I was out of
the house I'd time to cool off and think things out a little.

BIRLING [*giving him a drink*]: Yes, he didn't keep you on the run
as he did the rest of us. I'll admit now he gave me a bit of a scare
at the time. But I'd a special reason for not wanting any public
scandal just now. [*Has his drink now, and raises his glass.*] Well,
here's to us. Come on, Sheila, don't look like that. All over now.

SHEILA: The worst part is. But you're forgetting one thing I still
can't forget. Everything we said had happened really had
happened. If it didn't end tragically, then that's lucky for us.
But it might have done.

BIRLING [*jovially*]: But the whole thing's different now. Come,
come, you can see that, can't you? [*Imitating* INSPECTOR *in his
final speech*] *You all helped to kill her.* [*Pointing at* SHEILA *and*
ERIC, *and laughing*] And I wish you could have seen the look on
your faces when he said that. [SHEILA *moves towards door.*]
Going to bed, young woman?

SHEILA [*tensely*]: I want to get out of this. It frightens me the way
you talk.

BIRLING [*heartily*]: Nonsense! You'll have a good laugh over it
yet. Look, you'd better ask Gerald for that ring you gave back to
him, hadn't you? Then you'll feel better.

SHEILA [*passionately*]: You're pretending everything's just as it
was before.

ERIC: I'm not!

SHEILA: No, but these others are.

BIRLING: Well, isn't it? We've been had, that's all.

SHEILA: So nothing really happened. So there's nothing to be sorry for, nothing to learn. We can all go on behaving just as we did.

MRS BIRLING: Well, why shouldn't we?

SHEILA: I tell you – whoever that Inspector was, it was anything but a joke. You knew it then. You began to learn something. And now you've stopped. You're ready to go on in the same old way.

BIRLING [amused]: And you're not, eh?

SHEILA: No, because I remember what he said, how he looked, and what he made me feel. Fire and blood and anguish. And it frightens me the way you talk, and I can't listen to any more of it.

ERIC: And I agree with Sheila. It frightens me too.

BIRLING: Well, go to bed then, and don't stand there being hysterical.

MRS BIRLING: They're over-tired. In the morning they'll be as amused as we are.

GERALD: Everything's all right now, Sheila. [Holds up the ring.] What about this ring?

SHEILA: No, not yet. It's too soon. I must think.

BIRLING [pointing to ERIC and SHEILA]: Now look at the pair of them – the famous younger generation who know it all. And they can't even take a joke –

[The telephone rings sharply. There is a moment's complete silence. BIRLING goes to answer it.]

Yes? . . . Mr Birling speaking. . . . What? – Here –

[But obviously the other person has rung off. He puts the telephone down slowly and looks in a panic-stricken fashion at the others.]

BIRLING: That was the police. A girl has just died – on her way to the Infirmary – after swallowing some disinfectant. And a police inspector is on his way here – to ask some – questions –

[As they stare guiltily and dumbfounded, the curtain falls.]

END OF PLAY

The Linden Tree

A PLAY IN TWO ACTS

To J. P. Mitchelhill

My dear Mitch,

I hope you will accept, with my affectionate regards,
the dedication of this play. You were enthusiastic
about it from the first, and it took us back to the
Duchess Theatre again, in the happiest circumstances,
after an interval of nearly ten years, during which it
looked as if we should never work together in the
Theatre again. To have you on the management once
more, together with my friends of the Westminster
venture – and Dame Sybil and Sir Lewis Casson playing so beautifully – this has been happiness when I had
almost ceased to dream of finding it in the Theatre.
So far as the play itself has any virtue, it was a virtue
plucked out of necessity. The heaviest snowfall the
Isle of Wight had known for about a hundred years
found me down at Billingham, in a house hard to
warm and then desperately short of fuel. Besieged by
this cruellest of Februarys, I ate, toiled and slept in
one small room, and there the Lindens were born;
and for ten days or so, while I worked at the play, they
were almost my only company and the people I
seemed to know best. And then – what luck! – I was
back with you, back with the others, back at the
Duchess, and all went miraculously well. So please
accept the piece as a tribute to our friendship and
your love of the Theatre.

Yours ever,

J.B.P.

CHARACTERS

PROFESSOR ROBERT LINDEN
ISABEL LINDEN, his wife
REX LINDEN, his son
DR JEAN LINDEN, his eldest daughter
MARION DE SAINT VAURY, his daughter
DINAH LINDEN, his youngest daughter
ALFRED LOCKHART, University Secretary
EDITH WESTMORE, a student
BERNARD FAWCETT, a student
MRS COTTON, housekeeper

Synopsis of Scenes

The action takes place in Professor Linden's study, in the provincial city of Burmanley. Early spring, at the present time [1947].

Act One

Friday–
Scene One. Late afternoon.
Scene Two. Two hours later.

Act Two

Saturday –
Scene One. Afternoon.
Scene Two. Night, several hours later.

In each Act, between the Scenes, the curtain is lowered for a few moments only.

'The Linden Tree' was first produced at the Lyceum Theatre, Sheffield, on 23 June 1947, and subsequently at the Duchess Theatre, London, on 15 August 1947, with the following cast:

PROFESSOR ROBERT LINDEN	Lewis Casson
ISABEL LINDEN	Sybil Thorndike
REX LINDEN	John Dodsworth
DR JEAN LINDEN	Freda Gaye
MARION DE SAINT VAURY	Sonia Williams
DINAH LINDEN	Tilsa Page
ALFRED LOCKHART	J. Leslie Frith
EDITH WESTMORE	Carmel McSharry
BERNARD FAWCETT	Terence Soall
MRS COTTON	Everley Gregg

Produced by Michael Macowan

ACT ONE

SCENE ONE

PROFESSOR LINDEN'S *study. It is a large room, clean but shabby.
One door, preferably set obliquely and prominently between back and
left (actors') walls. Big bay window on right wall. A companion
window may be presumed to exist in fourth wall. Downstage* L. *is an
anthracite stove. Back wall and all available* R. *and* L. *walls are
covered with open bookshelves up to height of about five feet, with one
or two filing cabinets for lecture* MSS, *etc. A fairly large table, with
papers, books, pipes, tobacco jar, etc., rather downstage* L. *of centre.
A small table on back wall near door with telephone on it. As this
room is often used for seminars there are plenty of chairs about,
mostly oldish upright chairs near walls but also several shabby comfortable easy chairs nearer centre. Down* R. *a globe on stand. A few
good reproductions and perhaps an excellent original water-colour or
two on the walls. No domestic ornaments, and general effect that of a
scholarly, cheerful, untidy, and not well-to-do man.*

*It is afternoon in early spring, and rather coldish sunlight is coming
through window* R. *and fourth wall, giving plenty of light in the room
but not giving it any particular richness and warmth. At rise of curtain,
stage is empty and then* MRS COTTON *shows in* ALFRED LOCKHART.
MRS C *is the Lindens' woman-of-all-work and looks it. She is middle-
aged and has a curious confused manner, which must be played
seriously and not for laughs.* LOCKHART *is a precise, anxious, clerkly
middle-aged man, soberly dressed. He wears a light overcoat and
carries his hat.*

LOCKHART [*seeing where he is*]: Oh – I say, is this right?
MRS COTTON: Right? It's as right as we can make it. Nothing's
   right now, nor ever will be, if you ask me. Half the sitting-room
   ceiling come down yesterday – no warning – just come down in
   the night – and when I saw it, I stood there – ice-cold, turned to
   stone, I was – an' couldn't speak for ten minutes –
LOCKHART: I'm afraid I don't understand – I meant –
MRS COTTON: It took me straight back – see? Lived in Croydon –

an' went out one Saturday morning for a bit o' fish – and one o'
them buzz-bombs came – and when I gets back – it's all over –
finished for ever – all three of 'em – and the home of course –

LOCKHART [*sympathetically*]: Oh yes – I remember Mrs Linden
telling me. And so when you saw the sitting-room ceiling, it
reminded you –

MRS COTTON [*cutting in, massively*]: Turned to stone, I was – you
could 'ave pushed a dozen pins into me, I wouldn't have known
– couldn't speak for ten minutes. It's years since now – isn't it ?
– but sometimes I think to myself ' Suppose I'm still going for
that fish' – I'm waiting outside Underwoods really an' just
dreamin' – an' I'll go back an' everything'll be all right – Charlie
an' Gladys an' little George – just waitin' for me – having a good
laugh, I'll be bound –

LOCKHART [*embarrassed by this*]: Yes, I see what you mean. I –

MRS COTTON: No, you don't. Why should you ? I don't blame
you. [*More confidentially, and impressively*] Sometimes I feel
that if I could just turn a corner somewhere – or squeeze through
a narrow gap – it'ud be all right again – an' I wouldn't be 'ere in
Burmanley but in Croydon with everything all right – [*she
points to the window*] the sun's not the same now. Perhaps that
would be different. [*With sudden change of manner, sensibly*] But
you'll 'ave to see Mrs Linden in 'ere – 'cos of the sitting-room
ceiling, see ?

LOCKHART [*glad of this return*]: That's what I meant. I was afraid
you thought I'd come to see Professor Linden –

MRS COTTON: No, I 'eard you – Mrs Linden, you said. Besides
he's at the college on Friday afternoons, always – couldn't even
meet the family this afternoon. They've just come in a big car –
all the way from London. Plenty of petrol – money no object –
that's the son, Rex –

LOCKHART: Oh – is he here ?

MRS COTTON: Yes, with his two sisters. All smart as paint. She's
showing 'em their bedrooms. All excited. There'll be trouble
'ere this week-end. Ceilings comin' down – that's a start. You'll
see. It's the Professor's birthday today. Watch out for that. Big
changes comin'. I'll tell Mrs Linden you're 'ere. [*Moves nearer
door, then turns, confidentially.*] Don't believe all she says, she's
too excited. 'Cos Rex is 'ere. I'd 'ave bin the same.

[*She goes out, leaving* LOCKHART *bewildered. He stares about him a moment, tries a chair tentatively, then rises just before* MRS LINDEN *enters. She is a woman in her late fifties, not very smart but now dressed in her best, and with a brisk vivacious manner.*]

MRS LINDEN: Oh – Mr Lockhart, I hope you haven't been waiting long. Poor Mrs Cotton isn't – well – you know – quite –

LOCKHART: No, I gathered that.

MRS LINDEN: Only at times, when things happen to upset her. We've had an accident to the drawing-room ceiling. This house is really in a shocking condition, and Robert won't make a fuss about it to the bursar – it's University property, you know – *your* property.

LOCKHART: Shall I say something to him?

MRS LINDEN: I really don't think it matters now. Ten years ago was the time. But *do* sit down, Mr Lockhart. So good of you to call so promptly when you're so busy.

LOCKHART: Not at all. I enjoyed the walk across. The early tulips are out on College Green. Very pleasant.

MRS LINDEN: I've never cared for them. Tulips have never seemed like real flowers to me – more like something from a decorator's. All the children have just arrived, you know – Rex, Jean, and even Marion, who's come all the way from the very centre of France. Rex has just driven them down from London. So the whole family will be here this week-end – for the first time for years. Can you imagine what that means? No of course you can't – not really. Now – [*as she says this, confidentially, she sits fairly close to him and looks at him earnestly*] – I want you to consider this little talk of ours as being strictly between ourselves – very confidential. Even my husband doesn't know about it, and I'd much rather he didn't, if you don't mind.

LOCKHART: No – of course not – if you really think –

MRS LINDEN: Yes, I do – most decidedly. It's about him, this little talk. And I'm appealing to you not simply as the secretary of the University but also as a friend. And Robert and I have always regarded you as a friend.

LOCKHART: I'm very glad, Mrs Linden. And of course if there is anything I can do –

MRS LINDEN: Poor Mr Lockhart! How often have you to say that?

LOCKHART: About thirty times a day, at least. Including letters of course. But this time I mean it. Usually I don't.

MRS LINDEN: Yes – well –

LOCKHART [*encouraging her*]: Yes?

MRS LINDEN [*plunging in*]: Is there a definite retiring age for professors here at Burmanley?

LOCKHART: There *was*. Sixty-five.

MRS LINDEN [*pleased*]: Ah – I thought so.

LOCKHART: The late Vice-Chancellor ignored it. And of course during the war it was very convenient to keep on the older professors. But now –

MRS LINDEN: Yes – now? What is the attitude of this new Vice-Chancellor – I never remember his name –

LOCKHART: Dr Lidley.

MRS LINDEN: Dr Lidley. What's his attitude? He's not very old himself.

LOCKHART: About forty-five, I believe.

MRS LINDEN: I'm sure *he* doesn't want old professors.

LOCKHART [*hesitantly*]: Well – no – he doesn't.

MRS LINDEN: He doesn't like my husband, does he? [*As* LOCKHART, *embarrassed, does not reply.*] Oh – I know. Robert doesn't like him. And you needn't look like that, Mr Lockhart. I'm not talking to you now as the University official. You're here as a friend – and it's all in confidence. Dr Lidley and my husband don't get on, do they?

LOCKHART: Well, of course they represent two different points of view – about the University, I mean. Totally opposed, really. Professor Linden left Oxford to come here – didn't he?

MRS LINDEN [*emphatically*]: He did – much to my disgust – though it's all a long time ago. And he promised we'd get back to Oxford some time – and look at us! – but go on.

LOCKHART: Well, he's always wanted Burmanley to be as like Oxford as possible. Dr Lidley's quite different. He's been a very successful director of education in several cities. You might describe him as a high-pressure educationalist –

MRS LINDEN [*quietly, but firmly*]: Mr Lockhart, frankly I don't care tuppence what Dr Lidley is. The only time I met him he seemed to me one of those bright beaming bores. I hope I never see him again. And that's what I wanted to talk to you about.

LOCKHART: What – about not seeing the Vice-Chancellor again?

MRS LINDEN: It amounts to that, really. My husband is sixty-five today. He ought not to stay here in Burmanley any longer. He's tired. He's been here far too long already. He'll never keep up with these new programmes of work you're introducing. [*She breaks off to look hard at him, then softly*] Mr Lockhart, I can tell by the look in your eye that already – and quite recently – you've heard somebody else say what I've just said about my husband.

LOCKHART [*embarrassed*]: Really, Mrs Linden, that's not fair –

MRS LINDEN [*getting up*]: Wives can't afford to be fair.

[*As* LOCKHART *rises she regards him smilingly.*]

I think you're fond of Robert, aren't you?

LOCKHART: Yes. Most of us are – I mean, the older lot here.

MRS LINDEN [*very quietly, slowly*]: Well then, if you want to do him a kindness, you won't oppose any attempt, by the other side, to get rid of him. He ought to go. And though he's obstinate, he won't stay where he's not wanted.

LOCKHART [*staggered, stammering*]: But – but surely – if he himself –

MRS LINDEN [*cutting in, hostess now*]: Won't you have a cup of tea? It's here, I think.

LOCKHART: No, thank you. I must be getting back to my office.

[MRS COTTON *enters, either with a large tray or preferably pushing a trolley, with tea for five or six persons – bread and butter and cake – on it.*]

MRS COTTON: Family's just coming. I've told 'em it's ready. [*She goes out, leaving door open.*]

MRS LINDEN: Well, just stay and say 'How d'you do' to Rex and the girls.

[*Enter* JEAN, MARION *and* REX. REX *is the eldest, about thirty-five, good-looking, cool, humorous, very self-confident, well-dressed in an easy fashion.* JEAN *is a trim handsome woman in her early thirties, a clear-cut and rather cold type at a first glance, very much the professional woman.* MARION *is a year or two younger, pretty, softer, very well-dressed in French clothes.*]

REX [*to* LOCKHART]: Hello! Remember me?

LOCKHART [*shaking hands*]: Yes, of course, Rex. You're looking well.

REX: I'm feeling quite remarkable.

MRS LINDEN [*to her daughters*]: You remember Mr Lockhart, the University Secretary, don't you?

[*As they smile, she turns to* LOCKHART.]

This is Jean – now *Dr* Jean Linden, if you please, *and* on the staff of the North Middlesex Hospital. And this is Marion, who's come all the way from the centre of France, because now she's Madame de St Vaury.

REX: Really an old-world French aristocrat who wonders what Burmanley is all about.

MARION [*not pleased at this*]: Don't be an ape, Rex.

JEAN [*coldly*]: I know what he means, though.

LOCKHART [*hastily*]: It doesn't seem long since you were both schoolgirls – and now – well – makes me feel old. Wasn't there a René de St Vaury up here just before the war?

MARION [*smiling*]: Yes. Then I met him again in London, during the war, when he was with de Gaulle. And that's how it all began. We've been married four years – two children now –

LOCKHART: Splendid!

MRS LINDEN: You're sure you won't stay to tea?

LOCKHART: No thank you. Well – nice to have seen you all again.

[*Smiles and nods, and they all murmur* 'Good afternoon' *or* 'Good-bye' *and* MRS LINDEN *takes him out. The other three look at each other.*]

REX [*softly*]: I'd say that mother's up to something with poor little Alf Lockhart. I saw it in her eye. What about some tea?

MARION: Mother'll want to pour out. [*Surveys tray with disgust.*] Just look at it – ugh!

JEAN: Yes, fairly sordid. But we're all used to that. And what can you expect?

MARION: Well, that's what I mean. If one of our maids brought in a tray looking like that, René or his mother would have a fit.

REX [*taking a piece of cake*]: This is Labour England, ducky. Not your Catholic aristocratic old world, with a nice black market on the side. And not Jean's new world. [*He has been nibbling at the cake.*] If sawdust was easier to get, I'd say this cake was sawdust.

[MRS LINDEN *returns, smiling, closing door behind her.*]

Well, Mother, what are you up to with poor little Alf Lockhart?

MRS LINDEN: Just a little chat about your father. Now let's sit down and be cosy. You'd like some tea, wouldn't you, Rex?

REX: A cup, certainly.

JEAN: And so would Marion and I.

MRS LINDEN: Naturally, dear. But men don't always want tea – that's why I asked. I'm afraid this cake won't be very nice.

REX: It isn't. I've tried it. Stick to the bread and butter.

[MRS LINDEN *is now pouring out;* JEAN *and* MARION *are sitting near her; and* REX *hands bread and butter and cups, etc., and throughout the following speeches they are having tea.*]

MRS LINDEN: Such a shame you couldn't bring the children, Marion.

MARION: It really wasn't possible. And Belle-Mère was quite furious even when I said I'd like to bring them.

MRS LINDEN: She seems to forget they have another grand-mother –

MARION: No, that's not fair, Mother, when she and René are always suggesting that you should come and stay. We were talking about it one night last week when Father Honoré was dining with us – he's really very witty – and – [*She breaks off.*]

MRS LINDEN: Yes, dear?

MARION [*shortly*]: I'll tell you later. Don't let's bother about it now.

[MRS LINDEN *looks from her to* JEAN *inquiringly.* REX, *who misses nothing, takes it up.*]

REX: Marion's quite right, Mother. Only leads to trouble. She and Jean were at it on the way coming up in the car. And Father Who's-it is practically a detonator for Jean.

MRS LINDEN: Well, really, Jean – if Marion wants to talk –

JEAN: I didn't stop her. And Rex is exaggerating – as usual.

MARION [*heatedly*]: No, he's not. And if you're unhappy, Jean – it's not my fault, is it?

JEAN [*coldly*]: Unhappy? I'm not unhappy. What are you talking about?

MARION: Oh come off it. I'm not one of your hospital patients. Do you think I don't know you. You're miserable about something – I don't know what it is – so you're taking it out on me – or trying to do – just as you always did –

MRS LINDEN: Now, Marion, you shouldn't talk like that.

MARION: But it's true, Mother. And as soon as I say anything

that reminds her that I'm a Catholic now, she says something
hateful and hurting. No, Rex, I'm not going to start arguing all
over again. I agree with you – there's been too much already.
I'm simply going to say this. I became a Catholic at first simply
for René's sake. But now I'm more than glad I did. And the
more I see of the rest of you – no, not you, Mother – and – of
everything here – the more thankful I am that I am a Catholic –
and – and have a Faith – and – and belong to a community that
may be old-fashioned, as you call it, but is still civilized.
[*Defiantly to* JEAN] Now go on – call me a Fascist again –

JEAN [*coldly*]: Why – do you enjoy it?

MRS LINDEN: Now, stop it, both of you. If this is how you two go
on, then I agree with Rex – there mustn't be any more of it.

MARION: I'm sorry, Mother. I've finished.

MRS LINDEN: *Is* there something wrong, Jean? You're looking –
well – rather strained, dear.

JEAN [*curtly*]: I've been working too hard, that's all. We're all
overworked at the North Middlesex. And we're terribly short of
nurses – and domestic staff. Short of everything – except
patients. Oh – forget it.

MRS LINDEN: Couldn't you apply for some easier post somewhere?

JEAN: Not just now. But I'd like to find something not quite so
futile. Half the people we try to patch up might as well be dead –
they're only half alive –

MARION [*heatedly*]: I call that wicked – yes, downright wicked –

JEAN: I wouldn't call it anything, if I were you, unless you're
prepared to leave your delicious chateau and all your devoted
peasants and take night duty for a few months.

MARION [*heatedly*]: And that's –

REX [*cutting in, massively*]: Girls, turn it up. We've had enough of
it. We were asked up here for an urgent family reunion – business
and pleasure, I hope. And the Catholic–Communist debate is
now closed for the week-end.

MRS LINDEN: Just what I was going to say, Rex. And Dinah and
your father will be back soon –

REX: How is young Dinah – and why isn't she here?

MRS LINDEN: She's practising with the orchestra this afternoon
and nothing would induce her to stay away. She's very well and

happy, really, but still the oddest child you ever knew. More tea, anybody? It isn't very nice, I know, but poor Mrs Cotton, who likes nothing better than making tea all day long, really hasn't the least idea how to make it properly.

JEAN: Most of them haven't. They can't do anything properly.

REX: Don't care for the masses really, do you, Jeanie?

JEAN: No, of course not. That's why I want to see them turned into sensible civilized creatures.

[*The telephone rings.* JEAN *starts up, but* REX, *already standing, forestalls her.*]

REX [*as he goes*]: I'll answer it. I'm expecting a call. [*At telephone*] Hello! Yes, it is. Yes – speaking. Go ahead. . . . Yes, Fraser, Rex Linden here. . . . Yes, what did he say? . . . I see, well offer him twenty-five – cash down – as soon as he likes – if he walks straight out of the place, just taking his personal things and any sentimental bits and pieces, and leaves the rest. . . . Yes, twenty-five thousand – cold cash. . . . All right, ring me here later.

[*Comes away, looking pleased with himself, takes out cigarette-case, offering it to his mother and* MARION, *who shake their heads, then to* JEAN, *who takes one. He lights hers and his during following speeches.*]

MRS LINDEN: What was that about, dear? Some more of your mysterious business?

REX: No, not really. You remember my telling you about a nice little country place in Hampshire – small manor house with about ten acres, and all the comforts?

MRS LINDEN [*excitedly*]: You're going to buy it?

REX: You heard me. Twenty-five thousand, lock, stock and barrel. Sir Charles walks out, Mr Rex Linden walks in. I think he'll take it too, though he'd get far more if he auctioned everything. But he's in a hurry for the cash – wants to go to Africa.

MRS LINDEN: But, Rex darling, that'll be wonderful. And – you know – just at the perfect time. Goodness – I hope you *do* get it.

REX: I'll lay ten to one I do – and tonight too. You'll see.

MARION: But – can you afford to put down twenty-five thousand pounds – just like that?

REX: Yes. And quite a good deal more, ducky. I sound a vulgar type, don't I? Perhaps I am. It's a solemn thought.

MARION: But how do you make all this money, Rex? I don't

understand. What do you *do*? René was asking me that, the other day.

REX: I toil not neither do I spin.

JEAN [*dryly*]: We know that.

REX: I live on my wits and gamble with the boys in the City. A kind of racketeer really – free of tax too. A de-luxe model Spiv.

MRS LINDEN: Darling, nobody knows what you're talking about.

JEAN [*rising*]: I do. And he's right. What about these tea things?

MRS LINDEN [*rising*]: We'll clear and wash up ourselves – I really can't ask Mrs Cotton. I wish we could have gone out for dinner tonight, but really it's hopeless here.

[*They are now moving the trolley or tray and various tea things. As they move through door, front-door bell, not too close, is heard ringing.*]

MRS LINDEN: Rex, would you mind seeing who that is?

[*Stage is empty for a moment or two. Then* REX *returns with* EDITH WESTMORE, *a student, about twenty, carrying a cheap little case for books, note-books, etc. She wears spectacles, has untidy hair, rather shabby wrong clothes, but is not altogether unattractive and must not be grotesque or comic. She has a provincial accent, which must not be overdone, and has a strained manner, a mixture of shyness and defiance. Her general effect is likeable but rather pathetic.* REX's *manner with her has more charm than his lines might suggest.*]

REX: You'll have to wait, I'm afraid. My father isn't back yet, though I gather he's expected at any moment.

EDITH: Yes, I was at his lecture. I – we – well, there's another student too – we always see him at this time every Friday – we write an essay for him every week –

REX [*smiling*]: I know. Explain the Thirty Years War. Do sit down.

[*She does. He remains standing.*]

Good lecture?

EDITH [*with enthusiasm*]: Oh – yes. Wonderful. He makes it all seem so clear – and so exciting – and it's hard to take notes – and then afterwards – somehow – [*She hesitates.*]

REX: You can't remember a dam' thing.

EDITH: How do you know?

REX: I was a history student once. [*Produces his cigarette-case, a very expensive one.*] Have a cigarette while you're waiting.

EDITH [*hesitating*]: Oh – well – thank you.

[*Takes one. He offers her a light. She smokes rather awkwardly. He looks at her quizzically.*]

REX: You're using the wrong shade of lipstick, y'know.

EDITH [*helplessly*]: Oh – am I ? Yes – I expect I am.

REX: You need a darker shade. Do you mind my talking like this ?

EDITH [*rather dubiously*]: No – not really. It's a bit – embarrassing – of course. You live in London, don't you ?

REX: Yes, I'm a West End type now.

EDITH: Well, I haven't much time – to make myself look nice. And no money. I have a scholarship – and you can only just live on it, if you don't expect help from home – and I don't.

[*As he continues to regard her impersonally*]

Well – what else is wrong ? You seem a bit of an expert.

REX: I am. Now – suppose you take off your glasses –

[*She does.*]

and then pull your hair back – and then up – let me take your cigarette – no, not quite like that – farther back – then up –

[*He does, then, following his instructions, she pulls her hair back in a much more becoming fashion. She now looks quite different, quite attractive, and smiles at him uncertainly.*]

Makes a tremendous difference. You'd be surprised. Now any sensible young man would want to kiss you.

[*She does not react to this, but still holds her face up, smiling uncertainly.*]

I mean more or less – like this.

[*He bends down and kisses her, neatly and warmly but not passionately. When he steps back again, she releases her hair, gives a queer choking little sob, turns her face away, and fumbles for a handkerchief.*]

Oh I say. This is all wrong. I didn't mean –

EDITH [*cutting in, chokingly*]: No, it's not you. . . . I didn't mind . . . it's something quite different . . . suddenly I felt so miserable . . . as if everything is so hopeless . . . oh where's my rotten handkerchief ?

REX [*offering his*]: Take mine.

[*She does, and dabs at her eyes.*]

Why should you suddenly feel miserable – as if everything was hopeless ?

EDITH [*brokenly*]: I don't know – I'm a silly fool – it's all so muddled up –

REX: Never mind. What's the essay about this week ?

EDITH [*still weepily*]: Charles the Fifth.

REX: Here, try the cigarette again.

[*Gives it to her. She puts it in her mouth and now puts her glasses on again.*]

Do you care about Charles the Fifth ?

EDITH [*rather desperately*]: No, I've tried – and Professor Linden's so kind – and I must do well – they're all expecting me to, at home – and my essay is so dull and stupid –

REX [*softly*]: I'll tell you a secret about Charles the Fifth, if you promise not to mention it to my father.

EDITH [*a mess of smoking, half crying and laughing*]: All right. What is it ?

REX: Charles the Fifth doesn't matter a sausage. I haven't thought about him for years, and I'm having a hell of a good time.

EDITH: Yes, but it's different for you. There's no money at home – and I only just managed to get this scholarship –

REX: You stop worrying, and make the best of yourself and of everything else. What's your name ?

EDITH: Edith Westmore.

REX: Well, Edith, that's my advice to you. Start living. There isn't much time.

EDITH: Isn't much time for what ?

REX: For anything. And none for Charles the Fifth. He had his share. We'd better take ours while we can.

EDITH: It's all right talking like that. But I believe you're just making fun of me.

REX: I'm not. Never was more serious in my life. I tell you, there isn't much time.

[*There is a pause, while she looks at him dubiously and he stares quite sombrely at her. Then* DINAH *enters, carrying a 'cello case and a pile of music and books. She is eighteen, and a young eighteen, and a very clear eager personality, quite different from anybody else in the play, as if she belonged to another race.*]

DINAH: Rex!

REX [*who is clearly fond of her*]: Hello, Dinah! [*He goes up, kisses her on the cheek and rumples her hair, already untidy.*]

DINAH: Sorry I wasn't here when you came – did you bring Jean and Marion – ?

REX: Yes.

DINAH: Good. Well, I just had to go to orchestra practice.

REX: And how was it?

DINAH: Gosh! – we were awful. [*She now notices* EDITH.] Hello!

EDITH [*subdued*]: Hello!

DINAH: Isn't Daddy back yet? I think he's trying to buy some sherry. It's his birthday today and we're having a sort of family gathering.

EDITH: Perhaps I'd better go.

DINAH: I shouldn't, now you're here. Hang on a bit. Yes, we were quite peculiarly awful this afternoon. Were you ever in the orchestra, Rex?

REX: Yes, I played the triangle and the tambourine one term – about the time of the Great Depression. What is it murdering now?

DINAH: Dvorak's *New World*. And this afternoon we got all the parts boxed up, and one time Mary Stockfield – that's the other 'cello – and I were playing the third movement when everybody else had gone back to the first. I thought it sounded rather interesting – a bit like Bartok – but old Nubby, who's our conductor, hated it and danced with rage. How are Jean and Marion?

REX: Inclined to be quarrelsome types. Partly ideology. In the car it was like giving a lift to Thomas Aquinas and Lenin. And then for a bonus you have to add feminine sniffiness and odd jealousies. They're much better apart, those girls.

DINAH: I must go and talk to them. I hope you brought Daddy a lovely present. After all, you're the rich one in this family.

REX: I am and I did. A case of pipes – very special. Took a lot of finding, let me tell you –

DINAH [*who is still near door*]: Sh! I think he's here. [*Opens door and calls*] Daddy, they're here.

REX [*going towards door, calling*]: And this is me – Rex. [*Goes out, leaving door open.*]

[DINAH *smiles at* EDITH, *who rises rather nervously.*]

EDITH: I'm sure he won't want to bother with me tonight.

DINAH: Well, you can see – though it is all rather special tonight. Doesn't that gloomy boy usually come with you on Fridays?

EDITH: Yes. Bernard Fawcett. I don't know what's happened to him.

DINAH: Just brooding somewhere, I expect. Well, I must go and see my sisters. Haven't seen them for ages.

[EDITH *takes her essay out of her case, still standing up. Then* PROFESSOR LINDEN *comes in. He is carelessly dressed but has a certain distinction. He looks his age and is obviously rather tired, yet there is a kind of youthfulness about him.*]

PROFESSOR: Hello, Dinah! Good rehearsal?

DINAH: Awful!

[DINAH *exits.*]

PROFESSOR: I hope you haven't been waiting long, Miss Westmore. I hadn't forgotten, but I was held up. Do sit down. Where's Fawcett?

EDITH [*sitting down*]: I don't know, Professor Linden. I haven't seen him this afternoon.

PROFESSOR [*filling a pipe*]: Well, we'll have to do without him.

EDITH: Professor Linden, I thought – perhaps – as all your family are here – you probably wouldn't want to bother about us tonight.

PROFESSOR: No, no. But I won't keep you long, if you don't mind. Is that your paper? Thank you.

[*She hands it over. He lights his pipe before looking at it, sitting on edge of arm-chair.*]

EDITH [*timidly*]: Can I say – Many Happy Returns – ?

PROFESSOR [*smiling*]: You can – and thank you very much. Sixty-five, you know. I ought to feel something special, and I've been trying all day and can't manage it. The last time I felt something quite definite was when I was forty – and I've never felt quite so old since. Now then – [*He begins skimming through the essay with a practised eye, then breaks off to take up a portfolio and hand it to her.*] You'll find some reproductions of old Peter Breughel in there. Have a look at 'em. He's a great favourite of mine. Earthy and elfish at the same time. Real life but with bits of magic starting to work. Look at the Winter and the Summer and the peasants boozing and romping.

[*As she does, there is a knock.*]

Come in.

[BERNARD FAWCETT *enters. He is a rather dour, aggressive youth, who has a cold. He is shabbily dressed and carries some books.*]

FAWCETT [*thick and sniffy*]: I'm sorry I'm late. I went to the chemist's and couldn't get served.

PROFESSOR: I was late myself. And I'll have to cut you short tonight, I'm afraid. A family reunion here. Let's have your essay – and sit down.

[FAWCETT *hands over his paper, and sits down.* PROFESSOR *now glances quickly at this one, as he did at* EDITH's. *After a moment or two of this, he glances at* FAWCETT.]

Dull, isn't it ? [*Waving paper.*]

FAWCETT: I expect it is. When I have a cold I can't get interested somehow.

PROFESSOR: Miss Westmore couldn't either. All a long way off – and who cares ?

EDITH [*looking up*]: I'm sorry, Professor Linden.

PROFESSOR: How do you like those Breughels ? Fascinating, aren't they ?

EDITH: Yes – but I'd like to look at them a long time.

PROFESSOR: You can, if you like. Take 'em away with you. But the point is – that man was one of Charles the Fifth's subjects. And, allowing for old Breughel's temperament, you have to see Charles against that sort of background. Makes a difference, doesn't it ?

EDITH [*impressed*]: Why – yes – somehow I never thought –

PROFESSOR: No, you saw it as a lot of dim stuff in a book to be mugged up this week for old Linden. So did Fawcett. Didn't you, Fawcett ? With real life roaring all round you. Tell me – weren't you two both mixed up in that recent row about girl students at the Union ?

EDITH [*eagerly*]: Yes, I was. And I don't care what anybody says –

FAWCETT [*cutting in, alive now*]: Wait a minute, before you start talking. I'll bet the Professor doesn't know –

EDITH [*cutting in, sharply*]: Oh – I don't mind telling him how it all began. It wasn't our fault, not to begin with –

FAWCETT [*cutting in, louder*]: Of course it was. If you girls hadn't insisted –

EDITH [*cutting in, louder*]: We had a perfect right to insist. Look, Professor Linden, this is what happened –

PROFESSOR [*firmly*]: Miss Westmore, I don't really want to know.

EDITH [*disappointed*]: Oh – I thought you did.

PROFESSOR: No, I only wanted to show you both what history really is. And among other things – it's the row about the Union. And now it's come to life, hasn't it ? It's important. It's serious. It's urgent. And each of you is ready to talk for the next hour about it at full speed. Now remember what you felt when you were writing these things – dead as mutton – [*indicates the two essays*]. Let's forget about them, shall we ? [*Tears them up neatly and drops them into wastepaper basket. Then he rummages in his pockets, finally producing a square invitation card.*] This – is a ticket – to admit two – to a meeting – probably an Indignation Meeting – of the Burmanley Citizens' Vigilant Society – to be held tomorrow afternoon in the Town Hall. Our friend Professor Crockett is among the speakers, and Crockett's always worth hearing. Now I suggest you go together, note-book in hand, to this meeting, and each write an essay for me – On the Influence of Tudor England upon the Burmanley Citizens' Vigilant Society.

FAWCETT [*astonished*]: *Tudor* England ?

PROFESSOR [*firmly*]: Tudor England – and the Burmanley Citizens' etc., etc.

EDITH: But how can it ? I mean, there won't be any possible connexion between Tudor England – and – and this meeting –

PROFESSOR: Well, if there isn't, then say so. But I think there's sure to be. Even without going to the meeting, I can think of several possibly important links.

FAWCETT [*who has risen*]: We can try anyhow. [*Hesitates.*] Professor Linden, can I ask you something – ?

PROFESSOR: Yes. Charles the Fifth ?

FAWCETT: No, sir. What do you think's the best for a cold ?

PROFESSOR: My dear chap, for sixty years I've been dosed with everything, beginning with eucalyptus and steadily progressing to sulphur drugs – M. and B. – this and that. I suggest prayer,

fasting and patience – and don't encourage the wretched thing
by *enjoying it*, so to speak. Try to think about something else –
European History, for instance –

[*Enter* MARION, *who stops when she sees the students.*]

MARION: Oh – I'm sorry, Father.

PROFESSOR: No, come in, Marion. We've finished. I've cheated
them out of fifty minutes tonight.

[*As* MARION *comes forward,*]

Two of my students – Miss Westmore – Mr Fawcett – my
daughter, Madame de Vaury.

[*They murmur* 'How d'you do', *both students standing.*]

Now – Fawcett – here's the ticket. Tomorrow afternoon, both of
you. And if my subject still doesn't make any sense to you, look
in sometime after tomorrow afternoon and tell me about it.
Borrow the portfolio if you like, Miss Westmore.

EDITH [*taking it, with her other things*]: Thank you very much.

PROFESSOR: And the same time here next week, if you don't look
in before – for help. [*He goes to door, holding it open for them
smiling.*] And I liked your letter in the Rag, Fawcett. Quite
wrong, every word of it, but I liked it. And keep taking a peep at
old Breughel, Miss Westmore. Good night. Good night!

EDITH and FAWCETT [*as they go*]: Good night, Professor Linden.

[*They go out. He closes the door and smiles at* MARION.]

PROFESSOR: Well – now.

[*She kisses him on the cheek.*]

MARION: Many happy returns, Father.

PROFESSOR [*holding her arm*]: Thank you, Marion.

MARION: And I've brought you a very nice present. Two bottles
of very good Armagnac.

PROFESSOR [*delighted*]: Armagnac! My dear girl, what a wonderful present. I haven't tasted any Armagnac for six or seven years
at least. Every single sip will be a holiday in France.

MARION: It's hard to get even in France now. But René managed
it. He sends his love. He couldn't possibly get away – he wanted
to come, of course.

PROFESSOR: And the children?

MARION: Fat and flourishing. I've brought some photographs.
You'll see.

PROFESSOR: Of course I shall see. [*Looks at her appraisingly.*]

You're looking well, Marion. Happily settled there now? The truth, mind. Just between us.

MARION: Yes, I *am* happily settled now. It wasn't easy at first – harder than I made it out to be – they were all very kind but they made me feel a stranger – French people of that class are terribly clannish and close –

PROFESSOR: I know. It must have been like trying to push your way into a haystack. And René's mother looked a cast-iron Balzacian terror to me – a grenadier of the Old Guard.

MARION: Well, it's all right now. And the Church part of it has helped a lot. That and the children. So now I'm one of them.

PROFESSOR: I suppose that's possible, if it's what you want to be. And, I remember you always wanted something different – somewhere round the corner. And this must be it.

MARION: Yes, and I feel even better about it now that I've come back here. [*With sudden feeling*] Oh – Dad, it's no use – I must tell you. I hate it here. It's so messy and drab and slovenly. I never liked it, but now it's much much worse. Look at those two who just went out – they were bad enough before the war, but they weren't as awful as that pair. I hate to think of you, being here, with that scruffy half-crazy Mrs Cotton slouching about the house – and trying to teach history to dreary, shabby little half-baked students like those two. Just the very look of them – !

PROFESSOR [*mildly*]: They're not my brightest. But they're better than they look. Perhaps we all are now. I know something about them – where they come from – how they struggled to get here – the odds against their being any good at all – and – well, I can't agree, my dear. This is Burmanley, you know.

MARION: Yes, and I never want to see it again. No, never, never. You must come and stay with us from now on, Father. That's what René says too.

PROFESSOR: I'll try, though holidays abroad aren't easy.

MARION: But Daddy you look so tired – and –

PROFESSOR: And old. Go on, say it.

MARION [*gently*]: Well, you do look much older, Dad – older than you ought to look. When I think of René's Uncle Gustave, who's years older than you really. It's coming from Vaury – and the life there – [*She breaks off, looks at him uncertainly.*] Can I say this, Dad?

PROFESSOR: You can say anything you like, my dear.

MARION: Mother says you have some money coming to you now, from your endowment insurance. You could easily find some official excuse – health or a book or something – to drop everything here and come and live near us at Vaury.

PROFESSOR: And why should we do that, Marion?

MARION: Because it's a much better life than you find here. Better in every way. It's still part of the old civilized tradition, Father. Especially if you could do as I've done – and become a Catholic. I can see that Father Honoré was right – that's the secret – the Faith. That – and the land – and all the old tradition of living. [*Rather defiantly*] I mean it, Father. At first I did it all for René, of course, but now I know it was worth doing for its own sake. I couldn't live any other way.

PROFESSOR [*easily but with some gravity*]: That's your affair, Marion. I always said it was, and never tried to interfere, did I?

MARION: No. Mother did a bit, at first. But not you.

PROFESSOR: So if it's what you want, and it satisfies you –

MARION: More than that – makes me deeply happy –

PROFESSOR: Then that's all right. But you mustn't try to give it to me. Or to most of us. We tried it once – the peasants – the proprietors in their castles – the priests – the whole tradition – and then it didn't work. It doesn't work now, except in spots here and there. And those places really depend on other places, like Burmanley here, for instance. There's another side to the medal, Marion – a very dark side too. Sometimes as black as the shirts of Fascist bullies or the faces of the Moors let loose in Spain. You're living a very pleasant life, no doubt, my dear, but it can't solve a single major human problem –

MARION: It's solved mine.

PROFESSOR: But not mine – not ours – not the world's. No, my dear, I'd feel as if I were living in the Palm House at Kew. All right for a holiday – but –

[JEAN *enters. He turns and sees her.*]

Well, Jean!

JEAN: Hello, Father. Many happy returns!

[*They kiss.*]

I've brought you some books, I left them upstairs. Beckel's new social history is one of them.

PROFESSOR: Thank you, my dear. I'll enjoy disliking Beckel again – two parts Marx, one part Freud, a dash of Pavlov, and sprinkle well with sociological jargon. Now I spent half an hour this evening acquiring a bottle of what is probably not much better than cooking sherry. I'll go and uncork the muck for us. [*He goes out.*]

[JEAN *goes and sits down.*]

MARION [*after pause*]: How do you think father is looking?

JEAN [*with professional calm*]: Not too bad – he's sixty-five, you know.

MARION: You've seen him since I have. I had rather a shock. I think he looks tired – and older than he ought to look. I've just told him so.

JEAN: That must have cheered him up.

MARION [*bitterly*]: I suppose he's probably another of the people you think might as well be dead.

JEAN [*angry, but calm*]: Don't invent stupid insensitive things like that and then put them into my mouth. Though it's rather typical, that trick.

MARION: Typical of – what?

JEAN: Of you nice old-fashioned Christian souls. I've often noticed it.

[*They are silent for a moment, angry with each other, glaring.*]

MARION: I believe the only explanation is, Jean, that you're jealous of me.

JEAN: What? René and your stuffy little chateau –

MARION: No. But jealous of what I'm feeling – my peace of mind.

JEAN: We've got bottles and bottles of your peace of mind in the dispensary. We inject it into the bad cases –

MARION [*losing her temper*]: Oh – don't be such a conceited fool. *And* so childish!

JEAN [*angrily*]: Well – really – after the infantilism you've treated me to, for the last eight hours –

MARION [*angrily*]: Oh – shut up!

[*As they glare at each other,* DINAH, *who now looks tidier, enters with a tray with small glasses on it.*]

DINAH [*cheerfully*]: What you two ought to do is to take some whacking great wallops at each other – and then you'd feel better.

JEAN: I don't say you're wrong, but for all that – don't be cheeky.

DINAH: All right, but don't go and muck up Daddy's birthday between you. And, look here, what's the idea of everybody turning up for it this time?

MARION: Well, can't the family get together for once?

DINAH: Yes, of course. But there isn't somehow a nice Christ-massy getting-togetherness about all this – it's more like business – like characters in old plays and novels all coming to hear the will of the late Sir Jasper read out by Mr Groggins, the old family solicitor. So what's the idea?

MARION: It's to clear up one or two things. About Dad retiring – and so forth.

DINAH: He won't retire – and it looks like a plot to me. There's a plotty atmosphere about, particularly round Mother. [*She looks at them, and suddenly laughs.*]

JEAN: Now what is it?

DINAH: I suddenly remembered that time – oh, years ago when I was quite little – when we were staying in North Wales – and you two had a row about toothpaste or something.

MARION [*smiling*]: It was cold cream stuff for sunburn – and we fought – do you remember, Jean?

JEAN: Yes – and the stuff came out and went over everything.

DINAH [*sitting on arm of chair*]: That was a heavenly place – it smelt of whitewash and cows, and had gigantic fluffy brown hens – and I was just part of it – magic. That's what I don't like about growing up. You stop being part of places like that. You just look at them as if they were in a shop window. You're not swallowed up by them any more. And what do you get in exchange – by growing up?

JEAN: Consciousness – a more highly developed ego.

DINAH: I know. I can feel mine having growing pains. But I doubt if it's worth it. Marion, Mother said if you really want to add a few fancy French tastings and touches to the dinner, now's the time. And Rex is messing about in there trying to do something but I don't know what.

MARION [*rising*]: I can't be worse than Rex.

[*She goes out.*]

JEAN [*rising*]: Dinah, where's Dad?

DINAH: Trying to find the corkscrew. He always loses it.

JEAN [*quietly and quickly*]: I want to put through a call to the hospital. If I can get through, will you please rush out and hold Dad up a minute or two until I've had my call?

DINAH: All right.

[*As* JEAN *goes up to the telephone,*]

I'll bet this isn't hospital work, though – but some love business – some man you're miserable about –

JEAN [*at telephone*]: Is that Trunks? This is Burmanley – Two Five Eight One Three – and I want Northern – London – Five Four Eight Four. . . . Yes, I'll wait . . .

DINAH: Isn't it?

JEAN: Yes, it is.

DINAH [*coolly*]: I guessed it. I knew you were miserable anyhow. But this is more like Marion than you. I thought you considered this romantic sort of love a lot of silly old-fashioned rot.

JEAN: I do. But that doesn't make it any better, does it?

DINAH: No, I suppose it might make it worse. Because you couldn't *enjoy* being miserable.

JEAN [*bitterly*]: And might despise yourself too. [*To telephone*] Is that the North Middlesex? Dr Linden here – put me through to Dr Shalgrove, please. . . . [*To* DINAH, *urgently*] Go on, Dinah. Hurry – please!

[DINAH, *who has wandered up towards door, hurries out.*]

[*To telephone*] Dr Shalgrove, please. . . . Oh, Dorothy, this is Jean. Yes, I'm speaking from Burmanley. I must know about Arnold. Has he gone? [*With an effort*] I see. And no message for me at all – not a word? . . . I see – just gone – like that. . . . No, I'm all right . . . tomorrow night, I hope. . . . [*With a greater effort*] By the way, Dorothy, I forgot to leave a message to Crosfield – that he ought to look at that child in Five . . . yes, that's the one, and I'm not satisfied . . . yes . . . yes . . . good-bye, Dorothy. [*She puts down the telephone slowly, and comes down rather blindly, fighting her emotions. She sits down, trembling, gives a choked kind of sob, clenching her fists, fighting hard.*]

[PROFESSOR LINDEN *now enters carrying two different bottles, one of sherry, the other without a label. He gives a glance at* JEAN, *who has not looked round, and takes in her situation, so that we feel that his speech that follows is giving her a chance to recover. As he talks, he potters a bit with the bottles and glasses.*]

PROFESSOR [*beginning as he enters*]: Well, we've a choice of two aperitifs – my sherry, which may or may not be any good, and a mysterious concoction that Rex has brought, specially put up for him by one of his favourite barmen. It'll probably make us all roaring drunk. Except Rex, of course, who probably has it for breakfast. [*He pours out a little, and sniffs it.*] It smells like something that probably goes with Big Business in Shanghai. We'd better try it, I suppose. [*Slowly, while talking, he pours out several glasses of this stuff, of a dark amber shade.*] It's a curious thing about Rex. He does, with complete ease, all the things I wouldn't know how to begin to do – such as compelling important West End barmen to mix bottles of this stuff – hob-nobbing with head-waiters – sitting up late with millionaires – and making money just by making it. All the things I've probably secretly wanted to do all my life. Rex is just busy representing my unconscious self. You too, in a way, Jean, for all that opening up of people, and cutting and stitching inside 'em, which you do without turning a hair, is precisely what's awed and terrified me as long as I can remember. You and Rex – you're the Lindens in reverse, so to speak. Not Marion – she's too completely feminine. But there's Dinah, though. Now she's unblushingly blazingly happy, which is something most of us older ones haven't dared to be for years and years and years. It's as if human nature, which doesn't propose to give in, is now producing a new race, like Dinah, who can't be downed by anything.

JEAN [*not turning, muffled*]: There's a lot she doesn't know yet.

PROFESSOR: I don't believe it'll make any difference when she does. [*Hands her a glass, holding one himself.*] Now try this, my dear. And – your health, Dr Linden. [*Drinking.*]

JEAN [*doing her best*]: And yours – Professor. [*She takes a sip.*]

PROFESSOR: Got a warm disreputable flavour –

JEAN [*with an effort*]: I've – had it before – once or twice. [*She gives a sort of gulp.*] Oh – damn! You know something's wrong, don't you?

PROFESSOR: Yes. Tell me if you want to.

JEAN [*turning now, urgently*]: I can't. But I thought you guessed I wasn't feeling – very bright. Oh – I get so impatient with myself. Why can't we be as hard as steel ?

PROFESSOR: Because it would do us more harm than good. The dinosaurs had that idea – it was probably the only idea they did have – and so they grew more and more armour, thicker and thicker scales, bigger and bigger claws and spikes – all to be hard and tough and safe – until they were like hundred-ton tanks – and couldn't move, couldn't feed themselves, couldn't mate – and were done for. Then came the turn of the soft little monkey people, who could adapt themselves – us.

JEAN: And are we going to manage it ?

PROFESSOR: Probably touch-and-go. On the whole I think – Yes. But not by wanting to be as hard as steel. That's asking to be broken. [*He puts a hand on her shoulder.*] Jean, my dear – just take it easy.

[*Impulsively she turns and puts her cheek against his hand, and whispers.*]

JEAN: All right, Dad. I'll try. And – thank you.

[*Enter* REX, *carrying a handsome case of pipes.*]

REX [*holding out the case*]: Here they are, Dad. And easily the pick of the market.

PROFESSOR [*who has turned, taking case*]: Why – Rex, my boy – these are prodigious. Thank you – thank you. I didn't know there were such pipes any more.

REX [*taking glass*]: There aren't. I had to comb London for 'em. Collectors' pieces really. Been in that case for years and years, the chap told me. Well, Dad – cheers for the Birthday. [*He drinks, then smacks his lips.*] Very fond of this stuff.

[*Enter* MRS LINDEN, MARION *and* DINAH.]

MRS LINDEN: Mrs Cotton's just dishing up, but we've time for one of these drinks we've heard so much about.

REX [*gaily*]: There's Dad's sherry – or the stuff I brought, *Later Than You Think*.

MRS LINDEN: What do you mean, dear ?

REX: That's the name I gave it – the barman couldn't think of one. From the old Chinese saying – 'Enjoy yourself – it's later than you think.'

MRS LINDEN [*gaily*]: I don't know what you're talking about, darling, but give me just a little – please.

MARION: And sherry for me, Rex.

DINAH: Me too, please.

[REX *pours his stuff for his mother, while the* PROFESSOR *pours out sherry for the other two.* REX *then fills the glasses of* JEAN *and the* PROFESSOR *and his own again, throughout the following speeches.*]

MRS LINDEN [*happily*]: Well now, I call this a thoroughly sensible way for a family to behave –

REX: You mean – all tippling, eh?

MRS LINDEN [*beaming on him*]: I mean, being all together under one roof – instead of scattered all over the place. Well – now – [*preparing to drink*].

DINAH: We all drink to Daddy.

MARION: Yes, of course.

REX [*grinning*]: To the gnarled old trunk of the Linden tree!

MRS LINDEN: He's not gnarled. And anyhow – what about me?

REX: You're not the trunk – you're the roots –

MRS LINDEN [*who has had a sip*]: It's terribly strong – isn't it?

JEAN [*standing now*]: Yes, it always was. [*Drains her glass in one go.*]

MRS LINDEN: Jean, are you all right?

PROFESSOR [*hastily*]: Yes, she's all right. And I thank you for the Toast – [*burlesquing after-dinner speaker*] both for the terms in which it has been proposed and the way in which you have received it –

REX [*similar burlesque*]: Hear – hear!

[MRS COTTON, *wearing apron and looking hot and rather flustered, appears at door.*]

MRS COTTON: Well, I like to see everybody 'appy for a change – but you'd better go in an' eat that dinner 'cos it's in now an' getting cold –

[*She disappears, and laughing a little, the others all turn and move towards door, as curtain comes down.*]

    This is the end of Scene One.

    House lights do not go up, and curtain remains down only long enough for bottles and glasses to be cleared, curtains drawn across window R. *and lighting to be changed, for night.*]

SCENE TWO

[*When curtain rises again, it is two hours later. Stage is empty a moment, then* PROFESSOR, *carrying tray with bottle of Armagnac and several glasses, enters with* REX, *who is lighting a cigar. After* PROFESSOR *puts down tray – during first speeches – he lights one of his new pipes. There is an intimate after-dinner atmosphere between the two men.*]

PROFESSOR: Rex, being a parent I have to pretend to understand you, but as a matter of fact I don't. What do you do and what are you up to?

REX [*stretching out, comfortably*]: It's so simple that hardly anybody believes me. First, what do I do? Well, I make money – by buying stocks and shares – and then selling them at a handsome profit – all for myself, not for other people. I'm not a broker.

PROFESSOR: You must have some kind of flair for it.

REX: I have. But it's easy, believe me. You work ten times as hard as I do. And now I'm worth, well, what do you think?

PROFESSOR: I've no idea. More than I am, certainly.

REX: At least a hundred and fifty thousand, at this minute.

PROFESSOR: Good God! It's incredible. But how have you managed it – in this short time?

REX: Jock Mitchell was killed by the same mortar that knocked me out in Italy. He was my best friend. When I came home I found he'd left me all he had – but you know all this. I came in for a nice little packet of stocks and shares that poor Jock hadn't bothered about. After I recovered and was sent to the War House, I began playing about with 'em. Made money. Made more money. Got in the know. Paid no taxes, don't forget. Lived well, but still piled it up. Every time some bit of news made the fools in the City feel shaky, I bought. The minute they felt better again, I sold.

PROFESSOR: It couldn't be as easy as that.

REX: It was. Plus some information and perhaps, as you say, a flair for it. As to what I'm up to – that's quite simple too – I'm enjoying myself – while there's time.

PROFESSOR: You don't see it lasting, you mean.

REX: I don't see anything lasting. If you ask me, we've had it. And you can take your choice between a lot of Trade Union officials giving themselves jobs and titles or Tory Big Business screaming to get back into the trough. All the same racket. Either way we've had it. We can't last. And anyhow when the atom bombs and rockets really start falling, whichever side sends 'em, it's about ten to one we'll be on the receiving end here. I've sometimes thought of clearing out – South America, for instance, or East Africa – but somehow I feel that wouldn't do. So I'll take what's coming. But before then I propose to enjoy myself.

PROFESSOR [*regarding him steadily*]: I believe you're quite serious.

REX: Not a serious type as a rule – do a lot of clowning – but for once – and purely out of respect for you and this occasion – I'm in deadly earnest. What about some of Marion's Armagnac?

PROFESSOR: Sorry. I'd forgotten.

REX [*rising*]: I'll do it. [*Goes to pour out brandy.*]

PROFESSOR: Thanks. I don't agree with you, of course.

REX: Naturally. I didn't expect you to.

PROFESSOR: But we won't argue. That's not the point. I simply want to understand. All this of course is a reaction, first, from what you were before the war, and then from soldiering – the usual dose of post-war cynicism.

REX [*handing brandy*]: No doubt. But it's not a mood. It's permanent. For instance, not long ago, I broke with a young woman because she wanted us to marry and produce children. Nothing doing. So I broke it off – though I was very devoted to her. I wouldn't mention that to mother, by the way. She'd want to know all about it, and start worrying.

PROFESSOR: She would. And I could do a little worrying, myself. Doesn't it occur to you, by the way, that if we're drifting to disaster, you might try using some of your money and wits and energy in some kind of attempt to stop it.

REX [*after a sip*]: Damned good brandy!

PROFESSOR [*who has also tried it*]: Isn't it?

REX: You mean – politics, eh?

PROFESSOR: If necessary – yes.

REX [*feeling in his pockets*]: The other night I was reading some of Waley's translations of old Chinese poems, and one of them particularly took my fancy so I copied it out. [*He has found it now, and reads it out*] It's called *The Big Chariot*.

> 'Don't help on the big chariot;
>   You will only make yourself dusty.
> Don't think about the sorrows of the world;
>   You will only make yourself wretched.
>
> Don't help on the big chariot;
>   You won't be able to see for dust.
> Don't think about the sorrows of the world;
>   Or you will never escape from your despair.'

[*Puts it away.*] And I couldn't agree with him more. I wish I could dig that poet out of his grave and ask him to stay with me at Huntingdon House for a few weeks – we'd laugh ourselves sick. Don't look so depressed, Dad. You're not responsible for me any more, and you did your best to turn me into a fine thoughtful public-spirited citizen.

PROFESSOR: Perhaps I did it the wrong way. That's what I'm wondering. I'm not depressed. I'm wondering. You've changed completely. What happened? That interests me.

REX: First, losing Jock – and some of the other chaps. Then that spell at the War House – and war-time London. But even then I was still ready to put my shoulder to one of the back wheels of the big chariot – and be as dusty as hell – if somebody big enough had shouted 'Come on, chaps. Throw in everything you've got. Either we'll work miracles or go down fighting.' Something like that. The words don't matter. But the mood does, and the inspiration – just to have one good crack at it before the bombs came again – or perhaps they would never come if we showed the world a great example – gave 'em all hope again. Look – I'm talking too much – and most of it bullsh, I suppose –

PROFESSOR: No, it makes sense to me. You were ready – if somebody gave you a lift –

REX: Yes. But not a sausage. So I said to myself 'All right, Rex, you pack it up – earn some easy – and play.' And I do enjoy myself – don't you believe those people who tell you that you can't nowadays – they don't know enough. Oh – you can't in

Burmanley but you can where I live – if you know a few chaps and have the money.

[*Enter* JEAN. REX *turns and sees her. Just in time for a little serious conversation.*]

JEAN [*coming down*]: There'll be some coffee in a minute.

PROFESSOR: Have some brandy, Jean?

JEAN: Not just now, thank you. Is Rex telling you how to make money without working for it?

PROFESSOR: No, he's been explaining why he believes in making money without working for it. Eh, Rex?

REX: Fair enough. Mine's the Spiv philosophy now – only mugs work. It's everybody for himself, isn't it? Nobody's shown me anything else for the last few years. Most of the place looking like a fourth-rate factory and a dingy fun-fair – a nasty little mess of silly cheap newspapers, greyhound tracks, football pools, squealing capitalists, trades unionists on the make, sleep-walking civil servants, kids wanting to behave like touts or tarts –

PROFESSOR: Not much to enjoy then?

REX: Oh yes – if you just push it all away and forget about it. And that's where money comes in. You can buy a high wall or two – and bid for a little civilized amusement behind them. Look at Jean. I run into her now and again – with her boy friend – and they'd try to convert me. What's his name – I mean, the surgeon chap at your place?

JEAN [*very carefully*]: Arnold French. He's just left, by the way.

REX [*looking at her curiously*]: Has he now? I thought you and he –

PROFESSOR [*cutting in, deliberately*]: Convert you to what?

REX [*grinning, to* JEAN]: Tell him.

JEAN [*coldly*]: It doesn't matter. I don't want to talk about it. And Rex wouldn't want to talk so much if he didn't know he was all wrong, with his delicious undergraduate's cynicism and Epi-curean muck. We – I mean, I happen to believe in science and a properly planned community – and discipline – and work –

REX: And forced labour camps for anybody who won't join in –

JEAN [*coolly*]: Yes – and why not? I've no use for people who won't face a few hard facts –

REX: You haven't much use for people of any kind, my dear Jean, except a few interesting patients – and your handsome Arnold –

JEAN [*suddenly furious*]: Oh – for God's sake – shut up, you fool!

REX [*staring*]: Look – Jeanie – I'm sorry. I didn't realize –

JEAN: Oh – drop it. [*She recovers herself by a great effort. Then speaks in a low, bitter tone*] I'm just not going to run away and bawl in a bedroom.

PROFESSOR: There's probably something to be said for it, though. An old custom.

JEAN [*same tone*]: I don't like old customs. And I hate all the idiotic feminine fusses and tantrums – and I've seen enough of them. And what's the use of asking for a disciplined scientific society, if I can't even discipline myself – a woman with a good scientific training?

PROFESSOR: All right, my dear. Only don't imagine that a scientific training turned you into somebody from another planet. You're still just one of us, you know – the same old muddled emotional gang, who've been here for a few hundred thousand years. And don't try to fight all your feminine ancestors – there are too many of them. Better to come to terms with 'em.

REX [*getting up*]: And have some Armagnac now – do you good.

JEAN [*with a faint smile*]: All right, Rex. And – sorry for the outburst. [*He gets some brandy for her.*]

PROFESSOR: We have a new Vice-Chancellor here – a Dr Lidley.

REX: I know. What's he like?

PROFESSOR [*gloomily*]: He's an educationalist. He educationalizes – in quite a big dashing sort of way. It's something quite different from educating people – newer and much better. They'll probably have machines to do it soon, when they can import them from America. Two of my oldest friends here – Tilley and Clark – have already resigned. I believe he's hoping I'll go next. I won't say I see it in his eye, because he always gives me the extraordinary impression that he has two glass eyes, which must be wrong. But there it is.

[REX *and* JEAN *exchange glances, which* PROFESSOR *notices at once. He continues calmly.*]

Fortunately you two haven't that kind of eye. Far more expressive. But what exactly did those glances mean?

JEAN: We were wondering – at least I know I was – why you should think it worth while going on here.

REX: Right. Dad, why not pack it up now?

PROFESSOR: We can't all pack it up, as you call it, Rex. And one packed-up man in a family is probably quite enough. As for you, Jean, who are not a packer-up, well, I'm surprised at *you*.

JEAN [*softly*]: You're sixty-five now, Dad.

PROFESSOR: And one day, Jean, I hope, you'll be sixty-five – and then you may know what I'm feeling now –

JEAN [*contrite*]: Dad, please, I didn't mean –

PROFESSOR [*cutting in, but gently*]: I know you didn't, nobody does. They just say it, but don't mean what they think I think they mean. Mind you, I'll say this. Sixty-five is probably oldish for science. But history's different. You really know more about it – have the feel of it better – when you're sixty-five than when you're forty-five – or even twenty-five –

[*Enter* DINAH, *with a tray of cups filled with coffee.*]

Coffee, Dinah?

DINAH [*going to put tray down*]: Coffee it is. And I made it myself while the others were finishing the washing-up – and all talking about babies. There must be something wrong with me – un-womanly or something – because I hate talk about babies. Mrs Cotton told a mad *gruesome* story about a baby that turned blue in the blitz. Mrs Cotton's never come out of the blitz really. In a kind of way she loves it. [*Looks at the three of them sharply.*] You've been quarrelling here, haven't you?

REX [*getting up to help with coffee*]: No, we haven't.

DINAH: Well, that's what it feels like to me.

REX: You rather fancy yourself as the intuitive type, don't you?

DINAH [*coolly*]: Yes, I do. [*She takes a cup of coffee to* JEAN, *gives it to her, then impulsively bends down and kisses her on the cheek.*]

JEAN [*half-smiling*]: But why, Dinah?

DINAH: I just felt like it, that's all. Don't you go and imagine – just because you're a doctor now – you're high above all that sort of thing.

JEAN [*with a bitter smile*]: It might be better if I did.

PROFESSOR: No, it wouldn't. Otherwise, in a few years you might easily go sour. I've known several good clever people who went sour. After forty's the danger. If you're a professor, you call it sound scholarship, integrity and fastidiousness – but really they're old skim milk turned green. And then they begin to hate ordinary stupid people.

JEAN: And is that such a bad thing?

PROFESSOR [*sipping his coffee now*]: It's fatal. Even if we don't think we're ordinary stupid people ourselves – and we probably are – we're all rooted in ordinary stupid humanity. And try to cut your roots, and you're done for. Quite good coffee, Dinah.

DINAH [*solemnly*]: I added a pinch of salt.

REX [*who has tried his coffee*]: And a pretty big pinch too, young Dinah.

[*Enter* MRS LINDEN *and* MARION, *who are talking hard.*]

MRS LINDEN: Well, that's the trouble here now. Nobody cares how things are done – they just slop about and take the least possible trouble – and if you dare to complain, they don't hesitate to be rude at once – yes, at once.

MARION: I couldn't help noticing the difference, particularly this time. I don't say it's much better in the French cities, but in the country there's still a tradition – of taking trouble, and proper service, and politeness.

MRS LINDEN: Well, it's quite hopeless here now.

DINAH [*handing cups*]: I don't believe it *is* hopeless at all.

MRS LINDEN: You don't know what we're talking about, child.

DINAH: I do. People in shops – and waitresses – and all that. And I think they're all right – nice and matey – considering.

MRS LINDEN: You don't remember anything better.

MARION: Just what I was going to say. You're too young to be in this, Dinah.

PROFESSOR: I'm not, though. And I know what you mean. I remember when most of these people you're talking about were terrified that one or two complaints would throw 'em out into the street and back to the Labour Exchange. You could see that fear in their eyes, hear it in their apologetic voices, and I hated it so much that I never dared to make any complaints.

MRS LINDEN: You were always much too easy-going.

PROFESSOR: No, no. But now I can grumble like mad, and they can grumble back at me, and I feel much better about it.

DINAH [*proudly*]: Daddy had a blazing row with the man at the bookshop. Didn't you, Daddy?

PROFESSOR: Yes, but I thought he won on points. [*Catching his wife's eye*] What is it, my dear?

MRS LINDEN: Well, we're all here. I think we ought to talk about the money –

PROFESSOR: What money?

MRS LINDEN: The endowment insurance. It was your idea. But Rex knows all about it, and perhaps it would be better if he explained to the others.

REX [to his father]: I think it might, you know.

PROFESSOR: Well, you're the financial genius. Not that this needs one.

REX [specially to JEAN and MARION]: No, it's as simple as pie. For years and years, ever since we were in the nursery in fact, Dad's been paying premiums on an endowment insurance. I don't know how he did it on his princely salary –

PROFESSOR: There were always extras – royalties on my two or three books – outside examination fees – that sort of thing. But never mind about that.

REX: All right. The point is – now that he's sixty-five the money's due to arrive any moment. And the parents agreed that this was really a family insurance, for all of us to have some share if we needed it. That's partly why we're here.

PROFESSOR [with mild irony]: But we're quite glad to see you, even as shareholders –

MRS LINDEN: Now, Robert – this is serious –

REX: It's serious you should feel like this. We appreciate it. But apart from that, really it's all nonsense, you know. This money's all yours. We don't want any part of it.

PROFESSOR: We realize that you don't, my boy. But there are others.

REX: Well, let's see. [To JEAN and MARION] What do you say, girls?

JEAN: You can count me out. You spent a lot on my education – and the least I can do is to say I don't need any more money, and of course I don't.

MARION: Neither do I. I wouldn't dream of taking a penny. René and I are better off than you are.

DINAH [solemnly]: And I could probably manage somehow.

MRS LINDEN [hastily]: Don't be absurd, Dinah. We're not really talking to you.

DINAH: I don't see why not. A girl I know –

PROFESSOR [*cutting in, smiling*]: Your offer is noted, Miss
Linden, but not accepted. We shall be responsible for you for a
few years yet, whether you like it or not. [*To the others*] Now –
are you three quite sure ? Yes, you of course, Rex. But you two
girls –

JEAN: Of course we are.

MARION: And you need every penny of it yourselves.

MRS LINDEN: I knew that is what you'd all say.

PROFESSOR: Still, you had to be asked.

JEAN: You've your own future to consider. These are your savings
– almost all you have – and you're sixty-five –

PROFESSOR [*rather sharply*]: And still in full possession of my
faculties, and still Professor of Modern History in the University
of Burmanley.

MARION: Yes, but for how much longer ?

PROFESSOR [*again, rather sharply*]: Until I decide to resign the
Chair.

[*There is a ring at the telephone.* DINAH *runs to answer it.*]

DINAH [*at telephone*]: Hello! ... What ? ... Oh, yes he is – just a
sec. ... [*Turns, holding receiver*] It's for you, Rex. From London.

REX [*as he goes to telephone*]: This'll be Fraser – about the place in
Hampshire – you'll see. [*At telephone*] Yes – Rex Linden here.
... I thought he would ... probably tomorrow night. ... On
Monday if he likes. ... Yes, I'll do all that ... nice job, Fraser.
... 'Bye. [*Puts down telephone, turns, smiling.*]

MRS LINDEN [*excitedly*]: Rex – you've bought it ?

REX: I have. Behold the new owner and lord of the manor of
Four Elms, Childing, Hants. Four recept., ten bed, four bath –
billiard room, sun porch, hard tennis court, croquet lawn, large
garden, ten acres, small dairy – and butter for tea. You're all
invited.

DINAH: Gosh! – that's marvellous.

PROFESSOR: But you'll have to put some furniture and stuff into
it.

MRS LINDEN [*excitedly*]: No – everything's there – isn't it,
Rex ?

REX: Ready to walk into – even a man and wife on the premises.
It's a wonderful buy for twenty-five thousand, but I knew the
chap would never resist an offer of cash down at once.

MARION: But it's wasted on a bachelor. You'll simply have to get married now, Rex.

REX: Never. So don't try putting any of your old girl chums on to me. There's nothing doing. Incidentally, I don't propose to live there – only week-ends and holidays and so on. I'm keeping on my flat in Huntingdon House.

DINAH: You sound so grand. I can't ever believe you lived here.

PROFESSOR: This one didn't. It's another Rex who lived here.

JEAN: And perhaps we prefer him.

MRS LINDEN [*still excited*]: Now don't be silly, you two. Rex has done wonderfully well, and I'm proud of him. [*Turning to* REX] Now listen, darling – this settles it – you know?

REX: Yes, I think it does.

PROFESSOR: Settles what?

MRS LINDEN [*gaily*]: Shall we tell him? No, we'll wait a little while.

DINAH: There's plotting. I knew there was.

PROFESSOR: Well, I don't much like plotting.

MARION [*to* MRS LINDEN]: I know. And you might as well tell him now.

MRS LINDEN [*hastily*]: No, no, I have a special reason.

PROFESSOR [*lightly but with touch of gravity*]: I don't like the sound of this.

DINAH: We're out of it.

JEAN: Well, don't look at me. I don't know what it's about.

MRS LINDEN [*to* REX]: It makes just the difference – and settles everything perfectly.

PROFESSOR [*to* JEAN]: It's no use. Let's ignore them. Tell me, Dr Linden, what are your impressions of Burmanley after your recent absence from our city?

JEAN [*same manner*]: My immediate impression only confirms the opinion I have held for some time about your city – that it should be pulled down and then rebuilt, on some more civilized plan, as soon as possible.

[*The telephone rings.* JEAN *jumps up.*]

That may be for me. [*Goes to telephone.*]

DINAH: It won't be if you answer it. Somehow it never is.

JEAN [*at telephone*]: Yes, yes. . . . Oh! Yes, she is. . . . [*Turning*] For you, Mother. Mr Lockhart.

[MRS LINDEN *rises hastily, going to telephone.*]

PROFESSOR [*rising*]: Lockhart? That'll be for me. It must be Alfred Lockhart – of the University.

JEAN [*now returning*]: He said Mrs Linden quite distinctly.

MRS LINDEN: Yes?

PROFESSOR [*uncertainly, still standing*]: Oh well – if that's the case –

MRS LINDEN [*at telephone, eagerly*]: Yes, Mr Lockhart.... I see. ... You're certain?

PROFESSOR [*going up and across*]: Don't let him go.

MRS LINDEN [*turning*]: What? [*To telephone*] No, I was speaking to my husband.

PROFESSOR [*firmly*]: And I want to speak to him.

MRS LINDEN [*turning*]: Now, Robert –

PROFESSOR [*rather grimly*]: When you've finished, Isabel.

MRS LINDEN [*into telephone*]: He wants to speak to you.

> [*They look at each other for a moment as he takes the telephone.*
> MRS LINDEN *comes away but remains standing, looking rather tense.*]

PROFESSOR [*into telephone*]: Alfred – I don't want to know what you've been talking about to my wife – that's your business. But I'm wondering if you've anything you'd like me to know. .... Never mind being delicate about it, Alfred. We've known each other too long for that. ... No, I don't suppose you would choose this way of letting me know, but now I'm asking. ... [*Now he listens very gravely.*] ... I see.... No, no, I know that. ... But I don't propose to accept this, you know. No, not for a moment. I'll see you in the morning. ... By the way, was that what you were telling my wife.... Come on, now.... I thought as much. Well, you'll see me in the morning, Alfred – and I warn you, the fight's on. [*Puts down the telephone and looks hard at his wife.*] Isabel, I don't like the way that was done. Alfred Lockhart didn't sound happy about it either. Had you been speaking to him earlier?

MRS LINDEN: There's no need – to look and talk like that, Robert. I did have a word with him, because I wanted to know what might happen.

PROFESSOR: Why?

MRS LINDEN: Really, Robert – you needn't take that tone! I

wanted to know if possible while the children were here – so that if any arrangements had to be made –

PROFESSOR [*harshly*]: The only arrangements that have to be made are quite simple – I'm going to fight this decision by every possible means in my power.

MRS LINDEN: But why – why?

PROFESSOR [*curtly*]: Because there's work to be done here, and I'm still capable of doing it. [*Looks at the others, trying to smile.*] I've just been told that I shall be asked to resign my Chair. Officially because I've reached the official age limit, but we've had professors older than I am here for years now. Really, it's because I'm a nuisance. I'm too free-and-easy. I don't admire the mass-production and conveyor-belt system of education. I say *No* when important personages expect to hear *Yes*. And I propose to go on being a nuisance.

MARION: But, Dad, it simply isn't worth it – and if they don't want you, all right, what does it matter? You've done your share.

MRS LINDEN: Of course he has – more than his share – hanging on for years in this miserable place –

PROFESSOR [*with some warmth*]: You talk as if I were choosing a holiday resort. It's my life we're discussing. Or rather, we're not discussing – let's drop the subject. I'll go round in the morning, and point out that I still have a few friends round here.

REX: Now look, Dad –

PROFESSOR [*quietly*]: Drop it, Rex. No more, tonight. I've had rather a long day, and I don't want to lose my temper [*trying to smile*]. Besides, after all, it's my birthday.

DINAH [*eagerly*]: Yes, it is. And I think we ought to play *Black Sam*. We haven't played it for years, and this family always used to play *Black Sam* on all holidays and special occasions.

MRS LINDEN: Yes, dear, but now that everybody's grown up –

JEAN: No. I'd like to play *Black Sam* again.

REX: So would I. Though don't forget I nearly always win.

DINAH [*swiftly*]: You used to cheat.

REX: Certainly. Cheating's part of it, after the first hour.

MARION: Have you still got the cards and counters?

MRS LINDEN: They're about somewhere – but where, I can't imagine.

DINAH: The counters were up in somebody's bedroom the last time I saw them. Though I can't imagine why.

PROFESSOR: I think I know where the cards might be – at the back of one of the drawers in the dining-room.

DINAH: Well, you look for them, and I'll find the counters. You lot get the table ready.

[*She goes out with the* PROFESSOR, *shutting door behind them.* REX *and* MRS LINDEN *begin clearing papers and books, etc., off the study table throughout dialogue that follows.* MARION *and* JEAN *stand up and give them a hand too.*]

MRS LINDEN: I'm afraid your father's upset and annoyed – the news coming like that – but it's a good thing really. I'll have to talk him round, of course.

REX: Well, don't rush him. He's been here a long time –

MRS LINDEN [*dryly*]: Yes – and so have I.

REX: That's not the same thing.

JEAN: No, it isn't. But you seem to have settled something between you – what is it?

MRS LINDEN: To leave here at once – and stay with Rex. Your father wouldn't want to stay in the London flat – but now he needn't. He can stay in Rex's country house until perhaps later on, when we find some little place of our own quite near.

JEAN: And what about Dinah?

REX: D'you know, I'd clean forgotten about young Dinah.

MRS LINDEN: I hadn't. Dinah can stay on here in Burmanley until the end of the summer term – I know several people who'd be glad to let her have a room – and then she'd better try for Oxford or Cambridge, unless she decides to go to the Royal College of Music. And of course she'll be with us during part of her vacations, at least.

MARION: Well, it all sounds quite sensible to me. Though of course you must come and stay with us sometimes.

MRS LINDEN: Once we've left this wretched place, we can.

MARION: You've always hated it here, haven't you?

MRS LINDEN: Always – always. I ought to have *made* your father leave, years ago. He had several good opportunities. But then the war came – and it didn't seem worth while going then. But now Burmanley's finished with us – and we're done with Burmanley. This time I really mean it.

MARION: Don't weaken on that, Mother.

MRS LINDEN: Don't worry. I shan't. I'm getting older too – I'm nearly fifty-nine – sixty soon – and I refuse to live any longer like this. It isn't living. It hasn't been for years. Shabby, boring, dismal. What is there here for me now?

MARION: Nothing – so far as I can see.

MRS LINDEN: Rex agrees with me – don't you, darling?

REX: Absolutely. Pack it up, I say, and come and enjoy yourself while there's still time. And you leave it to me, Mother.

[*He winks at her and she smiles at him fondly.* JEAN *is looking gravely thoughtful.* MRS LINDEN *notices this.*]

MRS LINDEN: Well, Jean? You agree, don't you?

JEAN [*slowly*]: I don't know. I really don't know.

MRS LINDEN: That's not like you.

MARION: No, Jean usually knows it all – right off – bang!

JEAN [*sharply*]: Well, tonight for once, I don't. And it worries me. So just leave me out of it.

MRS LINDEN [*sharply*]: If it's your father you're thinking about, I'm just as anxious to get away for his sake as I am for my own. He's getting on – he's tired – most of his friends have gone –

MARION: And if his students are anything like the two specimens I saw here tonight, then they're not worth bothering about –

MRS LINDEN: And the University doesn't even want him here any longer – [*specially to* JEAN] – so there you are.

JEAN: I'm not arguing against you.

MRS LINDEN: No, but you're looking as if you might like to – as if – as if something was wrong, though you didn't quite know what.

JEAN: I've told you – this is one night when I don't find it easy to make up my mind – so leave me out of it.

REX [*who has been busy setting the table*]: Well, that's all set. Dinah's right. What the Linden family needs is an hour or two of *Black Sam* – cheating and all. Where are these cards and counters? [*He begins to take one or two upright chairs to the table.*]

[DINAH *now enters, carrying a box of counters, closing door behind her. She moves slowly and looks distressed.*]

Well, here are the counters, eh?

DINAH: Yes.

MARION: Can't Father find the cards?

DINAH [*tonelessly*]: Yes, he's found them.

REX: What's the matter?

DINAH [*her face working, distressed*]: I peeped into the dining-room as I came past. He didn't see me. He was just standing, holding the cards, staring at nothing. [*She gives a little sob. More distressed now.*] It was just as if I hadn't noticed him properly before. Suddenly – he looked so old – and tired – and so much by himself – as if everything was wrong and nobody cared – that I couldn't bear it – [*She gives a sob.*]

MRS LINDEN [*soothingly*]: Now, Dinah –

DINAH [*urgently*]: It isn't *Now Dinah* at all. Nothing to do with it.

MRS LINDEN [*sharper now*]: Now don't be stupid –

DINAH: I'm not being stupid. [*Looking at them, slowly*] He's so sweet – and it's his birthday – and he was so pleased when he knew everybody was coming – [*with sudden anger*] and you're all whispering and plotting – and it seems so bloody mean –

MRS LINDEN [*angrily*]: Dinah, I won't have you talking like that.

JEAN [*very sharply*]: Why shouldn't she if she feels like that?

MRS LINDEN: Please mind your own business, Jean.

JEAN [*crossing to* DINAH, *who is crying*]: This is my business.

[*Puts her arms round* DINAH, *who collapses against her.*]
All right, Dinah darling. You've said it now. All over.

DINAH [*muffled against* JEAN]: I'm sorry. I don't know why I said it. But it was seeing him like that.

REX [*at table*]: Look – turn this up, everybody. He'll be back any moment. Snap out of it, Dinah. Let's have the counters.

[*She gives them to him, and he pours them on the table, preparing to count them into heaps. With loud cheerful tone*]
Do you remember that time up in Cumberland when the farmer came in from next door and we made him play *Black Sam* with us?

DINAH [*eagerly*]: I can remember that, though I was too little to play. He had a huge whiskery sort of nose –

REX [*chuckling*]: He was left with *Black Sam* every time –

MARION [*eagerly*]: And he was so furious – do you remember, Jean?

JEAN [*beginning to laugh*]: Yes, what did he use to say?

REX [*quoting, in Northern accent*]: 'Well, lay me aht an' bury me, Ah've got dom' thing again – '

DINAH [*laughing*]: And then something happened to his collar, didn't it ?

JEAN [*laughing*]: Yes – yes – it suddenly *popped* –

MARION [*laughing*]: I know – I nearly died – the stud went –

REX [*quoting again, uproariously*]: And he said 'Sitha, tha's Black Sammed me clean aht o' me collar – '

[*As they laugh, in the way families do at their special jokes,* PROFESSOR *enters, carrying box of playing cards. He lights up when he hears their laughter, which is reminiscent of their young days.*]

PROFESSOR [*smiling*]: What's the joke ?

REX [*still laughing*]: That time – up in Cumberland – when the farmer played *Black Sam* –

PROFESSOR [*beginning to laugh*]: Oh yes – Joe Sykes – and he burst out of his collar – and he swore to me afterwards that you were all cheating –

REX [*laughing harder than ever*]: *But I was – I was –*

[*Here all the children give a yell. But suddenly* MRS LINDEN *has stopped laughing, and has turned her face away. As the laughter dies down,*]

PROFESSOR [*to his wife*]: What's the matter, my dear ?

MRS LINDEN [*turned away, muffled tone*]: No – it's nothing – don't bother –

[*They have all stopped laughing now, and glance curiously at her.*]

PROFESSOR: All right. Well, let's play, shall we ?

MRS LINDEN: No. I mean – you all play, of course. But I don't want to.

MARION: What is it, Mother ?

MRS LINDEN: I suddenly felt awful – hearing you all laughing again – and remembering what fun we used to have. Oh – I went back long before that holiday in Cumberland – to other holidays and times – to when you were all very little – and before that – when everything was beginning for us. [*She looks rather defiantly at her husband.*] I don't know what you tell those students of yours, Robert. But I'd like to tell them something – the truth, for once – the real truth.

PROFESSOR [*gravely*]: And what's that, Isabel?

[MRS LINDEN *now speaks with great sincerity and feeling, with a certain magnificence of manner.*]

MRS LINDEN: That everything just gets worse and worse – and it's time we stopped pretending it doesn't. Oh – I'm not just thinking about being short of things and having rations and queuing up. But when we were young – up to 1914 – the world was sensible and safe and kind – and even if people didn't have much money, they had most of the things they wanted. They could be happy in a simple easy way – because life seemed good. Oh – the very roads and the grass and the trees and the lilac in spring were different then, and you could notice and enjoy everything, and be quiet and peaceful. And then afterwards – after those years of great black casualty lists every day – it was never the same again – never the same. But it wasn't too bad – we still didn't know all the horrors and the cruelties and the miseries – and you could go away for real holidays – and the children were such fun. But then everything got worse and worse – and look at us now, just look at us – with only a few years more and all the colour and fun and life gone for ever – I tell you, it's heart-breaking –

DINAH [*eagerly*]: Oh, Mother, you're not fair. It's just because you're not interested, so you make it all seem dull and grey to yourself. It's all terribly exciting, really, and sometimes I lie awake at night – and think – and wonder – and can hardly bear it –

MRS LINDEN [*harshly*]: No, Dinah, you don't understand what I'm talking about – you're too young – much too young –

PROFESSOR: Yes, she's too young to understand what *you* feel. But she's given you the answer, just because she *is* young. And what am I to tell my students? That because I'm getting old and weary, they mustn't believe the very blood that's beating in their veins?

MARION: But there are such things as standards, Father. And Mother's quite right –

JEAN [*contemptuously*]: What – just because she's talking like any elderly member of a decayed middle class?

MRS LINDEN [*angrily*]: Oh – don't talk that pompous inhuman rubbish to me, Jean. I'm being real now. I'm not quoting books but talking about real life – and what I feel here – [*indicating her heart*].

PROFESSOR: Some things are worse, some things are better. And the sun will shine for Dinah tomorrow, my love, as it once shone for you, forty years ago – the same sun. And young families are still laughing somewhere at old farmers who burst their collars. And while there's time to lose the world, Rex, there's also time to save it – if we really want to save it. And there's also time – and of course it might be the last, you never know – for a Linden family game of *Black Sam*. Give us our counters, Rex – that's your job – [*He has now taken the cards out of the case*] while the old man, with his patience, shuffles the cards. Patience . . . patience . . . and shuffle the cards. . . .

[*He is now shuffling the cards,* REX *is distributing the counters in heaps, while the others begin to sit round.*]

SLOW CURTAIN

ACT TWO

SCENE ONE

The Scene as before, but it is afternoon again, with mild sunlight coming through the window. MARION, JEAN, EDITH WESTMORE *and* BERNARD FAWCETT *are all standing about, having a heated and noisy argument. Door is open and through it we hear* MRS LINDEN *and* REX *occasionally calling to each other, with a good deal of movement and bumping, and also we can hear, fragmentarily,* DINAH *practising bits of the 'cello part of Elgar's 'Cello Concerto. It is altogether a noisy messy sort of scene.*

FAWCETT [*an aggressive debater*]: How do you make that out? Just tell me that. How do you make that out?

EDITH [*heatedly*]: It's your business to make it out, as you call it. Not ours. [*Appealing to* MARION, *her ally*] Isn't it?

MARION [*nearly as heated as they are*]: Of course it is. They think they can come along with any piffling little argument against religion, and that we have to reply, when the best minds of the last two thousand years –

JEAN [*cooler than the other three*]: Wait a minute, Marion. We really can't swallow that.

FAWCETT [*disgusted*]: Of course we can't. Lot o' tripe, that's all. Yes, tripe!

JEAN [*louder now*]: The best minds have always been fighting the Churches tooth and nail. Just as they are today. And for the same old reason –

FAWCETT [*triumphantly*]: Exactly – the same old reason –

REX [*off, but near door, calling*]: What do you say, Mother? I know – but there's a hell of a row going on down here –

MRS LINDEN [*off, distant, calling*]: It's in the dining-room. *Din-ing Room!*

REX [*calling*]: Okay! I'll go and look.

MARION: Yes, and what is the reason?

EDITH [*backing her up*]: We know what it is. It's simply not to have any real moral responsibility –

MARION: To do what you like. And then you wonder why you're all so miserable –

FAWCETT [*shouting*]: Who said we're miserable? Were people any better off when they had Inquisitions and had to buy pardons and keep thousands of lazy priests and monks –

EDITH: How do *you* know they were lazy?

MARION: And anyhow people *were* better off. First, the scientists want to be free of religion, and now when they've invented atom bombs and think we'll all blow ourselves to bits with them, they're telling us it's a pity there's no religion –

JEAN: No, they're not, if they've any sense. What they're asking for is a properly planned and controlled world –

FAWCETT: Which you lot couldn't give us anyhow, and have done your best to stop –

MARION: How can you plan and control without any real authority to guide you? That's where the Church comes in –

EDITH: And if people don't worship God, then they'll worship the devil –

FAWCETT [*jeering*]: Superstition! Dope! That's all you're giving us.

MARION [*annoyed*]: Don't be so loutish.

FAWCETT [*to* JEAN]: There you are, you see. Bad temper now.

EDITH [*angrily*]: Well, you started it.

REX [*calling, as before*]: Are you sure it's a *brown* one? There's a *green* one here, that's all.

MRS LINDEN [*as before*]: No, darling – the *brown* one.

REX [*calling*]: And what about this basket thing? Do you really want it?

JEAN [*who apparently started earlier*]: Just a little elementary psychology is what I'd suggest. And somatic medical treatment too.

EDITH: What about them? Are they supposed to explain everything – what we're doing here at all, for instance –

FAWCETT: Well, can you explain that?

MARION: We can make a better shot at it than you people can.

JEAN: But don't you see that that kind of question is idiotic?

EDITH: No, I don't. It's what I've always wanted to know – ever since I can remember –

JEAN: Yes, of course it's a *child's* question – and that's all it is. We can explain how we came to be what we are – what physical and social forces –

MARION [*crossly*]: Oh – never mind about physical and social forces – they don't give the answer – they only explain how things work –

JEAN: Well, that's the only explanation that's sensible and necessary.

EDITH [*shouting*]: No, it isn't.

JEAN [*haughtily*]: I'll be much obliged if you won't shout at me like that.

FAWCETT: Can't face the argument. All alike.

EDITH [*to him*]: Oh – you shut up! [*To* JEAN] I'm sorry – I won't shout any more – but it always annoys me when people talk like that. Knowing how a thing works isn't knowing what it's for.

MARION: Exactly – and that's the mistake they all make –

JEAN: There's no *exactly* about it. Reality can't be *for* anything. It just *is*. You're talking out-of-date metaphysics – and don't even know it – that's your trouble.

MARION [*hotly*]: And your trouble is – you're so ridiculously conceited –

FAWCETT [*insufferably*]: Now – now – now – now!

MARION [*turning on him*]: Really – you're *insufferable*. Please be quiet.

[*Enter* MRS COTTON, *if anything odder than in the previous Act. She is smoking a cigarette and carrying a cup of tea.*]

MRS COTTON: 'Avin' a proper argy-bargy in 'ere, aren't you? Losing your tempers too, some of yer. [*To* JEAN *and* MARION] Your tea'll be ready soon. Dining-room. Packed up to go?

MARION: Yes. At least I have.

JEAN: So have I.

MRS COTTON: Your mother's makin' a proper job of it – an' keepin' Mr Rex on the run all right. Yer'd think she was goin' for good, the way she's throwin' things about – never saw such a mess upstairs – every drawer out of every chest. All gone straight to 'er 'ead. Excitement. I knew it would.'*Im* comin'. I'd 'ave bin just the same. [*Sits on edge of chair, takes a sip of tea, and looks at the others cynically.*] Well, get on with the argument. Don't let me stop yer. I like a bit of ding-dong.

MARION: No, I think we've had enough.

MRS COTTON: My 'usband wouldn't say more than ten words for two or three days, then 'e'd 'ave two or three bottles o' stout an' argue the point about anything – shout you down too. I used to grumble but I wish to God 'e'd come in now an' start shoutin' me down again – an' you too –

FAWCETT [*grinning*]: Perhaps we wouldn't let him.

MRS COTTON [*with contempt*]: 'E'd 'ave told you to run away an' play –

[EDITH *giggles*. FAWCETT *is annoyed*.]

FAWCETT: Here, wait a minute –

MRS COTTON: What for? [*To* JEAN] Who's this Cass Als?

JEAN: Cass Als?

MRS COTTON: That's right. Dinah come 'ome like a mad thing early this afternoon an' she shouts 'Mrs Cotton. Isn't it wonderful? I met a man at my lesson who used to know Cass Als'.

MARION: Oh – she means Casals – the great 'cellist –

MRS COTTON: That'll be 'im. Nearly off 'er 'ead with excitement 'cos she'd met a man who knew 'im. What it is to be young an' silly. She started practisin' right off then. Proper mad thing. Not knowin' what's in store. I was the same about Fox Trots, years an' years ago, when they'd just started – mad on Fox Trots – couldn't think about work or eatin' or sleepin' for Fox Trots . . . even the name sounds dam' silly now. [*Suddenly, to* EDITH] What are you mad on?

EDITH [*startled*]: I don't know really –

MRS COTTON: I'll bet yer don't. [*To* JEAN] Well, what about gettin' on with the Brains Trust 'ere? Not quite time for your tea yet, even though yer are 'avin' it early. What's the subject?

JEAN [*amused*]: A good old favourite. Science versus Religion.

MRS COTTON: Never fancied either of 'em really. 'Ad a sister that went religious, chapel, and an uncle that was a bit on the scientific side – insecks, chiefly –

[REX *appears at door. He is in his shirt-sleeves, carrying a suitcase in one hand, and a woman's coat and various oddments in the other. He has a cigarette, unlit, in his mouth, and looks rather ruffled.*]

REX: Put a light to this cigarette, somebody, please.

[FAWCETT *goes up to him, with lighter. He speaks now to* JEAN *and* MARION.]

MARION: Well, we're not really debating chapels versus insects.

REX: Thanks, old boy. Helping mother pack is no joke. [*Looking at them all*] You look a queer gang in here. Mrs Cotton, do you know anything about a little travelling clock?

MRS COTTON: No, I don't.

REX: Neither do I.

JEAN: I believe it's in my room. Shall I go –

REX: No, I'm going up – [*Goes out.*]

[*During all this scraps of 'cello playing, often repeating same passage, have been heard, with breaks. It continues now, though not heard above dialogue clearly.*]

EDITH [*rather shyly*]: But – in a way – it *is* chapels versus insects. I mean, *they* [*indicating* JEAN *and* FAWCETT] talk as if we were only a superior sort of insect –

FAWCETT [*impatiently*]: Oh – don't start all that old stuff. No-body's ever said anything of the sort.

MARION: No, you don't *say* it. But that's what you mean.

JEAN: No, we don't. The point is, if we study insect life, we know *exactly* what we're doing –

EDITH [*sharply*]: And we know what we're doing in chapels and churches –

MARION: We're behaving like spiritual beings –

FAWCETT: Or like superstitious savages –

EDITH [*angrily*]: Do savages have chapels and churches?

MARION: It's just savages who don't. And now they're turning themselves into savages again –

JEAN: On the contrary, we're using our reason and knowledge of scientific method –

MARION [*loudly*]: To blow everything and everybody to bits –

MRS COTTON: 'Ere, 'ere.

JEAN [*to* MARION, *angrily*]: Chiefly encouraged by *your* precious Church –

MARION [*angrily*]: That's simply not true –

FAWCETT [*rudely*]: Yes of course it is –

MARION [*angrily*]: No it isn't – and I'm not talking to you –

FAWCETT [*loudly*]: You can't reason with 'em. They won't listen to it.

MRS COTTON [*top of her voice*]: Go on, our side. Chapels versus Insecks. [*She laughs.*]

EDITH [*to* FAWCETT]: If you'd just be quiet a minute and not interrupt –

FAWCETT [*overlapping with her*]: Why should I be quiet? I've as much right to talk as you.

MARION [*angrily, overlapping too*]: Because you don't understand what we're talking about. You're not arguing, you're just shouting –

JEAN [*very loud, overlapping*]: Well, I know what I'm talking about. I've had all this out years ago –

EDITH [*cutting in*]: That doesn't make any difference. It doesn't prove you're right, does it?

JEAN [*together with* MARION, *as below*]: I say, we used to talk this stuff for hours when I was in college, years ago –

MARION [*together with* JEAN, *as above*]: No, but Jean always did know it all, and now she's a doctor, of course, naturally –

[PROFESSOR LINDEN *has entered, and his voice cuts them off.*]

PROFESSOR [*loudly*]: Just a minute!

[*They are quiet, attentive to him. He speaks quietly now.*]

Listen to Dinah –

[*The door is open behind him, and now we hear quite clearly, though at some distance, the 'cello playing the rich melancholy second subject of the First Movement of the Elgar Concerto. They are all very still. The music dies away. Short pause.*]

MARION [*quietly*]: What is that?

PROFESSOR: First Movement of the Elgar Concerto. I didn't know Dinah was doing the Elgar. She must have just started.

MRS COTTON [*softly*]: It sounds a sad piece.

PROFESSOR [*quietly*]: Yes, it is. A kind of long farewell. An elderly man remembers his world before the war of 1914, some of it years and years before perhaps – being a boy at Worcester – or Germany in the 'Nineties – long days on the Malvern Hills – smiling Edwardian afternoons – Maclaren and Ranji batting at Lords, then Richter or Nikisch at the Queen's Hall – all gone, gone, lost for ever – and so he distils his tenderness and regret, drop by drop, and seals the sweet melancholy in a Concerto for 'cello. And he goes, too, where all the old green sunny days and the twinkling nights went – gone, gone. But then what happens? Why, a little miracle. You heard it.

JEAN [*softly*]: Dinah playing?

PROFESSOR: Why yes. Young Dinah Linden, all youth, all eagerness, saying hello and not farewell to anything, who knows and
cares nothing about Bavaria in the 'Nineties or the secure and
golden Edwardian afternoons, here in Burmanley, this very
afternoon, the moment we stop shouting at each other, unseals
for us the precious distillation, uncovers the tenderness and
regret, which are ours now as well as his, and our lives and
Elgar's, Burmanley today and the Malvern Hills in a lost
sunlight, are all magically intertwined . . .

MRS COTTON [*to the others, proudly*]: When he likes, the Professor's a lovely talker.

PROFESSOR: That settles me. But that theme, you know – [*hums
it a moment*] you can tell at once it's a farewell to long-lost
summer afternoons. It's got a deep drowsy summerishness that
belongs to everybody's youth – it's telling you quite plainly that
now there aren't any such afternoons – the sun's never as hot,
the grass as thick, the shade as deep and drowsy – and where are
the bumble bees? God help me – I haven't seen a hammock for
years and years and years. I must tell Dinah. [*Half turns, then
checks himself.*] No, no, that'll keep. [*To the students*] What are
you two doing here? What about that meeting?

FAWCETT: We came to tell you. It's been cancelled.

EDITH: So as we had no other subject for this week's essay, we
thought we'd better tell you at once.

PROFESSOR [*thoughtfully*]: I see.

MARION [*to* MRS COTTON]: What about tea? I'll help.

MRS COTTON: Come on then.

[*They go out together.* PROFESSOR *looks at students.*]

PROFESSOR: You're probably both going to the Union show
tonight aren't you?

[*They nod and murmur* 'Yes'.]

Would it be a nuisance for you to slip in here afterwards? It
wouldn't? Then do that, please. So off you go. And I'm sorry
you had to wait.

[PROFESSOR *goes to door,* FAWCETT *following. But* EDITH
looks at JEAN.]

EDITH [*humbly*]: Dr Linden – I hope I didn't sound rude when we

were all arguing. Bernard always makes me lose my temper
when he attacks religion.

JEAN [*smiling*]: No, I didn't mind.

PROFESSOR [*as* EDITH *moves up*]: High time you lost your temper,
Miss Westmore. Pity I missed that. [*Confidentially*] I lost my
temper this morning, up at the University offices. Well, perhaps
I shall see you tonight –

[*He is now ushering the students through the door.* JEAN *lights a
cigarette.* PROFESSOR *returns, closing door.*]

JEAN: *Did* you lose your temper, this morning?

PROFESSOR [*with satisfaction*]: I did. I raised merry hell. I told
them they couldn't get rid of me simply by remembering we're
supposed to have an age-limit.

JEAN: So you think it's all over and done with.

PROFESSOR [*eyeing her*]: Don't you?

JEAN [*softly*]: No I don't.

[*Goes nearer to him.*]

PROFESSOR: I ought to write a letter or two.

JEAN [*now closer, softly*]: They can wait a minute, Dad. And we're
alone. Nobody listening. You can tell me. I'm not one of the
Get-Him-Out-Of-Here party.

PROFESSOR: Who is – or are – members of it?

JEAN [*still softly*]: Mother. Rex. Marion. Now confess, Dad, it's
not all as easy as you pretended, is it?

PROFESSOR [*with elaborate whisper*]: No – it isn't. Between ourselves, of course. [*Then in quite ordinary tone*] Nevertheless, I'll
settle it all right. Actually the battle's not over – may be going on
now. And I must write those notes – that wasn't an excuse not
to talk. [*Going to desk or work table, to write.*] Lidley probably
imagines from my grumpy manner that I haven't any friends
round here. He's wrong. I still have a few. And his own position
isn't as strong as he thinks, unless he has a string or two to pull
that I don't know about. He may have, of course. [*Sitting down
now, to begin writing.*] These notes are part of the campaign,
otherwise I wouldn't bother about 'em now.

[*He begins writing swiftly.* JEAN *watches him for a moment or
two, very thoughtfully. She opens her mouth as if to speak, then
checks herself.*]

Yes?

JEAN: Nothing.

PROFESSOR [*still writing*]: I thought you wanted to say something. If so, please say it. As Rex keeps telling us, there isn't much time.

JEAN [*after slight hesitation*]: I may be conceited – people keep saying so – but – well, I know you're a very wise old bird, Dad, and you always understood me best . . .

PROFESSOR [*looking up, putting pipe in*]: So?

JEAN: What's the matter with me?

PROFESSOR [*lighting his pipe*]: Not very much. Otherwise, you couldn't be doing the job you are doing.

JEAN: But there *is* something. *I* know that.

PROFESSOR [*coolly*]: Feeling miserable, aren't you?

JEAN: Yes. And hating myself.

PROFESSOR [*calmly*]: That's the trouble. You're resenting your own emotions. You're annoyed with yourself for being a woman. Quite wrong. After all, there's no escape from that. This man you're in love with. – Perhaps he isn't worth it. And you'll have to get over him. I don't know – and don't much want to. But just remember, you're a young woman, with a hundred thousand other women among your ancestors – and all the medical degrees in the world don't change that fact – and don't try to pretend to yourself you're a termite queen or a creature from Mars or something. Because you have to attend to bewildered sick women who perhaps enjoy their emotions – luxuriate in 'em – you refuse to give your own an inch of rope. And then they tear back at you like having a wounded cat inside you.

JEAN: Just about. But what can I do?

PROFESSOR: Buy a bottle of gin. Sit up with a girl friend. Split the bottle, tell everything, have a dam' good cry – and enjoy every minute of it. Then start again, on a better basis.

JEAN: For myself, you mean?

PROFESSOR: For yourself, and for the rest of us. Don't demand a world as efficient, sterilized and scientific as an operating theatre. We couldn't live in it if we got it. Don't confuse science with life. It's an abstraction – neat and quick, to get certain things done. That's all. Even if the bath water's distilled and heated to just the right temperature, it's still the baby that's important. Messy things too, babies. Always will be. You won't mind too much when it's yours.

JEAN: Let's have a long talk next time, Dad.

PROFESSOR [*beginning to write again, quickly*]: Yes, come up here alone, as soon as you can.

JEAN: But, Dad – I think I ought to warn you.

PROFESSOR [*still writing*]: Yes?

JEAN: Mother's more serious than you think.

PROFESSOR [*glancing up*]: She needs a change badly, of course. Burmanley's been a bit too much for her lately, I know. Don't blame her.

JEAN: It's gone farther than you think.

PROFESSOR [*looking at her now, quietly*]: You believe that, do you?

[*Enter* MARION, *holding door open.*]

MARION: Tea's in.

JEAN [*moving*]: I'm coming.

PROFESSOR [*writing*]: Early, isn't it?

MARION: Yes, but we shall be starting soon. But Mother said you needn't bother. She's having hers now, and she said she wanted to talk to you.

[JEAN *has now gone.*]

PROFESSOR: There – or here?

MARION: Here, I imagine. [*Hesitates a moment, drifting in a little.*] I hated that silly noisy argument we had this afternoon.

PROFESSOR [*still writing*]: You made a hell of a row about it.

MARION: What's the matter with everybody here?

PROFESSOR: All kinds of things.

MARION: No, I mean – why are you all so completely materialistic now?

[*He looks up at her questioningly. She continues, with more warmth.*]

As if nothing on earth mattered but production – and exports – and what people earned –

PROFESSOR [*mildly*]: We have to live, you know. And being poorer than we used to be, it's more of a problem.

MARION: But that's not all there is in life.

PROFESSOR: Not a bit. Only the start of it. The mechanics, so to speak.

278 THE LINDEN TREE

MARION: But it's all you seem to care about now. No, not you – yourself.

PROFESSOR: I know. Not me, but everybody else. Remember the miracle of the loaves and fishes – ?

MARION: Yes, of course.

PROFESSOR: Materialistic?

MARION: No, that's quite different.

PROFESSOR: The idea's the same. Spread it out and give everybody a fair share. It's never been done before, you know, not in a whole large society. Oh – there's been colour, grace, culture, philosophy, nobly spiritual lives – but always with a lot of poor devils, whole masses of people, left clean out, slogging away in the dark, ignored, forgotten. Is it materialistic and sordid not to ignore and forget them, to bring them all out into the light, to take their share?

MARION: Yes, but to talk and think about nothing else –

PROFESSOR [*jumping up*]: Wrong, yes. I keep saying so. But give us a chance, my dear Marion. Call us drab and dismal, if you like, and tell us we don't know how to cook our food or wear our clothes – but for Heaven's sake, recognize that we're trying to do something that is as extraordinary and wonderful as it's difficult – to have a revolution for once without the Terror, without looting mobs and secret police, sudden arrests, mass suicides and executions, without setting in motion that vast pendulum of violence which can decimate three generations before it comes to a standstill. We're fighting in the last ditch of our civilization. If we win through, everybody wins through. Why – bless my soul! – Marion – [*He is leading her to the window now, then pointing*] Look – you see that flat-footed dough-faced fellow . . . slouching along there –

MARION [*half-laughing*]: Yes. And I suppose he's the ordinary British citizen – the hero of the world –

PROFESSOR [*with sudden change of manner*]: That's what I'd hoped, but actually I see it's poor Atherfield, our professor of physics, who took some bull-headed wrong line of his own upon the isotopes of uranium, or whatever it was – and so missed his place on the atomic band-wagon. If we're all blown to smithereens, he won't have contributed anything to the explosion – and the poor chap's heartbroken. But I must post my letters. [*He hurries back to his desk or table and is putting letters in envelopes.*]

[*Enter* MRS LINDEN*; she is dressed ready for travelling, but not wearing a hat or heavy coat.*]

MRS LINDEN: Oh, there you are, Marion. Do go and finish your tea. Rex wants to start in half an hour.

MARION: All right, Mother, don't fuss, I'm quite ready. [*Exit* MARION.]

[MRS LINDEN *looks at the* PROFESSOR *steadily. He looks at her, then slowly rises, the letters in his hand.*]

MRS LINDEN: Did you hear anything more this afternoon, Robert?

PROFESSOR: No, my love. I have an idea that Lidley's busy with my protest at this very moment. Alfred Lockhart told me there might be some sort of meeting this evening. So I might have news later tonight.

MRS LINDEN [*gravely*]: You know what I think about it.

PROFESSOR: Yes. That even if they wanted me to, I'd be a fool to stay on. And as some of 'em don't want me, as I have to fight to keep my job, I'm out of my senses to stay. Right?

MRS LINDEN [*sits down*]: Yes. And Rex – and Marion – and even Jean, I think – agree with me.

PROFESSOR [*easily*]: Well, they could be wrong too. [*Pause, looks at her.*] I don't enjoy not having you on my side in this, you know, Isabel.

MRS LINDEN [*sharply*]: And do you think I enjoy it? I hate it. I hate it. But they never really liked you here – that's what you've never understood. It never was your place. I knew it – and you ought to have known it. All this is just another reason why I'm glad to go.

PROFESSOR [*lightly*]: You've had a particularly difficult time lately, I know, my dear. A change will do you good. Rex, who understands these things much better than I do, will see that you enjoy yourself. I'm glad you're going. When you come back, my little quarrel with Lidley and his set will be over, I hope – and we'll try to find some more help for the house.

MRS LINDEN: I'm not coming back.

PROFESSOR [*stares at her*]: You don't mean that.

MRS LINDEN: Robert, I mean every word of it. I'm not coming back. I'm leaving Burmanley for ever.

PROFESSOR: Never mind Burmanley. You're leaving *me*.

MRS LINDEN: I'm not leaving you. That's the point.

PROFESSOR: I don't see it.

MRS LINDEN [*with more urgency now*]: It's quite simple, Robert. You ought to retire – and you've been told to. There's nothing to keep us here. We can live with Rex for a time – he's very anxious that we should, and he can well afford to have us as his guests. Afterwards, if necessary, we can find a little place of our own. Everybody agrees that this is what we ought to do. It's perfectly obvious. But suddenly you've decided to be obstinate. *You* want to stay on here. But what about me? Have you ever thought about me?

PROFESSOR: I tried to, Isabel. And I realize it's not easy for you –

MRS LINDEN [*urgently*]: I never liked Burmanley from the first, but of course I put up with it – for your sake, always hoping that we'd soon be able to go somewhere else. During these last few years, with the older children away, with most of our friends dead or gone, with no proper help in the house, with all the rationing and queueing and drab misery, I've loathed every single day. And always I've been longing and praying for this time to come – when you'd have to retire – when we'd done with Burmanley for ever. Rex knew what I felt – he's always understood –

PROFESSOR [*lightly, but with underlying gravity*]: Rex the Tempter – it's a part that suits him – offering you breakfast in bed at Huntingdon House – then Bond Street – a nice little lunch somewhere – a theatre – a little bridge –

MRS LINDEN [*warmly*]: All right. And why not? Rex and I understand each other, always have done. And if he offers me those things – yes, and having my hair done properly – and looking at silly illustrated weeklies – and having a good woman's gossip – and sometimes spending money foolishly – and being nicely looked after –

PROFESSOR [*not sneering*]: Is that what you've always really wanted?

MRS LINDEN: No, it isn't, except somewhere at the back of my mind, like most women. What I've wanted is what I've had –

looking after you and the children – keeping this house going –
trying to plan good holidays for us all. And when it had to be
done, I did it – and did it gladly. But it hasn't to be done any
more. And now I don't want to spend another day in this
hateful place –

PROFESSOR [*in wondering melancholy tone*]: Hateful? Hateful?
It's just a city – full of people working, trying to get along – not
very different from us. Hateful?

MRS LINDEN [*almost tearful now*]: I don't mean I've never been
happy here. It was different at first. But it's hateful now – grey,
dismal – with a stupid shabby sort of life – all meaningless to me
– so that sometimes I've felt like a wretched ghost. You've had
your work – your students –

PROFESSOR: Yes, yes – I know it's easier for me – quite different.
But –

MRS LINDEN [*tearful, though not crying*]: And soon I shall be
sixty – all my life gone – Rex in London – Marion far away in
France. And I tell you I hate this drab gloomy world we've
made. Rex is right – the only thing to do is to laugh at it and then
forget it. And now he's been here again – and talked so much –
Marion too – if they went and left me here, I feel I'd die of
misery –

[*As she almost breaks down, he crosses to comfort her.*]

PROFESSOR [*comfortably, as he crosses*]: My dear, I'm sorry you
feel like this – I know it's been hard –

[*When he is about to touch her, she waves him away.*]

MRS LINDEN [*checking her emotion*]: No, Robert, please! Let me
say what I want to say. I'll be quite calm.

[*She makes an effort. He steps back. Then she speaks fairly
quietly and firmly.*]

No, I'm not leaving you. I'm leaving Burmanley. And I'm
doing it for your sake as well as for my own. I've tried to persuade you – so have the children – and now I'm doing the only
thing that I think may make you behave sensibly. But I mean
what I say. I'm going and I'm not coming back. If you stay here,
Robert, you'll stay here alone – and I don't think you'll want to
do that very long – thank goodness!

[*As he stands stiffly, she pleads a little.*]

Robert, please! This isn't a quarrel. I'm not leaving *you*.

PROFESSOR [*gravely*]: I think you are. A man stays where his work is and the woman stays with the man.

MRS LINDEN: And I did it for thirty-seven years. But you're no longer a man who has his work.

PROFESSOR [*bitterly*]: That's the most damnably hurting thing you've ever said to me.

MRS LINDEN: I'm sorry, Robert. I didn't say it to hurt you. But it's true – and you're hurting yourself because you won't admit it.

[*Enter* REX, *wearing an overcoat but no hat. He looks sharply at his parents, but takes an easy tone.*]

REX: Sorry to barge in. But I'd like to get off in about ten minutes. I've put most of the stuff in the car. Want to be alone?

MRS LINDEN [*rather wearily*]: No, it doesn't matter now. Come in, darling.

[PROFESSOR *goes over to the window and looks out, standing stiffly.* REX *and* MRS LINDEN *exchange a look, then she rises and they meet. He takes her arm and pats her hand with his other hand, affectionately. She smiles rather sadly at him.*]

DINAH [*off, just outside, surprised*]: But I didn't know you were going so soon.

MARION [*calling, farther off*]: In a few minutes.

DINAH [*off, as before*]: Gosh! – I don't really know what's happening about this family.

JEAN [*farther off, calling*]: Has anybody seen my little red bag?

DINAH [*calling*]: I'll have a look for it.

[*We hear her moving off whistling, the door being wide open.* MRS LINDEN *gently releases herself from* REX, *pulling herself together, but stands near him.* MARION *enters, ready to go, and looking very smart. She glances at her father's back, and then exchanges meaning glances with her mother and* REX.]

MARION [*softly*]: Dad – I hoped Mother would have persuaded you to come with us.

PROFESSOR [*after turning, quietly*]: Well, she hasn't, Marion. She tells me she's leaving Burmanley for good.

MARION: I know. And I think she's right. There's nothing for her here.

PROFESSOR: Except me. And some work still to be done.

MARION: I don't see that, Father. You needn't stay.

REX [*cheerfully*]: They don't even want you to –

PROFESSOR [*sharply*]: Rex – I've heard enough of that today.

REX [*who sees he is hurt*]: Sorry, Dad. I didn't mean –

PROFESSOR [*cutting in, curtly*]: All right.

MRS LINDEN: If your father felt he was behaving sensibly, he wouldn't be so touchy. But he knows he isn't. I do think he's behaving with ridiculous obstinacy.

PROFESSOR: Quite possibly what I do may not be very important, but I want to keep straight on doing it. I don't believe this is simply personal vanity – an elderly man not wanting to be put on the shelf. Although even now I don't fancy being one of the passengers, I'd rather be with the crew.

REX: Is that one for me?

MARION: *And* me?

MRS LINDEN: Well, if it is, it's absurd. Why shouldn't Rex –

PROFESSOR [*cutting in*]: This isn't an attack on Rex. Or on anybody else. You all seem to think I'm unreasonable and I'm trying to explain myself. After all we've heard during the past twenty-four hours, we know by this time that Burmanley's a gloomy, shabby hole that nobody but an old fool would want to do any work in. And why work anyhow if you needn't? That's been the line. And it doesn't appeal to me. I don't like the sound of it. There's death in it, somewhere. Down these fancy side turnings, although there seems more fun and colour and light that way, there are dead ends. I don't want to walk away from real life, give it up as a bad job. It's a pity just now that it's got a pinched look, frayed cuffs and down-at-heel shoes – whereas some coffins have satin linings – but I prefer to stay with it and help a bit if I can –

MARION: I don't see what this has got to do with anything we've said.

MRS LINDEN: And neither do I. And I don't believe it has. Has it, Rex?

[*She looks appealingly at* REX, *who does not reply but appears rather embarrassed.*]

PROFESSOR [*grimly*]: Well – Rex?

[REX *finally shrugs his shoulders.*]

My dear, your son is much too intelligent to reassure you.

MRS LINDEN [*sharply*]: Too good-mannered, you mean.

PROFESSOR [*sharply*]: His manners are excellent. I wish mine were half as good. But – if you will have it – what I *do* mean is that the whole lot of you, except young Dinah, are now busy turning away from life, giving it up. The Lindens are leaving the mucky old high road. And somebody's got to stay.

[*Enter* DINAH *and* JEAN. *The latter is ready for travelling.*]

DINAH: Mrs Cotton's *furious* because she says somebody's taken her tin of soap flakes.

PROFESSOR [*taking his letters*]: I must post these at the corner.

DINAH: I'll take them.

PROFESSOR [*beginning to move*]: No, thanks. I'm letting off steam. Better finish it off outside. [*He goes out hastily.*]

[*There is at once a certain slackening of tension.*]

JEAN [*to* REX]: Have I time to telephone to London?

REX: You have, but I wouldn't advise it. We'll make a stop on the road.

MRS LINDEN: Dinah darling, how would you like to come to London? We could probably arrange for you to go to the Royal College or the Academy of Music.

DINAH [*excited*]: And concerts! Wow! Of course that would be marvellous! But what's happening? Are we all going now? I haven't packed – or anything.

JEAN [*rather heavily*]: No, we're not. Dad isn't going. [*To her mother*] Is he?

MRS LINDEN [*rather sharply*]: No, he's not. And I was just going to explain that, Jean, if you hadn't interrupted.

JEAN [*pointedly*]: I'm glad.

MRS LINDEN: Don't interfere, please, Jean.

JEAN: I'm not going to.

REX: Look, chaps – drop this. We'll be off in a minute –

MRS LINDEN [*turning to* DINAH]: Your father's staying here – at least for the time being, though in my opinion he won't be here very long, even if the University doesn't insist upon his resignation. And I think they will, although he pretends they won't.

DINAH: Then I shall stay too. Daddy couldn't be here all by himself. Besides, I like it here, really. [*Looks at them all rather accusingly.*] What's been happening? Have you been saying things to him?

REX [*with grin*]: No, he's been saying things to us.

DINAH: Oh – that's all right, then. [*Looks anxiously at her mother.*] Do you think I'll be able to manage Mrs Cotton?

MRS LINDEN: Well, I never could.

DINAH: No, I'm better at her than you.

MARION [*worried*]: Mother – I know I agreed it was the best thing to do – but – well, Dinah and Mrs Cotton – I can't help feeling worried, you know – now that –

JEAN [*cutting in*]: I should think so, too.

MRS LINDEN: If I thought for a moment it was going to last, of course I'd agree with you. But it won't. And it's the only way. I told him plainly what I felt – but in his present mood I was just wasting my time. It really is the only way.

DINAH: What is? What's this all about?

REX [*as his mother doesn't reply*]: About Dad staying on here –

DINAH: Oh – we'll manage all right – you'll see –

[*Enter* MRS COTTON, *in a grim searching mood.* DINAH *turns and sees her.*]

Mrs Cotton – you and I can manage this house somehow, can't we – and look after the Professor?

MRS COTTON: Yes, we can. Manage better. [*Looks grim and searchingly at* MARION.] Wasn't it you that was drying some smalls on the cistern this morning?

MARION [*taken aback*]: No, it wasn't.

JEAN: They were mine – why?

MRS COTTON [*grimly*]: Well, it's a round biscuit-box really – with a dent in the lid and a picture of Clacton front round it – and full of my soap flakes –

JEAN: Well, I haven't seen it.

MRS COTTON [*grimly*]: That's what *you* say. One of you's taken it –

DINAH [*cheerfully*]: No, they haven't. It's still here somewhere – and I'll find it. You know I can always find things. And I promise.

MRS COTTON [*grumpily, going off*]: All right, so long as you say so. [*She goes.*]

[REX *looks at his watch.*]

REX: We ought to be going, you know. Is everything in the car?

JEAN: My case isn't. It's in the hall.

REX [*moving*]: I'll put it in. Then we ought to get cracking. There isn't much time. There isn't much time. [*Goes out.*]

　　[*As he goes,* JEAN *goes nearer* DINAH.]

JEAN: Dinah, if a telephone call comes for me, say I'm on my way back.

DINAH: All right.

JEAN: Say I ought to be up at the hospital about eight or half-past. Is it worth telling Mrs Cotton ? How is she about telephones ?

DINAH: She answers it, but she hates it – and so she says anything she feels at the time. As if a nasty-looking stranger had popped into the house.

　　[*Enter* PROFESSOR.]

PROFESSOR: Rex says you ought to be off.

MARION [*moving*]: We're coming now.

PROFESSOR: I'll be out in a minute.

MARION: Oh – dear!

DINAH [*moving with* JEAN]: What's the matter ?

MARION [*still moving*]: I don't know. But I feel rather sad now.

　　[*They go out leaving* PROFESSOR *and* MRS LINDEN *alone, not far from door, ready to move out.*]

MRS LINDEN: Will you be in tonight, Robert ?

PROFESSOR: Yes, unless there are dramatic developments over at the University.

MRS LINDEN: You're too optimistic about this business.

PROFESSOR: Why do you say that ?

MRS LINDEN: I have a feeling they want to get rid of you – and that they will. So don't expect too much. I'll ring you up from Rex's flat.

PROFESSOR: Good!

MRS LINDEN: But I meant every word I said, Robert. I'm not coming back. It's for your sake as much as mine. And this time you'll have to give in. [*As if about to break down*] Oh – Robert – I hate this –

PROFESSOR: So do I, Isabel. It's all wrong. [*He kisses her, lightly.*] You think I'm making a mistake. I think you are. But don't let's make a quarrel out of it, not after all these years. You're my wife. I love you very dearly.

MRS LINDEN [*as if about to change her mind*]: Oh – Robert – I'll – [*She hesitates.*]

PROFESSOR: Yes, my dear?

[REX *can now be heard calling, through open door, impatiently but gaily.*]

REX [*off*]: Come on, Mother. We're all set – the road's a-calling –

MRS LINDEN [*calling*]: I'm coming, darling. [*Changed again now, she looks sharply at* PROFESSOR.] I'll ring you tonight, Robert.

[*She turns and walks out, and, with something melancholy in the set of his back, he follows her. We then hear* DINAH *calling.*]

DINAH [*off*]: Yes, she is. She's here now.

[*There is a pause of a moment or two, then the telephone bell rings sharply. Then it waits a moment, and rings sharply again. Again it waits, then continues ringing.* MRS COTTON, *smoking a cigarette and looking annoyed, comes in to answer it.*]

MRS COTTON [*at telephone*]: Yes? . . . Who? Doctor? . . . *Professor* Linden lives 'ere. . . . Oh – that one. No, she isn't . . . just gone. . . . I don't know an' I don't care. . . . I sound bad-tempered 'cos I *am* bad-tempered.

[*As she bangs down the receiver, glares and blows smoke at it, the curtain is coming down for the end of Scene One. House lights stay down.*]

SCENE TWO

[*When curtain rises, a minute later, for opening of Scene Two, at night, several hours later, curtains are drawn across window and artificial lighting is on. This lighting should not be as general as it was in Act One, Scene Two, but more intimate, perhaps making use of large standard lamp downstage* L. *Door is half-open.* DINAH *and* MRS COTTON *are conferring.* DINAH *is holding several small shop-keeping books, while* MRS COTTON *is perched on arm of chair, still smoking a cigarette and holding a cup of tea. We feel that this housekeeping conference, for that is what it is, has been on some time.* DINAH *is puzzling over one of the small books, which she holds open, frowning at it, and* MRS COTTON *is watching her, and nothing is said for a few moments.*]

DINAH: Oh – dear – this rationing's difficult, isn't it?

MRS COTTON: 'Alf the time it isn't difficult – it's just bloody impossible. Minute I think o' them shops, up the language comes.
I come out with it at Frost's, greengrocer's Tuesday mornin', an
'e says 'You're no lady to talk like that'. An' I says 'I know I'm
not – but you're no greengrocer neither, though you've got it up
outside you are', I says.

DINAH [*consulting book*]: What's this about suet?

MRS COTTON: I don't know – but try to get it, that's all. An' your
Pa likes a bit o' suety stuff – every proper man does –

DINAH: I do too. Steak pudding – and treacle roll –

MRS COTTON: That's 'cos you're young. Lies on my stomach like
lead. But never mind what it says there about it. Just try to get
some, that's all.

DINAH: Well, I will – but the trouble is, I haven't much time –

MRS COTTON: Don't be silly. I'll do it, same as I did for your
Mum. Leave it to me –

DINAH: Well, I'd like to, Mrs Cotton, because I don't really
understand much about housekeeping, though I'll do my
best –

MRS COTTON: Well, your best an' my best an' all the shops' best –
won't make much dam' diff'rence, 'cos if we 'aven't got it, then
we can't 'ave it. 'Cept on the Black Market touch, of course.

DINAH: If somebody offered me chocolate on the Black Market
I'd take it.

MRS COTTON: So would I. Specially soft centres.

DINAH: Hard centres, I like. But then nobody ever does.

MRS COTTON: That's 'cos you're not in the know.

DINAH: Are you in the know, Mrs Cotton?

MRS COTTON: Not up this way, I'm not. Might be at 'ome. But
I'll bet I know one who is – an' that's your brother – that Rex.
An' I'll bet he has your Mum all fixed up nice on Black Market
tack – chickens an' cream an' eggs an' whisky –

DINAH: I don't think Mummie likes whisky –

MRS COTTON: I wish I didn't, 'cos I never see any, except that
'alf-bottle Bert sent me for Christmas.

DINAH [*with solemn air*]: Well now, Mrs Cotton, what about
tomorrow – ?

MRS COTTON: Sunday.

DINAH: Yes, I know. But I mean – meals an' things –

MRS COTTON: Don't you worry, we've enough stuff left over to do us nicely.

DINAH: Well, then, Monday – ?

MRS COTTON: It's only Saturday now – you needn't bother your 'ead about Monday. Leave it to me. An' don't look so solemn about it – 'cos it's no use – it's all 'it or miss, these days, an' mostly miss – an' if you start takin' it all serious, you'll soon be off your rocker. Matter of fact, 'alf the people nowadays *are* off their rockers, what with one thing an' another. Told you about my cousin, 'aven't I ?

DINAH: You mean the one who's married to two different men ?

MRS COTTON: No, that's poor Florrie – *she's* not all there neither. But this is another one, Agnes, married to a baker. Know 'ow it takes 'er ? [*In a loud whisper*] Saves tissue paper. Collects it an' saves it. Go miles, for some. Smooths it out – irons it sometimes – an' puts it away all nice. – Got at least a cupboard full.

DINAH: But why ?

MRS COTTON [*same whisper*]: Nobody knows. *She* doesn't know. Bit mental. That's 'ow it takes 'er. I tell yer, ducks, there's more an' more goin' queer – mental. Man called at the back door, Thursday – clean-looking oldish man with a beard – spoke quite refined – an' said 'e'd bin sent by the Prophet Enoch –

DINAH [*astonished, half laughing*]: The Prophet Enoch ?

MRS COTTON: True as I'm 'ere.

[*A distant ring, at front door.*]

DINAH: Somebody at the door. Do you think this might be one of them ?

MRS COTTON [*moving*]: Might be. I'll go. [*She goes out.*]

[DINAH *gives the book in her hand a last puzzled look, then puts it down.* MRS COTTON *now reappears at doorway.*]

MRS COTTON [*grumpily*]: Student.

[*She shows in* EDITH WESTMORE, *then closes door as she goes.*]

EDITH: Professor Linden told us to call here tonight after the Union show –

DINAH: He's out but he'll be back any minute. Do sit down. Where's what's-his-name ?

EDITH: Bernard Fawcett ?

DINAH: Yes.

EDITH: He'll be coming along. But I didn't wait for him. He isn't a friend of mine – I don't like him much.

[*She is now sitting down* – DINAH *just perches casually.*]

DINAH: I don't know him really. He always looks as if something or somebody has just upset him.

EDITH: Usually they have. [*She laughs, then hesitates.*] Is your brother still staying here?

DINAH: No, he drove back to London this afternoon. Did you meet him?

EDITH: Just for a minute or two, yesterday. He's very attractive, isn't he?

DINAH: I don't know really. – Yes, I suppose he is.

EDITH: It's surprising he isn't married, isn't it?

DINAH: He's not the type, I think. He couldn't bother settling down with just one person.

EDITH: Still – a lot of men seem like that, don't they? And then they do marry after all.

DINAH: Yes. I suppose it could happen with Rex. Probably some-body terribly glamorous – like a film star, that he could show off in expensive places. Rex is very clever in a sharp sort of way. Do you know a game called *Black Sam*?

EDITH [*rather despondently*]: No. We never played games at home.

DINAH: It's our Linden family game. We used to play it a lot. And last night we played it again. And it was just the same as it used to be. Rex won again. He always used to win. [*Begins laughing.*] And the whole last hour he was cheating, and we didn't know. He always did when we used to play it. And last night – Jean – that's my doctor sister, who's very serious and grown-up usually – was absolutely *furious* with him. People don't really change much, do they? Not inside themselves. And when they let themselves go again – when they're back with the family and are being silly – they're just the same as they always were.

EDITH: One of my brothers is quite different from what he was before the war. Now he won't look at you for a long time but then he suddenly stares – and laughs – in a meaningless sort of way. [*Hesitates a moment, then hesitantly*] Do you think – this lipstick – suits me – ?

DINAH [*rather astonished*]: I don't know. I'm not good on lipstick. [*Goes closer to her, inspecting her.*] No. Much too dark.

EDITH [*miserably*]: Oh dear! [*Then, bursting out*] Sometimes I
wish I weren't a girl. Don't you?

DINAH: I used to. But now I don't care – just don't bother about it.
[MRS COTTON *opens door. Same tone as before*]

MRS COTTON: Another student.
[BERNARD FAWCETT *enters, wearing a very shabby overcoat
and a muffler, but with no hat.* MRS COTTON *closes door.*]

FAWCETT [*gloomily*]: Hello!

DINAH: Hello! Father'll be back any minute. Won't you take off
your overcoat?

FAWCETT [*gloomily*]: No thanks.

DINAH: What's the matter?

FAWCETT [*irritably*]: These dam' colds I get. I had a bad one
yesterday – all the week, in fact. Then this afternoon I thought
it had gone. Now it's come back again. Head aches and can't
taste anything properly. But I'll smoke if it's all the same to you.

DINAH: Of course.
[FAWCETT *pulls out a clumsy-looking cherrywood, of the type
favoured by young students, and lights it rather awkwardly, then
puffs out smoke gloomily.*]

FAWCETT: That Union show was lousy.

EDITH [*mildly*]: I rather liked it this time.

FAWCETT [*rudely*]: You would!

EDITH [*sharply*]: Don't be so rude.

FAWCETT [*astonished*]: What?

EDITH [*still sharply*]: I said *don't be so rude.*

FAWCETT: What's the matter with you?

EDITH: I don't know why you boys think you have to behave like –
like louts – just because you've come to a university – because
you're students. If you could only see what you looked like – in
comparison – with – with – other kinds of men – you'd – you'd –

FAWCETT: Don't bother with it, Westmore. You sound to me as
if you've fallen for somebody.

EDITH [*hastily*]: I haven't – don't be stupid –

FAWCETT [*turning to* DINAH]: What's this about your father?

DINAH [*alert at once*]: What about him?

FAWCETT: Told another bloke who's taking history – chap called
Thring – I was coming on here to get next week's essay subject –
and he said I needn't bother. Because, he told me, there's a

strong rumour going round that your father's retiring – right
off –

DINAH [*sharply*]: Well, it isn't true.

FAWCETT: Very strong rumour, he said. 'Prof. Linden's had it'
he said.

EDITH [*hastily*]: Oh – for goodness sake, shut up.

FAWCETT: Why should I – [*he sneezes violently.*] Oh – blast!

DINAH [*who has been rigid, fiercely*]: And I hope it's 'flu – and the
kind that gives you awful pains in your inside and they make you
have castor oil –

> [*She has now stalked out.* FAWCETT *stares after her in
> astonishment, then looks at* EDITH.]

FAWCETT: Did she say she hoped it was 'flu?

EDITH [*fiercely*]: Yes. She was furious because you said that about
her father. 'Prof. Linden's had it'! What a way to talk! And
what a thing to say to *her*!

FAWCETT [*patiently, misunderstood*]: Look! Now what have I
done? I meet a bloke called Thring –

EDITH [*angrily*]: And I hope he has gastric 'flu too.

FAWCETT [*wrestling hard with his cold*]: Women! Girls! Women!
The more – more – more I see – [*another sneeze coming and he
wrestles with it.*]

> [EDITH *begins laughing. He glares at her.*]

How I admire your wonderful delicate sense of humour, Miss
Westmore!

EDITH [*laughing*]: If you only saw yourself. [*Laughs.*]

FAWCETT [*shouting*]: I don't want to see myself –

> [*Enter* PROFESSOR LINDEN.]

PROFESSOR: Well, Fawcett, if you don't want to see yourself,
there's no reason why you should, until you shave, tomorrow
morning. Good evening, Miss Westmore. And I apologize once
again for keeping you waiting.

EDITH: It's all right, Professor Linden.

PROFESSOR [*sitting down*]: Thank you. What with my family
coming and going – and other things – I seem to have completely lost my well-deserved reputation for punctuality. Well –
this afternoon's meeting of the Burmanley Citizens' Vigilant
Society was postponed – eh? And so, much to your relief, I
imagine I'll have to find another subject for next week's essay.

FAWCETT: Yes.

EDITH [*timidly*]: Professor Linden – ?

PROFESSOR: Yes ?

EDITH [*timidly*]: We shall be coming to you next week – I mean –

PROFESSOR [*rather sharply*]: I hope so. Why not ?

  [*They exchange glances, and he notices it. He gets up and moves
  a pace or two, impatiently, then more to himself than to them*]
Really – this is too bad. [*He turns to them.*] So you've heard
rumours that I may not be here next week – eh ?

FAWCETT: Yes. Only just tonight – at the Union.

PROFESSOR: I *see*. [*To* EDITH] And you too ?

EDITH [*unhappily*]: Yes – I did hear – something.

PROFESSOR: You oughtn't to have done. But it only proves what
I've said before – that a university is a mad village.

  [*They stare at him for a moment, and there is a pause while he
  reflects. Then, with more decision*]
You two are pretty average Burmanley History students and
here's a question I'd like to put to you, to be answered quite
truthfully. If you're merely polite about it, then you'll make me
sorry I asked it. [*Pauses, then quietly and impersonally*] Would it
really matter to you – if I wasn't here next week ?

EDITH [*involuntarily*]: Oh – dear !

PROFESSOR: A truthful impersonal answer, mind. Fawcett ?

FAWCETT [*steadily*]: No, sir, it wouldn't – not really. I get on all
right with Mr Pearse and Mr Saxon. I don't mean –

PROFESSOR [*quietly*]: Never mind about what you don't mean.
You gave me an honest answer. Now, Miss Westmore –

EDITH [*struggling*]: Oh dear ! – it's so difficult –

PROFESSOR: I could take that as an answer, if necessary.

EDITH [*struggling away*]: No, I mean I enjoy your lectures more
than anybody else's – and coming here for the essays – I don't
understand you always as I do Mr Pearse – but of course it
would matter terribly if you went –

PROFESSOR [*quietly*]: No, it wouldn't. You're giving me the same
answer.

  [*As she tries to apologize*]
No, please, Miss Westmore. If you try to apologize to me, then
I ought first to apologize to you – for asking such a question –
and we might be at it all night. [*With an obvious effort*] Well,

that's that. But – because we don't know what's going to happen
– that's no reason for not doing a bit of work, is it ? So let's get
back to the Sixteenth Century . . . the Sixteenth Century. . . .
[*He moves about a little, trying to concentrate.*] Yes – well.
Shakespeare's at the Globe Theatre, writing imperishable
masterpieces. Suppose you try to trace the connexion between
that glorious fact and the rise of the Lombard cities and the
development of the banking system.

FAWCETT [*dismayed*]: The banking system ?

PROFESSOR: Yes. You go back a century, of course. *Twelfth
Night*, *Hamlet* – here – and there, the Italian cities and the banking system. Letters of credit and loans at five per cent, at one
end of the chain, and at the other a crowded wooden theatre
near the Thames and the afternoon fading and a player with a
whitened face murmuring *Absent thee from felicity awhile*. That's
all.

FAWCETT [*as they rise to go*]: And if you're not here –

PROFESSOR [*rather sharply*]: I've not been told yet that I shan't
be, Fawcett. In fact, you may take it that I will be.

[*The telephone rings.* PROFESSOR *goes to answer it.*]

EDITH [*hissing at* FAWCETT]: Idiot!

FAWCETT [*indignant whisper*]: What for ?

EDITH [*same*]: Oh – shut up!

PROFESSOR [*at telephone*]: Yes ? . . . This is Professor Linden
speaking . . . all right. . . . [*He turns to the students looking old
and bleak now.*] This is a call from London and it may take some
time, so would you mind letting yourselves out ? And we meet
here, I hope, next Friday at the usual time.

EDITH [*moving out*]: Yes. Good night, Professor Linden.

FAWCETT [*moving out*]: Good night.

PROFESSOR: Good night. . . .

[*They go out, leaving door ajar. He now answers telephone.*]
Yes, Isabel – Robert here. . . . No, no news at all, but rumours
are flying round, of course . . . well, if it should be vanity,
it's already receiving a shock or two . . . no, not worth
talking about. . . . Do I ? Well, you never did like my telephone
voice, did you, my dear ? And I may be rather tired. . . . Mrs
Cotton ? I'll give her a shout, then we can go on talking. Just a
minute. [*Leaves telephone hastily and goes to door, calling*] Mrs

Cotton – Mrs Cotton – hurry! – telephone [*and then goes back
to telephone*]. I've called her. . . . No, don't worry about us.
Regarded from the splendours of Rex's flat, we probably seem
worse off than we really are. . . . Certainly, why shouldn't you
enjoy it, my dear. I'm glad. . . . Well, I was never good at
sounding glad on a long-distance telephone late on Saturday
night. . . . Yes, Isabel, I know, but that's how I feel and while
I still live at all, I have to live with myself.

[MRS COTTON *now appears.*]

. . . Let's leave it at that then, my dear – here's Mrs Cotton.

[*He hands her the receiver, which* MRS COTTON *takes grimly,
speaking into it in grim tone*]

MRS COTTON [*at telephone*]: This is Mrs Cotton. . . . Yes, Mrs
Linden – well, you said that this morning . . . oh, we'll manage.
. . . I'll tell 'em first thing Monday. – What ? . . . Oh –

[*She glances at* PROFESSOR, *who is standing not far away.*]

A bit pinched, I'd say – as if it was a colder night than it is, if yer
see what I mean. . . . Yes. – Oh, *she's* all right. . . . I tell yer, we'll
manage. . . . Tomorrow night, same time ? I'll tell 'im. 'Bye.
[*Puts down receiver as if she disliked it.*] She's goin' to ring yer
same time tomorrow night. Money no object. Mr Rex, I suppose. [*Sniffs dubiously.*] All this talkin' on telyphones – where's
it get yer ?

PROFESSOR [*rather despondently*]: I don't know. I'm not good at
it.

MRS COTTON: Not yuman, that's what's wrong with it. Oh –
there's a message for you.

PROFESSOR: Yes ?

MRS COTTON: Young woman – pal o' Miss Dinah's – brought 'er
some gramyphone records – an' a message for you at the same
time – works in 'is office, I think –

PROFESSOR: Whose office ?

MRS COTTON: That Mr Lock'art. She said 'e's comin' to see yer
tonight – might be any time now –

PROFESSOR [*slowly, softly*]: I see. Well, Alfred Lockhart's an old
friend of mine – and – [*looking her in the eye*] Mrs Cotton – how
much whisky is there left ?

MRS COTTON [*with innocent air*]: Not much. Might be a couple o'
pub doubles – and yer know what they are now –

PROFESSOR: There ought to be more than that.

MRS COTTON: There isn't. Soon goes.

PROFESSOR [*softly*]: It does. You couldn't – by any chance – have had any lately, could you ?

MRS COTTON [*after giving him a nod*]: Just a nip – yesterday morning – when that ceiling come down – an' reminded me, you know – just 'ad to 'ave a nip.

PROFESSOR: Yes, fair enough. I'd have done the same.

MRS COTTON: Ah – you an' me, Professor – we can get on all right – live an' let live – that's our motto.

PROFESSOR: Something like that. Well, bring what's left of the whisky and a couple of glasses for Mr Lockhart and me. We've a ceiling coming down too.

[*Sound of gramophone, distant and behind closed door, comes through now.*]

MRS COTTON: Right. 'Ear that ? Music. She's at it. [*Smiles with some tenderness.*] Talked to me tonight in 'ere about 'ouse-keepin' an' shoppin' an' all that – wants to look after yer properly, she does – bless 'er!

PROFESSOR [*gently*]: You must look after her, Mrs Cotton. I know you're fond of her.

MRS COTTON: As if she was my own. Kid got me from the first go off – one reason why I stayed. That Dinah, Professor – she's growin' up of course –

PROFESSOR: Yes, seventeen.

MRS COTTON [*solemnly*]: Eighteen. But she still lives in the land o' childhood, where you an' me's forgotten.

PROFESSOR [*astonished*]: My dear Mrs Cotton, it's true of course but what an extraordinary thing for you to say –

MRS COTTON [*complacently*]: 'Eard a chap say it top of a tram – one Easter Monday – an' it stuck in my mind. Crossin' the river we was – packed of course – an' it was rainin' a bit an' sun shinin' all at the same time – way it does about Easter – an' everything suddenly so bright an' shiny I could 'ave laughed an' cried. So when I 'eard 'im say that it stuck in my mind. Yer know ?

PROFESSOR [*softly*]: Yes. And perhaps, after all, we're not forgotten.

[*As if the door is now wide open, the gramophone can now be heard, clearly but still distantly. It is the Casals recording of the final movement of the Elgar 'Cello Concerto – the passage, before the very end, in which earlier themes are recalled poignantly.* PROFESSOR *begins listening intently.*]

MRS COTTON [*quietly*]: I'll get yer that whisky.

[*She goes, and as he listens near the open door, he is joined by* DINAH, *in a fine state of excitement.*]

DINAH [*in a loud whisper*]: That's Casals. You didn't think it was me, did you?

PROFESSOR: I wondered, but I couldn't think how you'd got the BBC symphony orchestra into the dining-room.

DINAH: Wouldn't it be marvellous if you could? Just pack them up in a magic little box?

PROFESSOR: They're in one now. Last movement, isn't it?

DINAH: Yes, and I'll never be able to play it properly for ages and ages – if ever. Listen – [*the music comes through poignantly*] he's remembering the earlier themes now, Daddy, and saying good-bye to them.

PROFESSOR [*quietly, almost to the music*]: Wandering through the darkening house of life – touching all the things he loved – crying Farewell – for ever – for ever –

[*After a moment, there is heard a ring at the front door.*]

DINAH [*crossly*]: Oh – bother! I'll go. [*Hurries out.*]

PROFESSOR [*going to doorway, calling*]: If it's anybody but Alfred Lockhart, I can't see them. [*Going out to look.*] Oh – it *is* you, Alfred.

LOCKHART [*calling*]: Yes.

PROFESSOR: Come up. Dinah, when you've finished with the gramophone, you'd better go to bed.

DINAH [*as she hurries past doorway*]: All right, but I'm a bit excited.

[PROFESSOR *now ushers in* LOCKHART, *who wears a dark overcoat and carries a dark hat. He looks grave.*]

PROFESSOR [*still near door, not closed*]: Alfred, you're wearing your undertaker's look tonight. Won't you take your coat off?

LOCKHART: No, thanks, Robert. I mustn't stay long.

[MRS COTTON *appears with a tray on which are two glasses, small jug of water, and whisky decanter with small amount of whisky in it.*]

MRS COTTON: 'Ere it is, what's left of it – so make the most of it, I say. [*Goes to put tray down.*]

PROFESSOR: Thank you, Mrs Cotton. And there won't be anything else tonight. So – good night.

MRS COTTON [*moving out*]: Good night. An' I'll try an' get that young madam off to bed too. [*She goes out and closes the door behind her.*]

PROFESSOR: A little whisky, Alfred?

LOCKHART [*gravely*]: I'd rather get the official part of my visit over first, if you don't mind, Robert.

PROFESSOR: I thought there must be an official part.

[*They have now sat down.*]

LOCKHART: I'm not enjoying this. That's why I wanted to get it over tonight.

PROFESSOR: Go ahead.

LOCKHART [*steadily, impersonally*]: I've been instructed by the Vice-Chancellor that in the circumstances he will not press for your immediate resignation – though he deplores – and he particularly asked me to tell you this – the attitude you have adopted and trusts you will reconsider your decision –

PROFESSOR [*cutting in*]: Alfred, I can't listen to any more of this jargon or watch you pretending to be a Civil Service dummy. What have they agreed to? Do I stay as I am?

LOCKHART: No.

PROFESSOR [*shocked*]: What?

LOCKHART: It's a compromise. I expected it, as I hinted this morning. You give up the Chair and most of the work but you can stay on an Emeritus level – no examining – off the Board of Studies – about half-salary – a little more perhaps –

PROFESSOR [*angrily*]: God! – Alfred – it's an insult –

LOCKHART: It's what I expected.

PROFESSOR: But was there a proper meeting?

LOCKHART: Yes.

PROFESSOR: But what about Drury and Hamilton – and my lot – ?

LOCKHART: They were there. Didn't like it. Hamilton said what he thought – he was pretty fierce. But they had to give in.

PROFESSOR [*quietly*]: We'll have that whisky now, I think. [*Gets up and begins pouring it.*] And don't keep on being official,

Alfred. You and I have known each other for over twenty years
– skirmished and fought together – and tied up each other's
wounds – eh?

LOCKHART [*calm and mild*]: Yes. And I'm not being official any
longer. To hell with 'em. And I'm sick of this job. I'll find a way
out – and soon too.

[*Takes the glass* PROFESSOR *gives him.*]

Thanks, Robert. Can you spare it?

PROFESSOR: No, and neither can my housekeeper.

LOCKHART [*calmly*]: It'll taste all the better. [*Looks solemnly over
his glass.*] Skoal!

PROFESSOR [*raising his glass*]: Salut!

[*They drink solemnly.*]

LOCKHART: I'll say what I tried to tell you this morning. You
shouldn't have given them this chance. You should have walked
out. Your wife was right –

PROFESSOR: You behaved badly there, Alfred, lending yourself
to female intrigue. Isabel, by the way, has gone to live with Rex,
and says she's never coming back here.

LOCKHART: Bad in theory, but right and sensible in practice –
trying to force your hand. You ought to join her on Monday.
Tell the VC he can keep his Emeritus nonsense. I'd enjoy
taking him a message in your best style, Robert.

PROFESSOR: I'd two students here tonight, Alfred. Average types
– Fawcett and the Westmore girl – so, like a fool, I did a Gallup
Poll on them – would it really matter to them if I did go? I
gathered it wouldn't. So far as they are concerned, I might as
well be in Rex's super-flat tonight, swigging his excellent Black
Market whisky.

LOCKHART: That's where I'd be.

PROFESSOR [*softly*]: No, you wouldn't, Alfred, you old liar. What
about the job that Masterton, the motor chap offered you, last
year, with an expense sheet as long as your arm? You turned it
down – to toil on here.

LOCKHART: I was a fool.

PROFESSOR: I'm the same kind of fool. And insult or no insult,
students or no students, wife or no wife, I'm staying –

LOCKHART [*rather angrily, for him*]: But why? What in God's
name do you think you can do here now?

PROFESSOR: Be an old nuisance. Make senile mischief. Throw large spanners into their godless works. I'll grab the pick of the history honours people and show them what life's done so far with this gaudy little planet. I'll give lectures that have about as much to do with the syllabus as Brock's fireworks. I'll contradict every dreary little lie about humanity that Pearse and Saxon and the rest can cook up. I'll –

LOCKHART [cutting in, rather sharply]: Don't go on, Robert. Because I think you're bluffing.

[PROFESSOR, who has been on his feet during his last speech, turns away, hurt, but not wanting LOCKHART to see he is hurt. LOCKHART, however, guesses this and rises, moving nearer PROFESSOR. The latter turns and looks at him, reproachfully.]

LOCKHART: I'm sorry. Even if I thought that, I oughtn't to have said it.

PROFESSOR: If you can think it, then you'd better say it – even tonight. But perhaps I was bluffing a bit – whistling in the dark perhaps. Let's put it like this, then. I've been here a long time – I like the glum mucky old place. And times are hard, Alfred – we've got to keep on if we can. And there might be something I could help to do here, before the light goes. A touch of colour. A hint of wonder. An occasional new glance at old stuff. A bit of insight. Or is it the characteristic vanity of the Emeritus type?

LOCKHART: No, it isn't. You've all that to give. If they'll let you.

PROFESSOR [a trifle bleakly, at first]: Yes, there's that. And it's not so much men – as machines – that we have to beat. The new educational machine here, for instance. And generally – the capital-industrial machine – and now the Trade Union machine and the Civil Service machine.

LOCKHART: Right.

PROFESSOR: I was telling my family, who don't care a damn, that we're trying to do a wonderful thing here. And so we are. But somehow not in a wonderful way. There's a kind of grey chilly hollowness inside, where there ought to be gaiety, colour, warmth, vision. Sometimes our great common enterprise seems only a noble skeleton, as if the machines had already sucked the blood and marrow out of it. My wife and family tell me to go away and enjoy myself. Doing what? Watching the fire die out of the heart, and never even stooping to blow? Here in Burmanley – with Dinah and her kind – and a few friends and allies – I can still blow a little – brighten an ember or two.

LOCKHART: The young and the old are the best now, Robert. There's a lot of rotten dead stuff in the middle –

PROFESSOR: But perhaps there always was, and the young and the old were always the best. Nearer the door in and the door out, and with more spirit to spare. The world's too much with the middles, who are busy looking for promotion and a seat on the Board.

LOCKHART: Robert – you look tired – cold too. Go to bed and don't bother seeing me out –

PROFESSOR [*exasperated*]: Damn it, man, I'm sixty-five – not eighty-five –

LOCKHART [*moving rapidly, decisively*]: Good night.

[*He is out before* PROFESSOR *can get near him. As* PROFESSOR *is at door, we hear a rather desolate door-slam off.* PROFESSOR *now comes down and may here make change to more intimate lighting still, with most of stage in shadow.* PROFESSOR *moves slowly and wearily, and now for first time looks really dispirited. He sits down in light, rather heavily, puts a pipe in his mouth but does not smoke it, but stares rather desolately, perhaps with his head in his hands.* DINAH, *now in pyjamas, slippers, thick dressing-gown, enters very quietly, closing door softly behind her, and looking concerned at sight of her father brooding there, slowly comes down.*]

DINAH [*softly*]: Daddy!

PROFESSOR [*looking up*]: Hello, Dinah. Thought you'd gone to bed.

DINAH: I started – but – [*lets this trail off. Then softly*] You looked so miserable sitting there –

PROFESSOR [*neither denying nor agreeing*]: I was brooding a bit. There *are* times – [*He breaks off.*]

DINAH [*encouragingly*]: Yes?

PROFESSOR [*with a sheepish grin*]: Well – let's say – there are times. Leave it at that.

[*She glances with concern at him, then settles in large arm-chair, not far from where he is sitting, preferably up at desk or table.*]

Here, young woman – settling down?

DINAH: Will you do something specially to please me?

PROFESSOR: I might.

DINAH: Do you remember – you read us once – a bit of that book on history you started writing ? Will you read some of it again – the beginning –

PROFESSOR: You don't want that stuff.

DINAH: I do. I *need* it. *You* need it. And if we don't have it, I'll go to bed and be miserable – and you'll go on being broody and lonely down here. So – please!

PROFESSOR [*in pretence of grumbling tone*]: All right then – if I can find the thing –

[*She settles back, as he brings the MS out of drawer, puts on a pair of spectacles, and then begins to read – quietly but impressively.*]

'History, to be worthy of the name, should bring us a stereoscopic view of man's life. Without that extra dimension, strangely poignant as well as vivid, it is flat, and because it is flat it is false. There are two patterns, endlessly being superimposed on one another. The first pattern is that of man reproducing himself, finding food and shelter, tilling the land, building cities, crossing the seas. It is the picture we understand now with ease, perhaps too easily. For the other pattern is still there, waiting to be interpreted. It is the record of man as a spiritual creature, with a whole world of unknown continents and strange seas, gardens of Paradise and cities lit with hell-fire, within the depths of his own soul. History that ignores the god and the altar is as false as history that could forget the sword and the wheel. Nor does the former belong only to the first youth of a civilization –' [*Breaks off to say quietly, glancing up*] I don't like 'former' – can't imagine – [*his voice gets softer and slower*] how I came to write it. . . .

[*For now standing up, quietly, he sees that* DINAH *is fast asleep. He looks down smilingly for a moment. As he quietly sits down again, takes out a pen and crosses out a word or two in the MS, the curtain is slowly descending.*]

END OF PLAY

*Contemporary ... Provocative ... Outrageous ...
Prophetic ... Groundbreaking ... Funny ... Disturbing ...
Different ... Moving ... Revolutionary ... Inspiring ...
Subversive ... Life-changing ...*

What makes a modern classic?

At Penguin Classics our mission has always been to make the best
books ever written available to everyone. And that also means
constantly redefining and refreshing exactly what makes a 'classic'.
That's where Modern Classics come in. Since 1961 they have been an
organic, ever-growing and ever-evolving list of books from the last
hundred (or so) years that we believe will continue to be read over and
over again.

They could be books that have inspired political dissent, such as
Animal Farm. Some, like *Lolita* or *A Clockwork Orange*, may have
caused shock and outrage. Many have led to great films, from *In Cold
Blood* to *One Flew Over the Cuckoo's Nest*. They have broken down
barriers – whether social, sexual, or, in the case of *Ulysses*, the
boundaries of language itself. And they might – like *Goldfinger* or
Scoop – just be pure classic escapism. Whatever the reason, Penguin
Modern Classics continue to inspire, entertain and enlighten millions
of readers everywhere.

'No publisher has had more influence on reading habits than Penguin'
Independent

'Penguins provided a crash course in world literature'
Guardian

The best books ever written

PENGUIN ⊙ CLASSICS

SINCE 1946

Find out more at www.penguinclassics.com